The Imaginary War

The Imaginary War

Civil Defense and American Cold War Culture

Guy Oakes

New York   Oxford
Oxford University Press
1994

Oxford University Press

Oxford   New York   Toronto
Delhi   Bombay   Calcutta   Madras   Karachi
Kuala Lumpur   Singapore   Hong Kong   Tokyo
Nairobi   Dar es Salaam   Cape Town
Melbourne   Auckland   Madrid

and associated companies in
Berlin   Ibadan

Library of Congress Cataloging-in-Publication Data
Oakes, Guy.
The imaginary war : civil defense and American
cold war culture / Guy Oakes.
p. cm.
Includes bibliographical references and index.
ISBN 0-19-509027-6
1. Civil defense—United States—History—20th century.
2. Nuclear warfare—History—20th century.
3. United States— Military policy.
4. Deterrence (Strategy)—History—20th century.
5. Cold War. I. Title.
UA927.023 1994   363.3'5'097309045—dc20
93-46098

1 3 5 7 9 8 6 4 2

Printed in the United States of America
on acid-free paper

Acknowledgments

Thanks are due to Doyle McCarthy and Arthur Vidich for their comments on sections of an earlier draft of this project and to Andrew Grossman for many conversations on national security and civil defense during the Truman presidency. Helpful suggestions for revisions of the penultimate draft were made by two readers for Oxford University Press. For advice on sources, I am indebted to Dennis Bilger of the Harry S Truman Library and Dwight Strandberg of the Dwight D. Eisenhower Library. As always, I am grateful to the staff of the Guggenheim Library, Monmouth College. My research was supported by the Jack T. Kvernland Chair, Monmouth College, and by grants from the Harry S Truman Library Institute and Monmouth College.

Contents

Introduction   *3*

1. National Security and National Morale   *10*

The Berlin Crisis: The Soviet Threat and Nuclear Strategy   *10*
The Soviet Atomic Bomb: Nuclear Strategy and National Will   *17*
National Security and the Problem of National Will   *21*
Civil Defense and National Will   *30*

2. Managing Nuclear Terror   *33*

National Will and Nuclear Terror   *33*
The Problem of Panic   *34*
The Cold War System of Emotion Management   *46*
The Social Psychology of Emotion Management:
   American Society in World War III   *71*

3. The Cold War Conception of Nuclear Reality   *78*

The Construction of Nuclear Reality   *78*
Crisis Mastery   *79*
Operation Alert   *84*
Operation Alert: The Movie   *96*

4. The Nuclear Family   *105*

The American Family Under Nuclear Attack   *105*
Civil Defense and the Regimentation of Family Life   *113*
Radioactive Fallout and Nuclear Housekeeping   *117*
The Cold War Ethic   *129*

5. The Antinomies of Cold War Culture   *145*

The Dilemma of Emotion Management   *145*
The Paradoxes of Nuclear Crisis Management   *152*

**Epilogue: Liberal Propaganda and the Exigencies of National
Security**   *165*

Notes   *169*

Index   *189*

The Imaginary War

Introduction

Alert Today–Alive Tomorrow, a film produced by RKO for the Federal Civil Defense Administration in 1956, opens in the seemingly innocuous but uncomfortably ominous fashion characteristic of Alfred Hitchcock, the camera slowly panning down from a sweeping panorama of a small American town to focus on a single residential street. The houses all are remarkably alike—modest, two story, white frame, with scrupulously trimmed lawns. As the announcer observes, "It could be any street, any town, USA." Homeowners are engaged in light gardening. Parents walk their young children along the sidewalks. One neighbor assists another with some yard work. The streets are immaculate, the residents neatly dressed and friendly, the children well behaved and smiling. This is the postwar paradise of the American middle class, in which everyone is well-off, white, and civil—a triumph of residential real-estate development, landscape architecture, and social homogeneity.[1]

The announcer employs a tone of chatty informality, bringing viewers into the narrative and including them in the stereotypical scenes of small-town life depicted in the film, as if they lived on this particular street. "Wherever you are," he suggests, "you're probably part of an old-fashioned, home-bred spirit of . . . well, do you mind an old-fashioned word? Let's call it neighborliness." Neighborliness means "helping the guy next door," sharing responsibilities, and "not minding a bit." Men on their way to work share a daily car pool. Their wives share the latest news over the backyard clothesline. One neighbor lends another his lawnmower. Everyone on the street, it seems, is animated by the original ethic on which the United States is said to have been founded, for the audience learns that "this country was practically built by this neighborly feeling." In the reconstruction of American history presented in *Alert Today–Alive Tomorrow*, the American nation was possible because its people recognized that their common needs could be met only if burdens were shared. Accordingly, the experiences that formed the American character were local gatherings where communal bonds were created in acts of neighborliness and mutual assistance. In roof-raising parties, the men of the community gathered to help families accomplish what they could not do alone: erect a house or a barn. In quilting bees, the women made bridal trousseaus for the daughters of the community. In constructing forts, pioneers practiced mutual defense against attacks by Native Americans, the "Indians." And in joining wagon trains, settlers established a joint enterprise without which the movement across the Great Plains and the conquest of the West could not have succeeded.

But what does the American tradition of neighborliness and community effort have to do with the hydrogen bomb? the announcer asks rhetorically. Now more than ever, viewers are told, Americans must learn to help one another in order to meet the common challenge of national survival. The key to the cooperative endeavors required for survival in the nuclear age is civil defense, which is essential to protect the hopes and values that Americans cherish, the ideals that "weave business, industry, and livability into the accustomed tapestry of the American scene." In documenting the relation between the American communal ethic and civil defense against nuclear attack, the film highlights the civil defense organization of Reading, Pennsylvania, and its 8,000 volunteers. Readingites of all classes and stations of life—blue-collar workers, businessmen, bankers, nurses, and "Junior League women"—sign up in the thousands for the civil defense services that will save the community in the event of a Soviet nuclear assault: rescue teams; hospital, nursing, and ambulance units; auxiliary police and fire departments. Everyone pitches in to do his or her part, and local businesses cooperate by donating equipment and supplies. Thus the people of Reading work together in a remarkable display of patriotism, public spirit, community pride, personal responsibility, and mutual assistance.

Readingites treat the threat of a nuclear attack as a managerial problem. The larger objective of the community's survival is reduced to its component parts, each of which is shown to be amenable to a solution by teams of trained citizens who have mastered the necessary techniques and learned to work effectively in tandem. A group of volunteers loads the components of a 200-bed emergency hospital into large trucks, which are then driven to a designated emergency site.

There, the audience is told, thirty-three additional volunteers assemble the entire hospital in only four hours. Reading also has a special rescue team composed exclusively of women. Middle-aged matrons outfitted in white jumpsuits and helmets practice emergency rescue routines, gamely taking on dangerous assignments and jobs that require heavy lifting, so that when the real attack comes they will be prepared.

A dozen or so men and women, wearing the same white jumpsuits and identified as the Reading auxiliary police corps, line up at the firing range of the Reading Pistol Club. The instructor demonstrates the proper stance and firing technique as the volunteers watch. Then each takes his or her turn with the revolver. But why an armed civil defense militia? In the aftermath of a nuclear attack, who would be the targets of the Reading auxiliary police? The announcer answers this question with the bland observation that when these volunteers complete their course, they will have the training to "check possible panic." In a nuclear emergency, it seems, the citizens of Reading may pose a threat to civil order in spite of their magnificent civil defense organization. This means that precautions must be taken to maintain order, by the threat of force if necessary. In a morale-shattering nuclear crisis, the auxiliary police will exercise what the announcer describes as "a strong stabilizing effect on the jittery populace."

In *Alert Today–Alive Tomorrow*, the background music alternates between rapidly bowing violins and military music reminiscent of World War II newsreels. Both suggest determined, purposeful, and incessant activity. Reading civil defense is on the march. In the thermonuclear era, the audience is told, "survival is possible, but only if you and your neighbor are willing to help each other."

Alert Today–Alive Tomorrow introduces the main themes that formed the American civil defense ethos of the 1950s and pulls out all the stops on which civil defense propaganda played: domestic privatism and the house-proud ethic of the postwar middle class, anxieties about personal and national security, fears about nuclear war and apprehensions over the breakdown of social order in a nuclear attack, and the appeal to putatively traditional and small-town virtues of self-help, mutual assistance, and community spirit, which would continue to stand Americans in good stead even in the extremities of nuclear war.

During World War II, the United States was not occupied as Europe was, not invaded as the Soviet Union was, or not bombed as Great Britain was. Nor was there any plausible suggestion that the home front might be subjected to any of these acts of war. As a result, it has been said that Americans were obliged to fight the war at a distance and "on imagination alone."[2] Within months of V-J Day, civil defense strategists began to make plans to mobilize the American public for World War III; and by the late 1940s, these plans included preparations for a Soviet nuclear strike against the United States. Thus Cold War civil defense planning posed the much more daunting problem of fighting an imaginary war.

By 1950, the American objective of containing what was perceived to be an otherwise irresistible expansion of Soviet power was tied to the strategy of nuclear deterrence. If the Soviets threatened war in Europe, the United States would guarantee peace, if necessary by nuclear retaliation against the Soviet homeland.[3] Deterrence depended on the Soviet conviction that the United States would respond to an attack on Western Europe with atomic weapons: If the armored divisions of the Red Army moved through the Fulda Gap, atomic bombs would fall on Moscow and Leningrad. As students of the early Cold War have stressed for some years, this policy was based on domestic prerequisites. It was necessary to rally the country and coordinate its institutions in order to sustain what President John F. Kennedy retrospectively called "a long twilight struggle" in support of a new conception of national security. In the nuclear age, the project of safeguarding American interests would be interminable in principle, unprecedentedly expensive, and uniquely dangerous.

There is a substantial literature on the economic and political requirements of Cold War mobilization,[4] but it has not been generally appreciated that containment by means of deterrence also rested on moral foundations. If the attempt to preserve peace by threatening nuclear war produced the very consequence it was intended to avert, the American people would be required to pay the price ultimately exacted by this strategy. If the price of freedom proved to be nuclear war, would Americans be willing to pay? The answer to this question depended on whether Americans believed that even if deterrence failed, the consequences would still be tolerable. Even if the American threat to counter Soviet provocations by employing atomic bombs led the Soviets to respond in kind, the results would not be catastrophic. Otherwise, American resolve to fight a nuclear war could not be expected to hold.

The instrument chosen to convince the American people to pay the price for the failure of deterrence was civil defense. Americans would accept the risks of nuclear war only if they could be assured that a nuclear attack on their own cities would not be too costly. This depended on a demonstration that at a minimum, they would survive and, following a reasonable interval of reconstruction, return to their familiar preattack lives. The civil defense programs of the 1950s represented an attempt to produce this demonstration by persuading Americans that they could be trained to protect themselves from a nuclear attack. As the government repeatedly admonished, in the event of nuclear war the public would be largely responsible for defending itself. "Civil defense" meant precisely that: the defense of the public by the public. There were two versions of this policy: one official, public, and optimistic; the other unofficial, clandestine, and cynical. The optimistic interpretation held that Americans could actually manage their own survival. The purpose of civil defense was to provide them with the information and training necessary for nuclear crisis management. The cynical interpretation held that although the state could not protect the American people in a nuclear attack and they could not be expected to protect themselves, they could at least be persuaded to believe that self-protection was possible.

There is a sense in which both interpretations advocated the same position, but on the basis of quite different arguments. Optimists supported self-protection because it would work. Cynics supported this policy not because it would work. It would not. But if the public believed in self-protection, the moral underpinnings of American national security would be secure. From the cynical standpoint, civic defense did, indeed, have the purpose of protecting the public, but in a rather circuitous sense. Civil defense would convince Americans that they could protect themselves. This conviction, in turn, would provide the necessary support for deterrence, which would protect the American people by preventing a nuclear war. The real objective of civil defense, then, was not to protect the public in a nuclear attack. This was impossible. Rather, civil defense would forestall such an attack by creating a popular tolerance for deterrence. But Americans would tolerate deterrence only if they believed that in the event of its failure, they would still survive. This meant that it was necessary to promote civil defense not primarily as a means of legitimating deterrence, but as a means of ensuring survival. If civil defense could be marketed on this basis, tolerance for deterrence would follow and the ultimate purpose of civil defense would be achieved.[5]

This book is not a history of American civil defense in the 1950s, and thus it does not attempt to tell a story. On the contrary, it analyzes the relationship of national security and civil defense to civic ethics in the early years of the Cold War. Because the book advances a single extended argument, some comments on how I propose to develop this argument as well as a brief sketch of the plan of the ensuing may be helpful at this point.

Like World War II, nuclear war depended on an uncertain variable: American national will, always a fickle and unpredictable entity for foreign-policy makers. In the early years of the Cold War, American national security was believed to depend on the strength of the American character. As Chapter 1 shows, foreign-policy planners had grave doubts that the American public could pass the test for world leadership in the nuclear era, and these doubts led national security strategists to sketch the lineaments of an ethic appropriate to the demands of the Cold War.

A Cold War ethic would sustain the determination required to risk nuclear war and to form the resolve needed to underpin national security policy. The civil defense programs of the 1950s may be understood as an institutional strategy to forge this ethic and to solve the moral problem posed by the mobilization of the home front for nuclear war. This strategy had three components. Chapter 2 delineates the program of emotion management designed to control American fears of nuclear attack and put them to work in fighting the Cold War. Chapter 3 explores the world of nuclear attack, which civil defense planners envisioned as a large-scale social problem that could be solved by American managerial rationality—careful planning, organization, and training. Chapter 4 reconstructs the production of the Cold War ethic and its basis in the mythology of the home—the ultimate sanctuary of traditional American values, reconceptualized as the final redoubt in World War III. Emotion management would channel public anxieties about nuclear war into civil defense activities, convincing Americans that their fears of annihilation were groundless. The representation of a nuclear attack on the United States as a limited and manageable disaster, not fundamentally different from a flood or a hurricane and amenable to the strategies and tactics of crisis mastery, would persuade Americans that they could protect themselves in such an attack by learning the requisite civil defense procedures and techniques. The construction of an ethic that interpreted civil defense as a moral obligation of every household and construed the practices demanded by family preparedness as civic virtues indispensable to the American way of life in the nuclear age would produce the ultimate moral foundation of national security through nuclear deterrence.

One of the most fascinating aspects of the civil defense program was the tension between the official conception, promoted to the public as self-protection for survival, and the unofficial conception, which held that self-protection was a vain but not utterly futile illusion, useful and even necessary to produce the public resolve necessary to prosecute the Cold War. Chapter 5 examines how the conflict between the official and the unofficial conceptions emerged in the thinking of President Dwight D. Eisenhower and his national security advisers. The concluding remarks trace some of the tensions between liberal propaganda and the strategic premises of Cold War civil defense.[6]

Although my argument is not a narrative, its premises depend on the construction of narratives, exercises in fictionalization that frame the experience and institutions of the American people in stories with morals intended to confirm the assumptions and support the objectives of civil defense: the story of how Americans could be expected to respond to a nuclear attack if they were left to their own devices and not subjected to the discipline of civil defense training; the story of American society under nuclear attack, which formed the basis of the national civil defense preparedness exercises performed between 1954 and 1960; and the story of the American family and the foundation of Cold War civic ethics in domestic life that was articulated in the civil defense home-protection manuals of the 1950s.

Construed most narrowly, this study examines selected aspects of civil defense policy in the Truman and Eisenhower presidencies. Viewed more generally, it analyzes certain features of the moral and institutional history of the first decade of the Cold War in America. Construed most generously, it charts some of the connections that link public policy, propaganda, marketing, and public ethics in American society. The declaration of the end of the Cold War became an instant media cliché, whose banality obscured the institutionalization of Cold War culture in American life—a process that cannot be expected to end with the dramatic finality of the fall of the Berlin Wall or the collapse of the Soviet Union. If this study can claim a relevance beyond the limited scope of the period and the materials it investigates, it is because certain of the consequences of the Cold War remain as powerful forces on the contemporary scene.

1

National Security and National Morale

The Berlin Crisis: The Soviet Threat and Nuclear Strategy

The Berlin blockade of 1948 and 1949 was the first nightmare of post-war American foreign policy planning. The Red Army, it seemed, was poised to overrun Western Europe. America's European allies would be occupied or neutralized, subdued by Soviet power or seduced by Communist ideology. The United States would be forced to maintain a garrison state within its own borders, its economy ruined and its most sacred values destroyed. Although the Cold War did not begin with the Berlin crisis, the blockade was the first conflict with the Soviet Union that led American planners to fear that World War III could be imminent.

Since mid-1947, the Western Allies had been troubled by repeated, although apparently uncoordinated, Soviet provocations—petty harassments that compromised effective administration in the Western sectors of Berlin as well as more consequential challenges that contested the Allies' right to maintain a military and political presence in the city. In the spring and summer of 1947, newspapers controlled by the Soviets began to publish rumors that the Western powers might withdraw from the city, a tactic calculated to discourage Berliners from supporting democratic reforms and Western programs generally. It also raised the worrisome possibility that Berliners perceived as too close to the West or as unacceptably offensive to the Soviets might be subject to reprisals after a Western withdrawal.

In August 1947, the Soviets accused the United States and Britain of plotting to incorporate their sectors of the city into their respective zones of occupation in the western part of Germany. In February 1948, the Soviets prevented British representatives from attending a German political meeting in the Soviet sector, arguing that Berlin as a whole was part of their zone of occupation. Consistent with this doctrine, they also began to control civilian rail traffic between Berlin and western Germany, ostensibly to protect the Soviet zone against penetration by what were termed "subversive and terrorist elements."[1] In March, new restrictions were imposed on Allied traffic between Berlin and western Germany on the grounds that stricter measures were necessary to curtail black-market activity.

On April 1, the commissioners of the Atomic Energy Commission (AEC) were advised that the developing crisis in Berlin might lead to war. Suggestions were entertained to remobilize the civilian atomic-bomb assembly groups that had armed the Hiroshima and Nagasaki bombs at the end of World War II. There was also discussion of recalling to the United States the atomic-bomb assembly teams at the American nuclear-testing area in the South Pacific so that they would be available for duty in Europe in the event of a military emergency. Finally, some consideration was even given to postponing the upcoming SANDSTONE tests of a new type of mass-producible atomic bomb in order to preserve the nation's modest nuclear stockpile for use in war.[2]

Throughout May and June 1948, the Soviets incrementally increased searches, restrictions on the movement of goods and persons, and interference with Allied personnel. They also began to limit Allied air access to Berlin and to suspend food deliveries to the Western sectors of the city. On June 18, the Western Allies published the first currency-reform law for Germany, which was applicable to the Western zones of occupation but not to Berlin. Following this announcement, events moved swiftly. The Soviets responded on the same day with new traffic restrictions in Berlin, allegedly to protect their zone of occupation from an influx of devalued currency. On the next day, the Soviet military governor of Berlin declared that the entire city was part of the Soviet zone, and on June 21 and 22 the Soviets announced currency reforms that would apply to their own zone, which now would include Berlin. On June 23, the Western military governors answered by introducing the new Western currency into the three Western sectors of the city.

On June 24, the Soviet blockade began. Passenger rail travel to and from the Soviet zone was suspended. All official Western vehicles were refused entry into the Soviet zone. Even pedestrian traffic from west to east was interdicted. Since most of the electricity for Berlin was produced by plants located in the eastern part of the city and the Soviet zone, the Western sectors of the city lost most of their electric power. The Soviets also announced that all food transported to Berlin from eastern Germany would be distributed only in the Soviet sector, which left the Western sectors without dairy products as well as fresh meat and vegetables.

On June 25, General Lucius Clay, the American military governor of Germany, decided to transport essential supplies to the Western sectors of the city from air bases in western Germany. Thus began the celebrated airlift, which quickly became a central motif in the political mythology of the Cold War and an early source of nostrums concerning the payoffs of standing up to Soviet intransigence. Less celebrated, although not unnoticed, was President Harry S Truman's decision, made only three days after the airlift began, to send two B-29 squadrons to Germany. By June 30, there were thirty B-29s at American air bases in Germany. On July 15, the National Security Council (NSC) decided to send sixty B-29s to bases in Great Britain.[3] Although the *New York Times* described the flight of the B-29s to Britain as a routine training mission, every policy maker in the East and the West knew that the superfortress was the aircraft that had dropped the atomic bombs on Japan.[4] Indeed, it was the only aircraft in the American inventory that could be outfitted for atomic weapons.

The dispatch of B-29s to bases in Britain and Germany could be understood as sending a variety of messages. It demonstrated to Berliners and western Germans that the Western Allies, and the Americans in particular, could be relied on to stand firm in their commitments to the German people regardless of Soviet intimidation. It indicated to the American people the seriousness of the Berlin crisis and its possibilities for igniting a war with the Soviet Union. Finally, it could be interpreted in several ways by the Soviets. The flight of the B-29s was an early and important reversal in the postwar military demobilization of the United States and represented a significant increase in its retaliatory forces, which were negligible during 1946 and 1947. The American decision on the B-29s also suggested that any Soviet measures beyond those already taken would not be tolerated by the Western Allies. If the Soviets made further efforts to dominate Western Europe, they risked the atomic bombing of their cities. In order to protect Western Europe from Communism, it was necessary to save Berlin from Soviet domination. To counter the Soviet attempt to absorb Berlin into the Communist bloc, it was necessary for the United States to insist on its rights of occupation and access. In order to secure these rights, the United States was prepared to risk World War III, in which the Soviet Union would be threatened with atomic bombs.

In Cologne, the *Rheinische Zeitung* articulated this last and most serious message with unmistakable clarity. The paper noted pointedly that the Soviet foreign minister, V. M. Molotov, was "not likely to forget that the 90 Superfortresses stationed in Germany, when loaded with atom bombs, represent a destructive force which is four times as great as the entire Air Force of the United States in the Second World War."[5] According to this view, the B-29s demonstrated the absolute determination of President Truman and Secretary of State George C. Marshall to defend the American presence in Berlin regardless of the consequences.

In a secret telegram dated July 20, three days after the arrival of the B-29s in Britain, Marshall explained this policy to his ambassador in London. In order to protect its rights in Berlin, the United States was willing "to use any means that may be necessary." The presence of the Western Allies in Berlin and their occupational and supply duties in the Western sectors of the city were guaranteed by "unquestioned right." Marshall insisted that there were no circumstances under which the United States could be forced to withdraw, "whatever methods may be employed by the Soviet Military Commander." Although the United States did not want war, it could not tolerate indefinitely provocations and brazen encroachments on its military rights and obligations. Indeed, Marshall warned darkly that "methods of coercion, irrespective of their motivation, obviously can lead to war if the Government applying such methods continues to pursue them to the end."[6]

The military component of the policy to employ any means necessary to defend the American position in Berlin was a Joint Chiefs of Staff (JCS) plan produced in December 1948 and based on the assumption of a war with the Soviet Union during the Berlin airlift. A major premise of the plan was the use of atomic weapons "to the extent determined to be practicable and desirable." The principal targets of the American atomic offensive were seventy Soviet cities, whose destruction was expected to "cripple" Soviet industry as well as communication and control networks.[7]

In sum, the Berlin crisis focused the attention of American national security planners on the importance of countering Soviet expansion. In response to the Soviet blockade, the United States took advantage of its nuclear monopoly to discourage Soviet military action unacceptable to the West. Although the United States was not willing to go to war to break the blockade, it was willing to risk war by undertaking the airlift. American atomic bombs were not used against the Soviets to break the blockade. That was the purpose of the airlift. Rather, the United States employed its nuclear monopoly as a threat to prevent the Soviets from interdicting the airlift.

The atomic bomb seemed an ideal solution to the problem of checking the Soviet Union without incurring the immense costs, unacceptable on both political and economic grounds, of engaging the Red Army with comparable conventional forces. In 1948, American officials transposed an argument that linked economic welfare, national will, and the capacity for national defense from the sphere of international relations to the internal conditions for American national security. In 1947, American leaders had attempted to assess Europe's recovery from World War II. The question was whether the European nations, weakened by war and threatened by political disintegration and economic collapse, would be able to thwart Communist aggression and subversion. The assumption was that economic prosperity, public morale, and the capacity for national defense were closely connected.[8] Nations with debilitating economic problems might lose confidence, not only in the future, but in themselves as well. This would result in political impotence and the inability to resist Soviet intimidation. Prosperous nations, however, would develop a self-confident public spirit and a will to defend themselves against enemies, external or internal.

In 1948, American leaders brought this argument home to the United States, ironically the nation on which they were counting in some desperation to rebuild Europe. In the plan for European recovery framed in Washington, it was American economic goods and political resolve that would inspire the Europeans—economically prostrate, politically unstable, and psychologically intimidated—to save themselves from Communism. But what about the American economy, which had forged the arsenal of democracy in World War II and was expected to propel the economic forces that would achieve postwar prosperity? If the American economy were undermined, the United States could not play its pivotal role in the new international order. Indeed, given the relations among economic growth, national will, and national defense postulated by American leaders, a weakened American economy would leave the United States itself defenseless.

There were no military Keynesians among Truman's principal advisers in the White House, the Treasury, and the Bureau of the Budget. Chief among the fiscal conservatives in the Truman administration was the president himself. Three considerations were especially troubling to Truman and his financial advisers: the huge public debt incurred during World War II, the high rate of postwar inflation, and fears that the country might lapse back into a depression.

These factors led Truman to make a balanced budget one of the primary objectives of his presidency. In the words of Secretary of Defense James Forrestal, Truman was a "hard-money man," intent on presiding over an administration that would balance its budgets and even generate surpluses that could be used to reduce the national debt and control postwar inflation. Military expenditures would weaken rather than strengthen the economy. From the standpoint of Washington officialdom in 1948, there were two ways to finance large postwar military budgets: high taxation and deficit spending. Both were regarded as unacceptable. If a larger defense bill were paid with higher taxes, the risk would be a recession and possibly even the return of a depression. Higher taxes would also impose burdensome federal regulations on the economy. The result would be socialism and a garrison state; in other words, the destruction of the American work ethic and its entrepreneurial spirit—the demise of the American way of life that the government was attempting to save by waging the Cold War. But if higher defense costs were covered by deficit financing and printing more money, the risk would be inflation. Sustained deficit spending would produce chronic economic instability and, in the long run, might even bankrupt the economy. Such a policy would be even more dangerous than the external threat of Communist aggression. In grappling with the problem of financing national security, Truman and his advisers therefore faced a dilemma. In the presidential campaign of 1948, Truman not only promised a $15 billion limit on defense spending, but even claimed that the economy could not sustain military expenditures in excess of that amount.[9] The economy was the engine of national prosperity and security, and excessive defense spending would damage this engine, perhaps irreparably. The victory of the United States in World War II was due primarily to its ability to exceed the combined production of both its adversaries. Higher levels of defense spending would squander the economic resources of the nation, which meant that the next war, if it came, would surely be lost.

In light of these strictures, what means for countering the Soviets were at the disposal of the American military establishment? In the face of presidential as well as congressional diffidence concerning defense spending, the military interpreted its objective as the achievement of American national security within narrow fiscal limits that ruled out the expansion of conventional forces. Under these circumstances, there seemed to be only one way to oppose the Soviet threat: the atomic bomb. The Joint Chiefs argued that Truman's $15 billion ceiling would not provide the resources needed for a large-scale, World War II–style response to a Soviet offensive. That is, within the limits of Truman's budget, the United States would be reduced to lobbing atomic bombs at the Soviet Union from distant air bases in Britain and Egypt—assuming that it retained sufficient manpower to protect these facilities. In short, the American perception of the Soviet threat to Western Europe, Truman's hard-money policy, and the inability of the White House, Congress, and the military establishment to reach an agreement on the means for financing a conventional defense of Western Europe made the atomic bomb the keystone of American national security.[10] In 1948, the atomic bomb emerged as the first of many subsequent American attempts during the Cold War to get a bigger bang for the buck.

Nuclear weapons delivered by long-range bombers made it possible to subject a nation to virtually instantaneous and unparalleled destruction. The military forces of an adversary would be powerless to repel

such an attack, which meant that the United States could horribly damage the Soviet Union without defeating, or even opposing, its formidable army. Finally, all this could be achieved without initiating an
elaborate and expensive mobilization of human and material resources.
A credible threat to punish the Soviet Union by means of atomic bombs
could be detached from much less intimidating threats to engage
its vast forces in the field; this meant that the threat to punish could
serve as a means of inhibiting behavior unacceptable to the United
States. Therefore, it seemed that nuclear weapons were the ideal deterrent to Soviet probes, incursions, or general assaults into areas regarded by American leaders as lying outside a tolerated sphere of Soviet
influence.

The atomic bomb would not be flaunted aggressively. In the colorful language of James F. Byrnes, Truman's first Secretary of State,
the bomb was "the gun behind the door": As long as your adversary
knew you had it, he would be restrained from acting contrary to your
declared interests even if you did not use it.[11] At least this argument
could be taken seriously as long as the United States enjoyed a monopoly on nuclear weapons. Without their own nuclear weapons, the
Soviets could not respond in kind, thereby neutralizing the American
nuclear deterrent by nullifying the ability of the United States to make
good on its threats.

This reasoning—a strategy of deterring Soviet aggression by relying
on the atomic bomb—was employed by the NSC in 1948. In response
to the Communist takeover of Czechoslovakia and the Berlin crisis, the
NSC began work in May 1948 on a policy governing the use of nuclear
weapons. Its deliberations were concluded on September 10 with NSC
30, "United States Policy on Atomic Warfare." This was the first postwar U.S. government document to approve the use of atomic bombs
in warfare. Following a tortuously scholastic discussion of the conditions under which the use of atomic weapons should or should not
become a matter of public deliberation, the authors of NSC 30 decided
to withdraw this issue from public debate. Although there would be an
official policy on the use of atomic weapons, it would not be made
public. The NSC's reasoning on this point was tied to its view of the
bomb's deterrent value. The Soviets should not be given

> the slightest reason to believe that the U.S. would even consider not to use
> atomic weapons against them if necessary. It might take no more than a
> suggestion of such consideration, perhaps magnified into a doubt, were it
> planted in the minds of responsible Soviet officials, to provoke exactly that
> Soviet aggression which it is fundamentally U.S. policy to avert.[12]

According to this view, the B-29s in Britain and Germany demonstrated the boldness of American policy, enhanced the credibility of
the American atomic threat, and compensated for the modest size of

the American atomic arsenal. In fact, no atomic bombs made the flight across the Atlantic. The B-29s sent to Britain and Germany were not loaded with atomic bombs, and these aircraft had not been outfitted so that they were—in the air force jargon of the time—"atomic capable." But even if the B-29s had been suitably modified, the entire inventory of atomic bombs in the American arsenal during the summer of 1948 was too small to supply even one bomb for each of the B-29s in Europe. At the height of the Berlin crisis, the United States possessed only about fifty atomic weapons, none of which had been assembled. Finally, there were no atomic bombs in either Germany or Britain throughout the entire Berlin crisis. Thus the United States could not have acted on its implicit threat to respond to further Soviet belligerence in Germany by using atomic weapons.[13]

When the airlift continued without Soviet military interference, however, officials at the highest levels of the Truman administration concluded that the American atomic deterrent had produced its intended effect. Marshall claimed that "Soviet officials must now realize that the use of this instrument would be possible and hence the deterrent influence now [is] perhaps greater than before."[14] As Forrestal noted, Marshall thought that "the Soviets are beginning to realize for the first time that the United States would be ready to use the atomic bomb against them in the event of war."[15] Truman was considerably less restrained, going so far as to maintain that without the American atomic deterrent, "the Russians would probably have taken over Europe a long time ago."[16]

The Soviet Atomic Bomb: Nuclear Strategy and National Will

But what if the American atomic deterrent and the alleged willingness of the Truman administration to use the atomic bomb in a war over Berlin had been confronted by a Soviet atomic arsenal and counterthreats by the Soviets to deploy against the United States the same weapons the Americans contemplated using against them? Without its nuclear monopoly, would America have been ready to risk war over Berlin? In the words of Forrestal, the period framed by the American nuclear monopoly marked the "years of opportunity" for American foreign policy. If the American economy could outproduce the world, if its navy could secure sea-lanes for international trade, and if its leaders could threaten enemies of the new international order with the atomic bomb, then the United States would be able to adopt an aggressive foreign policy and assume otherwise unacceptable risks in rebuilding the world economy and restoring the balance of power.[17] What would happen when the years of opportunity ended and the Soviets developed their own atomic weapons? Would Americans possess the determination needed to face the extraordinary dangers of a permanent crisis in national security if these dangers included the possibility of a nuclear attack on the United States? When the years of opportunity lapsed, would American policy makers still be prepared to counter Soviet moves with the same confidence?

In December 1947, the Joint Strategic Plans Committee of the JCS drew up the "Estimate of Probable Developments in the World Political Situation up to 1957" as a guide for military planning. The "Estimate" accurately predicted that international efforts to control atomic energy would fail, producing a nuclear arms race of indefinite duration: "The increasing probability that at least two opposed nations will possess atomic weapons by the middle of the period, will probably result in a tense and excitable state of world public opinion—possibly in a species of world hysteria—wherein minor political incidents are exaggerated into political crises."[18] Would American firmness hold when the comparatively comfortable period of nuclear monopoly was transformed into an unpredictable race with the Soviet Union for supremacy in nuclear weapons? What was the relation between national security and national will in American life? If national security depended on the resolve of the American people to support the containment of Soviet expansion by means of nuclear deterrence, how would they respond when they discovered that the ultimate cost of deterrence might be the atomic bombing of their own cities? American policy makers had good reason to think seriously about these questions in the autumn of 1949.

On Monday, September 19, 1949, a panel of American atomic-energy experts concluded that the fission isotopes in radioactive samples picked up by U.S. Air Force reconnaissance flights over the North Pacific were indeed products of a Soviet atomic test. The age, composition, and dispersion of hundreds of fission samples collected over a wide expanse of the Northern Hemisphere indicated a single large fission reaction. As Robert Oppenheimer wrote in his draft of the panel's report, the evidence was "consistent with the view that the origin of the fission products was the explosion of an atomic bomb on August 29."[19] The Soviet Union had developed its own atomic bomb.

The problems posed by the Soviet atomic bomb were immediately apparent to American officials. Indeed, in 1946, Arnold Wolfers had already produced a brilliant and prescient analysis of the implications of Soviet atomic weapons for American national security. Wolfers argued that when Soviet military technology reached the nuclear threshold, the result would be a "truly revolutionary change" in the military predicament of the United States. From the late nineteenth century to 1945, American national security was guaranteed by several factors. Continental isolation and the protection afforded by thousands of miles of ocean separated the United States from its nearest potential adversaries. A strong navy and the ability to mobilize vast industrial resources meant that even when it was necessary for the United States to enter wars, it could do so largely on the strength of its economic assets, using human surrogates supplied by other nations. Because these engagements transpired on foreign battlefields, the United States did not suffer the collateral destruction that occurs in any war. But a Soviet nuclear force would destroy these traditional bases of American security and bring this period of military history, with all its advantages for the United States, to a terrifyingly swift conclusion. America might be able to avoid future military defeats, but it would never be able to fight a major war without risking the devastation of its population and the destruction of its economy. The result, Wolfers contended, was profoundly unsettling. America was emerging from a unique position of geographically and economically guaranteed security into "a kind of earthquake zone which will be rendered livable for our urban populations only by the hope and confidence that the outbreak of another war will be prevented."[20]

On October 12, some three weeks after the detection of the Soviet atomic device, the State Department Policy Planning Staff was apprised of the military consequences of a Soviet atomic threat. The Policy Planning Staff was told that if the Soviets, armed with atomic weapons, were able to occupy Western Europe, then the United States would not be able to marshal the forces required to expel them from the continent. The result would be a stalemate, the prolongation of which would not favor the United States. This meant that it was necessary to avert a Soviet invasion of Western Europe, which the United States could not do with conventional armaments. The only alternative was to threaten the Soviets with nuclear weapons should they contemplate such an invasion. As a deterrent, how effective would such a threat be? The certainty of nuclear retaliation would not prevent the Soviet Union from using its own atomic bombs if this seemed to be the course dictated by pragmatics and national interest. Although the question of whether the United States would actually resort to atomic weapons in war had never been definitively resolved, the dependence of American military strategy on the atomic bomb apparently made this question moot. The use of atomic weapons by the United States in a major war with the Soviet Union was regarded as "almost a foregone conclusion."[21] Thus the unfolding political and military logic of the Cold War appeared to reveal the horrifying prospect of a third world war waged with atomic bombs.

A month later, on November 16, 1949, Air Force Chief of Staff Hoyt Vandenberg delivered the judgment that in only a few years the Soviets would have a large stockpile of atomic weapons. With fifty or sixty, they could strike the United States with deadly effect.[22]

In January 1950, a JCS paper, "Need of Defense Measures Against Increasing Threat of Atomic Attack Against the Continental United

States," maintained that the Soviet atomic bomb marked a watershed in American military history, comparable to Pearl Harbor and Hiroshima. It considered the possibility that the atomic bomb, which the United States had used to end World War II, might in the future be turned against the United States "in a new type of Pearl Harbor attack of infinitely greater magnitude than that of 1941."[23] In a few months, the Soviets would have 10 to 20 atomic bombs, a stockpile that would increase to between 70 and 135 by mid-1953. A parallel report by the Central Intelligence Agency (CIA) claimed that the Soviets would have 100 Nagasaki-type bombs by 1953 and 200 by the end of 1955. The CIA judged that the delivery of 200 such weapons on selected American targets could completely destroy the economic and political structure of the United States.[24]

On January 31, 1950, President Truman called for a reassessment of American national security objectives in light of the Soviet atomic bomb and the new dangers it posed for the United States.[25] This reexamination became one of the most important documents of the Cold War: NSC 68, innocuously entitled "A Report to the President Pursuant to the President's Directive of January 31, 1950." Nuclear war with the Soviet Union was a somber theme repeated throughout NSC 68, like the baseline of a Verdian tragedy. The Soviet Union was said to have a substantial atomic stockpile and the means to launch "devastating surprise attacks on certain vital centers of the United States and Canada."[26] The uncompromising Communist ideology of world mastery and the Soviet acquisition of atomic weapons meant that "every individual faces the ever-present possibility of annihilation."

The conjunction of the international Communist movement and a Soviet nuclear-weapons program marked a unique moment in history. In the Cold War, the United States was engaged in a deadly "total struggle" in which it risked "total defeat" at the hands of a totalitarian power.[27] Not only American security but also the fate of civilization itself rested in the balance.

Were Americans prepared to resist Soviet expansion under these dramatically altered conditions? After September 1949, every American scenario for the use of nuclear weapons was based on the answer to this question. Deterrence depended on the credibility of the American nuclear threat. The plausibility of the claim that Soviet bad behavior would be punished with atomic bombs rested on the assumption that the United States was prepared to back up this claim, despite the prospects of Soviet nuclear retaliation. Did Americans have the resolve to fight a nuclear war and suffer its consequences? After September 1949, deterrence entailed the possibility that the Soviets might counter American attempts at intimidation by launching a nuclear attack of their own. Such a response might be based on a variety of perceptions and motives. Perhaps the United States could be defeated in a surprise attack, an atomic Pearl Harbor. Or perhaps the Soviet Union, because it could not sustain a protracted economic and technological struggle with the United States, would strike before such a contest began to take its toll on the Soviet economy. Were Americans ready to assume these risks?

There were, of course, methods for handling the grim possibility of a Soviet first strike, but they would subject Americans to new and harrowing tests of resolve. For example, the United States might launch a preemptive strike against Soviet airpower and other nuclear-delivery forces. When alerted to an imminent attack, Americans bombers would destroy most of the Soviet air force on the ground. As a result, the Soviets would face the unimpeded destruction of their cities and their economy, which would vastly reduce their ability to damage the United States. Such a maneuver was calculated to discourage the Soviets from launching a nuclear offensive, by reducing its attractiveness to the vanishing point. If the United States could employ this tactic, however, so could the Soviet Union. Under these circumstances, would the United States demonstrate the fortitude to do so? An American commitment to this stratagem would give the Soviets the best of reasons to adopt a preemptive first-strike doctrine of their own. Indeed, it would be essential in order to preempt the putative preemptor. Did Americans have the nerves for this sort of gamble?

National Security and the Problem of National Will

These questions raised the issue of the moral prerequisites of the United States' national security policy. In the parlance of the time, this issue was conceived as a problem of national will or morale, a matter of considerable apprehension on the part of American leaders in the early years of the Cold War. The attempt by the United States to exercise global power and to secure world peace in its contest with the Soviet Union depended on its ability to project a credible threat to fight a nuclear war. The plausibility of this threat was based on the moral resources of the American people. Did they possess the resolution to face the new perils of the Cold War? Were they prepared to make the hard sacrifices that would be exacted in a nuclear war? National security planners were not optimistic about the answers to these questions. Their doubts were grounded in a severe judgment of the American character. Americans were childish and selfish. Because of their addiction to pleasure, they had become frivolous and irresponsible. A life of mindless consumption had led to moral corruption and decadence. Americans were weak, lacking the toughness needed to oppose a powerful and ruthless enemy in the hazardous world of the Cold War.

Henry L. Stimson

This contemptuous view of the American public was part of the cultural capital of the postwar national security establishment and one of the key premises in a compendium of moral assumptions that underpinned the planning of the Cold War. It was originally expressed in the Olympian rhetoric of Henry L. Stimson's valedictory to the Truman cabinet as Secretary of War. In his final remarks to the cabinet on September 7, 1945, Stimson observed with immense satisfaction that the United States had just brought a great war to a victorious conclusion. The courage of its people as citizens and soldiers was universally acknowledged. But, Stimson reminded the cabinet, this was not the conception of the American people that generally prevailed in peacetime. On the contrary, the conventional view of the American character, which Stimson attributed largely to movies and newspapers, was decidedly unflattering.

The United States was typically perceived as a "frivolous, selfish, pleasure loving country which did not take the business of living in a rough international world seriously." As a result, potential adversaries repeatedly underestimated American patriotism and courage. Stimson warned the cabinet that this perception was not far from the truth. The American drift into isolationism following World War I was the consequence of a public spirit of hedonism and irresponsibility, an unwillingness to measure up to the serious demands of the times. The formation of the Axis powers, Japan's assault on Pearl Harbor, and Germany's ultimate plans to attack the United States all could be traced, at least in part, to these peacetime tendencies of American life. Isolationism in foreign policy was an expression of public indifference and moral weakness. Because the enemies of the United States understood this, they concluded that "we were too engrossed in lives of pleasure and internal interest and too oblivious of what was going on in the outside world to be of any account in their calculations." If this peacetime ethos of civic apathy and private self-indulgence persisted, it would result in a dangerous misconception on the part of other nations:

> They will not only regard us as unprepared, which will be true, but they will also regard us as too irresponsible ever to take the trouble to prepare or to defend ourselves. They will form the same impression of our young men that our movies and our other peacetime expressions regularly give them.

This meant that it was necessary to transform the peacetime ethic of American life and at the same time demonstrate to the world that Americans took their public obligations seriously. A hard school was required, in which Americans would learn to practice in peacetime the more stringent virtues they needed to avoid war. The stakes, Stimson argued, could not be higher. Because the United States had become the leader of the world, "it is of enormous importance that the real character of America should be understood." The ability of the United States to assume the position of world leadership depended on how seriously the country took this role and "what she is willing to sacrifice to make it a success."[28]

In Stimson's farewell address, it is not clear whether hedonism, decadence, and irresponsibility are distinctive features of the American character, fabrications of the press and the film industry that misrepresent the American ethic, or consequences of the impact of newspapers and movies on American life. These uncertainties are resolved in a pessimistic fashion in the more pejorative reflections on American civic ethics by two of the most influential members of the postwar national security elite. John Foster Dulles and George F. Kennan, otherwise antagonistic in their views on how to achieve American security in the emerging international order, had made similar assumptions about the moral laxity of their fellow citizens and its impact on the American position in world affairs.

John Foster Dulles

After 1945, John Foster Dulles was the most authoritative voice on foreign policy in the Republican party. During the 1948 presidential campaign, he was New York Governor Thomas E. Dewey's principal foreign policy adviser and his presumptive Secretary of State. In 1950, Dulles wrote a little book entitled *War or Peace*, which outlined his suggestions on how to avoid war with the Soviet Union. Dulles painted a troubling picture of American society, strikingly ill-equipped to face the new challenges posed by the end of World War II. The public mood was fearful. For the first time in its history, the nation seemed on the defensive. How had this happened? The answer was "materialism." The American dependence on things material, which Dulles did not specify more closely or analyze in more detail, had led to a variety of infirmities: intellectual confusion, moral corrosion, a loss of the "spiritual loyalties" that provided the basis for American individualism and its ethic of self-control, and a vulnerability to subversion by hostile forces that would eventually destroy the American way of life.

The ultimate cause of the postwar moral bankruptcy of American life was a loss of religious faith. Four years earlier, Dulles had made his debut as a cold warrior in a two-part *Life* magazine article, in which he stressed the moral and spiritual foundations of American national security and their importance in defeating Communism.[29] This article did not express Dulles's later pessimism concerning the decline of national

moral resolve. However, under a full-page photograph of a Congrega-
tional church service in Plymouth, Massachusetts, complete with an
oversize American flag draped high above the congregation, he urged
that a spiritual rededication was "the most significant demonstration"
that the American people could make to show the Soviet Union that
the United States remained committed to its fundamental principles.[30]

In 1950, Dulles interpreted the collapse of American moral vitality
as the consequence of a cleavage between religion and conduct, faith
and works. This was why contemporary Americans had lost the virtues
that made America great: the commitment to hard work, both as a
matter of duty and a source of self-satisfaction, and the inner discipline
of industry and frugality. What was responsible for this cleavage?

Dulles's answer to this question lay in the decline of the spiritual
strengths that were responsible for American greatness. At one time,
belief in inalienable rights and responsibilities prescribed by a divinely
ordained moral law and commitment to free institutions built on this
spiritual foundation had inspired the American people. These values
created the American destiny, the vision of a unique and divinely in-
vested national mission, which was the source of a "spiritual, intellectual, and economic vigor the like of which the world had never seen."
What had gone wrong? In Dulles's metaphysics of history, the American experiment was ironically done in by its own success. As the country's economic power increased, its spiritual vitality waned. Americans
lost their breadth of vision and sense of mission. "We appeared to be
less concerned with conducting a great experiment for the benefit of
mankind and to be more concerned with piling up for ourselves material advantages." In the end, Americans failed the "severest test that
can come to a people, the test of prosperity."[31]

Dulles interpreted the degradation of American moral standards in
the language of the Puritan paradox of the spirit and the world: the
quest for "the Kingdom of God and His righteousness" and its corruption by wealth, "the rust that corrodes men's souls."[32] A community
inspired by the fervor to do God's will in this world inevitably develops
the virtues essential to material success. A society founded on these
virtues will achieve wealth, even luxury, since it produces but does
not consume the products of its labor. What happens when the spiritual ethic of industry and frugality confronts the affluence it has un-
intentionally but inevitably created? Dulles's answer recalls Max
Weber's interpretation of the relation between the Protestant ethic and
the spirit of capitalism, as well as John Wesley's homily on the paradoxical relation between piety and mundane success. According to
Wesley:

> I fear, wherever riches have increased, the essence of religion has de-
> creased in the same proportion. Therefore I do not see how it is possible,

in the nature of things, for any revival of true religion to continue long. For religion must necessarily produce both industry and frugality, and these cannot but produce riches. But as riches increase, so will pride, anger, and love of the world in all its branches.[33]

The material products of the spiritual energies of life acquire a new moral status. No longer insignificant and unimportant by-products, they become the end and purpose of life itself.

Thus for Dulles, the history of the American character was a tragedy. The inner dynamic of the religious ethic that had animated the original American dream had destroyed itself. The spiritual energies that had created the American character had led to an accumulation of wealth that sapped these same energies. As a result, the old American ethic of spirituality became, in the ironic phrase Max Weber used to characterize the tragedy of Protestant asceticism, "the power which ever seeks the good but ever creates evil." By fostering an ethos of materialism, commercial life pursued according to the regime of the spiritual ethic corrupted the moral conduct that this regime demanded. The moral qualities grounded in this ethic, the virtues of individual initiative and personal accountability, were inevitably weakened. This meant that American national security, which ultimately rested on these same virtues, was also undermined.

George F. Kennan

In his pronouncements on American moral decline, his contempt for the quality of American public life, and his disdain for the ordinary American, George F. Kennan was unquestionably the most unrestrained member of the national security establishment during the early years of the Cold War. Soviet specialist, architect of the early containment policy, and State Department foreign policy strategist, Kennan, reflecting on the same questions, reached conclusions about the problem of American national will strikingly parallel to those of Dulles. However, Kennan's views were based on quite different premises. If Dulles's moral pessimism represented a theological conception of American history as a struggle between the forces of light and darkness, spirituality and materialism, Kennan's pessimism expressed a lament for the passing of the old middle class of independent farmers, merchants, and craftsmen and a nostalgic veneration for its typical locus, the small town and the village of the early twentieth century. Kennan was convinced of the superior virtues of this class and their importance in maintaining the characteristic traditions and institutions of American life.

What were the moral imperatives of American national security? What ethical conditions had to be satisfied in order for the United States to prevail in the Cold War? In facing the Soviet challenge, what strengths did Americans require? What weaknesses would prove fatal in the struggle with Communism? Writing in the early 1950s on his reencounter with American life after nearly twenty-five years as a diplomat posted in various European cities, Kennan thought he had the answers to these questions. He knew what the Cold War would exact from the American people. To his dismay, he also knew why they would fail to measure up to its demands. Kennan was persuaded that the most important factor in deciding the outcome of the Cold War was the quality of American civilization, its "spiritual distinction."[34] The quality of a civilization was determined by the moral character of its people, and the moral character required to persevere in the Cold War demanded self-discipline, resolution, and a willingness to face hardships and accept sacrifices.

In Kennan's judgment, it was quite unlikely that his fellow citizens would meet the heroic demands of this ethic. This was because of the deterioration in the quality of American life produced by the distinctive processes of modernization: the growth of population, industrialization, urbanization, and commercialization. The main objection to modernization did not lie in these processes themselves, which were not intrinsically pernicious. Rather, the modernization of American life was objectionable because of its pace and scope. In the United States, modernization occurred in an uncontrolled and unfettered fashion. Admitting no limits, it was unconstrained by traditions and established values. The real American vice was not modernity but excess, which compromised discipline, diminished the capacity for self-control, and enfeebled the moral faculties generally.

In Kennan's diagnosis of the American psyche, it was above all the city that represented the decline of ethical standards. In the late winter of 1950—at the same time his conferees at State and Defense were laboring over the successive drafts of NSC 68 that would substantially modify his view of containment—Kennan was dispatched on a journey by train from Washington to Mexico City. His chief observations on this voyage across America were devoted to the American city as a place of unqualified corruption. In Kennan's mind, the ultimate moral antithesis of the city was the small, independently owned and managed farm. The farm is a source of physical and emotional health, practical wisdom, and communal responsibility. Farm life also expresses the harmony between humanity and nature cultivated by a respect for the land. Without self-imposed limits on greed and rapacity, the moral equilibrium represented by the farm would be impossible. Kennan conceived of the farm as a fragile artifact of civilization that establishes a wholesome relation among its animals, the land, and its human inhabitants, who find there comfort, coziness, and reassurance.[35]

Upon waking in his sleeping compartment to the pale reflections of an early Sunday morning in February, Kennan recorded in his diary that a farm, "secure in its humility and its submission," can stand the chill light of a winter dawn. For the city, however, the dawn is "sinister and pitiless," exposing its pretenses, its ugliness and transience. As his train passed through an anonymous city—"what city I did not know, nor did it matter"—Kennan noticed only the oily scum on the water, the "desolation of factories and cinder-yards and railroad tracks," and the "mute slabs" of skyscrapers.[36] The trouble with the American city seems to be the trouble with the American spirit—its debasement by unlimited growth, immoderate change, and their consequences: waste, destruction, and the abandonment of what is solid, traditional, and stable.

Kennan's passage through urban America is a lamentation on the degradation of life and the corruption of the soul produced by the city. St. Louis is represented by seedy-looking men leaning against closed, dilapidated storefronts; the slime on the gray water of the Mississippi River; sooty old buildings; "grotesque decay"; shabby lots "strewn with indecent skeletons" of blight, debris, and befoulment.[37] The picture is even more dismal in Chicago, where Kennan travels a year later to deliver his celebrated lectures on American diplomacy. Again, he arrives by train on a Sunday. His stomach is queasy; the taxi is battered and dirty; his hotel is a pile of "besooted ornateness, springing like a mushroom out of a sea of cinder lots, traffic, filling stations, and long streets of one-floor brick saloons."[38] To Kennan, the morals of the people seem to reproduce the filth and revulsion of their surroundings. In a park, two soldiers attempt to pick up a pair of unkempt young women, who respond to their suitors with a stream of profanity. A boy on an embankment heaves fist-size, skull-splitting rocks at a child below. Kennan takes refuge in a drugstore to order lunch. As luck would have it, the soda-fountain counter is dirty, no one waits on him, and a man with a broom pushes a heap of refuse under his feet. In a Fellini-like daze, overwhelmed by the indecency and brutality he has witnessed, Kennan gives up and wanders back to his hotel, depressed, troubled by his lack of confidence in his people, and in despair of his country.

Thus did the philosopher-diplomat conceive the passing of the small town of his youth, or at least of his fantasies: the seat of the old middle class and the virtues of republican culture. And yet when Kennan encountered actual human specimens of small-town life—as opposed to idealized citizens of the mythological towns of his imagination—he was more often than not appalled. In a young Missouri state politician, luckily unaware that he had been fixed by Kennan's merciless anthropological scrutiny, he is able to detect intellectual confusion, ignorance bordering on moral irresponsibility, a lack of inhibition and reserve, an absence of conviction and principles, a "bewildered complacency," and a "restless vacuous curiosity." Encountering a cit-

izen of Indiana, Kennan is repelled by mindless vulgarity, a lack of
restraint and propriety, crude provincialism, and plain bad manners—
evidence of the collapse of an entire moral culture.[39] It seems that these
representatives of America, caught at mid-century under Kennan's un-
forgiving gaze, have already been irredeemably corrupted by the city.

It was not the older cities of the Middle West, however, that epi-
tomized for Kennan the decay of American moral life but southern
California, which he saw as the apotheosis of a new American impotence. Like so many others, Kennan went to California and found the
future of America. Unlike so many others, he did not experience California as a new promised land where the problems of the future would
either disappear or find their solution. On the contrary, California represented the moral abyss of the future, made more imperceptible and
terrible by its seductive comforts and lack of hardship. Here the experiment in self-government would come to an inglorious and contempt-
ible end as a result of the collapse of its moral foundations. Kennan's
California was characterized by three features that anticipated what he
saw as definitive tendencies of American life in the twentieth century:
"motorization," freedom from political restraint, and freedom from
want.

California represented the zenith of the motorization of America,
where dependence on the automobile for the performance of virtually
all activities had become most complete. In southern California, "the
revolutionary process of motorization has made a clean sweep of all
the patterns of living and has overcome all competition." Established
communities and forms of life were disrupted by the automobile and
the transformations it effected. The "abject dependence" created by the
universalization of automobile transportation led to an impairment of
human faculties and potentialities. Powers of reflection were anesthe-
tized and emotional sensibilities distorted. Californians became both
helpless and thoughtless and, in the long run, increasingly childlike:
"fun-loving, quick to laughter and enthusiasm, unanalytical, unintel-
lectual, outwardly expansive, preoccupied with physical beauty and
prowess," unpredictably and capriciously aggressive, driven by the protection of status through conformity, "and yet not unhappy." In the
California dream of eternal youth and beauty, Kennan saw the American dream of "childhood without the promise of maturity."[40] Faced
with hardship and crisis, the children of the sun, being only children,
would be found wanting. Individual autonomy and civic responsibility,
the paramount virtues of the American liberal tradition, were finished.
A newer and softer breed of American, incapable of meeting the harder
and more exacting standards of that tradition, would pursue a life of
mindless self-indulgence and ethical shallowness that it called "happiness." Thus was Kennan led to his melancholy view of American

moral culture in the early years of the Cold War as "blind, willful, doomed, and not very interesting."[41]

As early as his famous "Long Telegram" of February 1946 from Moscow, in which Kennan first traced the outlines of the policy of containment, he stressed "the point at which domestic and foreign policies meet" and the sense in which American national security rested on the civic virtues of its people. Here Kennan linked his concerns about the moral resilience of the American people with the question of whether they had the strength required to prevail in the contest with the Soviet Union. In summarizing his view of Soviet international conduct and the policy it called for on the part of the United States, Kennan noted that an adequate response to the Soviet threat depended on the "the health and vigor" of America itself. Pursuing this organic metaphor with considerable abandon, Kennan compared Communism to a "malignant parasite" that can live off only bodies that are already diseased. This meant that national security is not merely a matter of adopting the correct diplomatic and military strategies. It also has a domestic basis and, above all, a moral foundation in the determination and steadfastness of the American people. Every effort to build the "self-confidence, discipline, moral and community spirit of our own people," Kennan argued, "is a diplomatic victory over Moscow worth a thousand diplomatic notes and joint communiqués."[42]

Kennan returned to the issue of the moral requirements of national security in the famous "X" article published in *Foreign Affairs* in 1947. Here the struggle between the United States and the Soviet Union was characterized as a test of the worth of American nationhood. How would this worth be judged? What factors would decide whether the United States could pass the test posed by its postwar challenges? Kennan's answers to these questions were cast in vague allusions to the importance of measuring up to what was best in American traditions and proving that the United States was a great nation actually worth saving. Americans had to prove themselves capable of carrying the heavy burden that history had imposed on them. This called for "spiritual vitality," without which they would be unworthy of "the responsibilities of moral and political leadership that history plainly intended them to bear."[43] In the final analysis, the Cold War was not governed by a Bismarckian *Primat der Aussenpolitik*, an immanent and self-propelling logic of international relations. On the contrary, the role that the United States was destined to play in world affairs depended ultimately on the quality of American society itself and the moral character of its people.

Writing in October 1949 in his capacity as director of the State Department Policy Planning Staff, Kennan prepared a memorandum on the popular appeal of Communist ideology and propaganda. Moving with apparently equal facility between amateur philosophy and armchair sociology, he maintained that the insecurities of contemporary American life and the anxieties expressed by so many Americans could be explained by the breakdown of communities, local neighborhoods, private associations, and families. In all these groups, individuals had formerly found "the illusion of security through the sense of belonging."[44] This illusion was broken by urbanization, the inevitable consequence of the advance of American technology and industry. The growth of the American city destroyed the social formations on which the moral stability and the psychological comforts of American life were based. The result was a crisis in American democracy. Because Americans had lost their moral compass, they were no longer the masters of their own souls. They lacked the will to make the decisions and face the consequences on which their fate depended. A "chasm" had emerged between the national myth of the United States as a society of free and responsible citizens and the political realities of American life. Indeed, Kennan went so far as to claim that the ultimate question of the possibility of America that Lincoln had raised in the darkest days of the Civil War—whether any nation "so conceived and dedicated can long endure"—remained in doubt. But if the foundations of American moral strength had crumbled, how could a new structure of national security be erected? How can we be justified, Kennan asked, "in regarding ourselves as fit for the leadership of others? All our ideas of 'world leadership,' 'the American century,' 'aggressive democracy,' etc. stand or fall with the answer to this question."[45]

Civil Defense and National Will

The link between national will and national security that Dulles and Kennan pondered in an abstract fashion in their reflections on the philosophy of history also entered national security planning in a much more concrete and pragmatic fashion. While Kennan was musing over the moral corruption of American life on his journey from Washington to St. Louis, his colleagues assigned to the national security policy review requested by President Truman were discussing early drafts of NSC 68 with a highly select group of consultants. In these sessions, the unsatisfactory state of the American character and the question of what to do about it were critical issues. A recurrent theme was the challenge to American national resolve represented by Soviet nuclear weapons. What practical measures were required to instill a new sense of purpose in the American people? After reading a draft of NSC 68, Robert Oppenheimer considered with Paul Nitze the problematic relation between national "moral fiber" and national security.[46] In a later meeting, Chester Bernard, management theorist and president of the Rockefeller Foundation, emphasized the importance of marshaling public support for the new risks that NSC 68 would impose on the country in the name of national security. Bernard argued that a major problem in winning this support was deciding how much information about atomic weapons and national security should be made public and how it should be framed.[47]

The signal importance of propaganda that would firm up the resolve of the American people and increase their tolerance for the tough and increasingly dangerous measures contemplated against the Soviet Union was stressed throughout the comments on early drafts of NSC 68. In order to rally the public behind American objectives in the Cold War, the mere release of secret information, even if it included a complete and unsanitized account of the effects of nuclear weapons, would not do. Although it was necessary for Americans to grasp what was at stake in the conflict with the Soviets and why the United States could not afford to lose, this was not sufficient. Their hearts had to be moved as well. In order to equip the American people for this struggle, it was imperative to build up their courage and steadfastness. Only then would they be prepared to assume the risks entailed by the strategy of deterrence.[48]

These ambitious objectives required changes no less sweeping than the reeducation of American moral sensibilities, the regeneration of the allegedly waning spiritual resources of the American people, and the creation of a new civic ethic tailored to the requirements of the Cold War. What were the specific measures by means of which these changes would be accomplished? A two-step strategy was contemplated. The government would initiate a psychological "scare campaign," laying out what the public needed to know about the sobering facts of nuclear war and the hazards America faced in opposing a Soviet Union armed with nuclear weapons. Once the fears of Americans were aroused and they were shaken out of their apathy, the government would move immediately to the second step: a program of "public information" designed to persuade the American people that victory in the Cold War was not merely a matter of which side had the bigger air force, the more powerful nuclear weapons, or the superior military strategy. In the final analysis, the outcome of the contest with the Soviets would depend on the American people themselves: their ability to conquer the new and terrible fears created by the possibility of nuclear war and their determination to make the sacrifices that were the burden of world leadership in the nuclear era.[49]

This strategy was adopted by the Truman administration in 1950. During the Eisenhower presidency, it was revised, articulated more coherently, and systematically implemented. The primary instrument chosen for its execution was civil defense. The federal civil defense programs of the 1950s thus represented an institutional means of solving the problem of national morale and securing the moral underpinnings of nuclear deterrence.[50]

2

Managing Nuclear Terror

National Will and Nuclear Terror

In the early years of the Cold War, American national security planners arrived at an interpretation of the probable reaction of the American people to a nuclear attack on the United States. They argued that the public would respond to the prospect of nuclear war with expressions of panic or terror. Such a response, however, was inconsistent with the role that the planners had reserved for the American people in the contest with the Soviet Union. The policy of containment by means of deterrence required the public to exhibit credible expressions of determination to fight a nuclear war. Acting on this interpretation, civil defense specialists developed a plan to bring the public psychology into conformity with the requirements of national security policy. This plan was a comprehensive system of emotion management designed to suppress an irrational terror of nuclear war and foster in its stead a more pragmatic nuclear fear. Once the passage from nuclear terror to nuclear fear had been completed, civil defense organizations would be in a position to employ nuclear fear in their programs of human resource management. Properly channeled, nuclear fear would motivate the public to deliver the support regarded as essential to deterrence.

Emotion management translated the moral problem of national will into a problem of mass psychology: How could nuclear terror—an irrational fear of nuclear war—be prevented, and how could the resolution necessary to confront a nuclear attack be formed? The solution to this problem was civil defense. The self-control that Americans learned in civil defense training would eliminate the moral deficits that made them such unsatisfactory weapons in the struggle against Communism. The discipline of civil defense would cultivate the toughness they needed to meet the demands of the Cold War. As a result, American national security would rest on a solid moral foundation despite the risks entailed by deterrence.

The Problem of Panic

Early civil defense theory held that anxieties about nuclear war would create an extravagant emotional response. The American people, terrified by weapons that seemed to place at risk not only human life but an entire way of life and perhaps even life itself, would take no steps to protect themselves. Nuclear terror signified a breakdown of emotional control that precluded the confident self-possession and proficiency that civil defense theorists regarded as appropriate responses to the bomb. Once in the grip of uncontrollable fears, victims of nuclear terror would become completely egocentric and amoral. Either they would hazard a blind and irrational flight to save themselves, oblivious of their obligations and the needs of others, or they would lapse, equally irrationally, into a state of confused inaction and stupor. In either case, nuclear terror would destroy the emotional restraints and moral sanctions that tie individuals to their routine roles and responsibilities. As a result, the norms that underpin the social order would collapse.

Nuclear terror could subvert the strategy of deterrence in either of two ways. It could create the impression that nuclear weapons are so absolute and horrifying that any defense against them would be impossible. This would result in an apathetic public. Or it could encourage Americans to embrace the "one world or none" ethic, the view that nuclear weapons should be withdrawn from sovereign American control and placed under the authority of an international body. This would result in a pacifist public. Either contingency would destroy the basis of the United States' Cold War national security policy.

Civil defense theorists framed their conception of nuclear terror by reference to what they called the "problem of panic," which was said to pose immense, even incalculable, obstacles to the formation of national morale. As early as 1946, nuclear scientists warned that in the next war, panic could prove to be an even more formidable weapon than the atomic bomb. Nobel laureate Harold C. Urey warned that the Soviet Union might not need forty or fifty atomic bombs in order to neutralize the American ability to retaliate, that the atomic bombing of only a few cities could create a nationwide panic that would make further resistance impossible.[1]

The analysis of the first postwar American atomic-bomb tests also stressed the probable impact of an atomic attack on the moral and psychological resilience of the survivors. In July 1946, the American government carried out OPERATION CROSSROADS at its nuclear-testing area in the Marshall Islands. Three detonations were planned. The first, code-named ABLE and carried out on July 1, was designed to ascertain the effects of an atomic bomb exploded in the air on a fleet of warships. The second, code-named BAKER and carried out on July 26, was intended to determine the effects of an underwater atomic explosion on the same fleet. A third test, CHARLIE, was canceled without explanation, apparently to avoid depleting the American supply of fissionable material.[2]

On June 30, 1947, the JCS Evaluation Board submitted its top-secret final report to the president on the results of OPERATION CROSSROADS. The Evaluation Board consisted of two generals, two admirals, and a chairman, Karl Compton, a distinguished physicist, Manhattan Project alumnus, and president of MIT. The Evaluation Board concluded that the principal virtue of the atomic bomb as a military weapon was its power to "break the will of nations and of peoples." In order to achieve this effect, it was not necessary to drop a single atomic bomb; the mere fact of the existence of nuclear weapons would be enough to terrorize a nation that believed it was threatened by atomic attack. This meant that in spite of—or perhaps precisely because of—the immense destruction that could be produced by an atomic bomb, its primary military value was moral and psychological. World War III would not be decided by the question of which adversary won the battle of neutralizing the military forces, destroying the resources, and killing the people of its opponent. On the contrary, the war would be won by the side that exploited most effectively what the Evaluation Board called the "psychological implication" of the bomb: its capacity to terrify and demoralize potential victims.[3]

In August 1947, less than two months after the Evaluation Board submitted its assessment of OPERATION CROSSROADS, the Joint Chiefs prepared a plan for war with the Soviet Union with the colorful code name BROILER. The main premise of BROILER was an "air-atomic" campaign against Soviet cities early in the war. Bombing Soviet cities with nuclear weapons was intended to take advantage of "the maximum psychological effect of the atomic bomb." This effect would be achieved by creating "chaos and extreme confusion" as well as "an increased element of hopelessness and shock."[4] The Soviet home front would be demoralized not merely by the magnitude of destruction, but also by the uncertainty concerning what might happen next and the panic that was likely to ensue as millions of people attempted to escape the effects of the atomic blast. The bomb would decide the outcome of the war by means of a direct and ruthless assault on the Soviet people that would crush their determination to resist. Therefore, BROILER regarded the atomic bomb not only as a weapon of mass destruction, but also as an instrument of mass terror.

Civil defense theory transposed this doctrine of nuclear terror along lines already implicit in the JCS Evaluation Board's report on OPERATION CROSSROADS. In this transposition, the psychological strategy of nuclear warfare devised by American military planners for BROILER was attributed to Soviet war planners. The assumptions of BROILER, conceived by American strategists for war against the Soviet Union, were ascribed to putative Soviet war plans for an atomic offensive against American cities. Following the logic of BROILER, such an attack would panic the American people, destroy the morale of the home front, and guarantee a swift Soviet victory.

This was the dominant logic of all the principal civil defense–planning documents produced in the early years of the Cold War. In 1946, the Social Science Research Council formed the Committee on Social Aspects of Atomic Energy to study the social problems posed by atomic energy. The committee was composed of prestigious academics such as the strategic theorist Bernard Brodie, the sociologist William Ogburn, and the nuclear physicist Isidor Rabi. Its initial product was a monograph written by Ansley Coale, then a graduate student in economics at Princeton, on the question of reducing the vulnerability of the United States to an atomic attack. One of the issues addressed by the study was the problem of public morale, which was perceived as a determinant of both military strength and national security. Could the first few bombs dropped on American cities shatter the nerves of the American people, even though the actual damage they produced might not be significant? Suppose, for example, that the atomic bombing of Chicago and New York caused people in other parts of the country to panic when they sighted one lone aircraft overhead. Would the result be "aimless, even hysterical activity, or flight," a "troublesome handicap to war activity after the first bombs were dropped"? After the first nuclear strike against the United States, would "nuisance raiders" flying over industrial plants paralyze the work force? Further research was recommended to determine what might be done to make sure that neither "hysteria nor defeatism" became a major impediment to the American effort in a nuclear war.[5]

The same thinking was incorporated into civil defense planning by the military establishment. On November 25, 1946, the War Department established the Civil Defense Board, which was charged with defining the responsibilities of the federal government for civil defense and determining how civil defense operations should be organized to meet these responsibilities. The board was composed of six generals and six field officers, each representing the various interests in civil defense of the armed services. It was chaired by General Harold Bull, Eisenhower's Chief of Operations during World War II: thus the "Bull Board" and the "Bull Report."

The Bull Board held hearings between December 2, 1946, and February 28, 1947, issuing the Bull Report, which was classified as confidential on the latter date. It was declassified on January 13, 1948, and published, with the appendices deleted, on February 2, 1948, as *A Study of Civil Defense.*

The Bull Report held that in the next war the United States might be subjected to surprise aerial bombing that would not only devastate the economy, but also destroy "the will and ability of the people to resist."[6] The Bull Report envisioned the American social order as a fragile edifice endangered by internal forces of disloyalty and sabotage that threatened to disintegrate the society from within. Insidious and clandestine, these forces were potentially even more dangerous than an overt threat of external military attack, preparations for which could be detected in advance. In a military emergency, the United States would encounter not only a visible enemy abroad, but also invisible fifth-column subversion at home. In light of these considerations, it was necessary to bolster public determination to combat the forces that threatened internal disintegration. This meant it was imperative to take every reasonable precaution to ensure that "our will to fight for our national security be maintained."[7]

On March 27, 1948, following the unification of the military services in the Department of Defense, the Secretary of Defense established the Office of Civil Defense Planning, whose purpose was to draft a national civil defense plan. Its first director was Russell J. Hopley, president of Northwestern Bell Telephone in Omaha. The Hopley Report was much more ambitious than the twenty-four-page Bull Report. With 301 pages, thirty-two chapters, and seventeen organizational charts, it outlined a model state civil defense organization, analyzed the various specializations essential to civil defense, and proposed a functional division of labor based on these specializations as well as a political division of labor among federal, state, and local civil defense authorities.

Published in October 1948 as *Civil Defense for National Security,* the Hopley Report also stressed the importance of controlling the panic that was expected to accompany a nuclear attack. Although the Hopley Report advocated crisis relocation—the swift evacuation of urban populations—as a crucial civil defense measure, it noted that "fear and panic render large groups almost unmanageable and could easily destroy the effectiveness of the best laid transportation plan."[8] In order to combat panic, the Hopley Report proposed a national public-information campaign. Its authors embraced the optimistic liberal doctrine that public enlightenment would solve even the most intractable problems of moral and political psychology. Panic is caused by fear, and fear is a consequence of ignorance. Thus the solution to the problem of panic is public information about the effects of a nuclear attack and what can be done to prepare for them. "Panic arises from fear, but knowledge and understanding help to dispel fear, thus enabling the individual to meet the situation calmly."[9]

The National Security Resources Board (NSRB), an agency created by the National Security Act of 1947, assumed responsibility for civil defense planning in March 1949. The NSRB conducted its own study of civil defense and in September 1950 submitted a report entitled *United States Civil Defense*, known in the federal government as the Blue Book because of the color of its cover. Following the doctrine on panic outlined in the Bull Report and the Hopley Report, the Blue Book maintained that panic was perhaps the most serious problem of social control associated with a nuclear attack. Because panic would pose immense difficulties for law enforcement, the Blue Book recommended that law enforcement officers, including auxiliary police, receive special training to "handle panic situations." Police training in panic control should include practice drills with public participation. In the interest of national security, the American people were expected to acknowledge their moral and psychological weaknesses and cheerfully collaborate in their own surveillance and regimentation by the police.[10]

On December 1, 1950, President Truman issued an executive order creating the Federal Civil Defense Administration (FCDA) in the Office for Emergency Management. On January 12, 1951, Congress passed the Federal Civil Defense Act of 1950, which established the FCDA as a separate agency in the executive branch, with its own civilian administrator appointed by the president. On November 3, 1950, less than a month before the FCDA became operational, two consultants, Dean R. Brimmhall and L. Dewey Anderson, submitted to the NSRB a brief study for the new agency on the "sociological problems of civil defense from the field of morale."

The consultants regarded public morale as the ability to resist panic. The purpose of their memorandum was to identify questions concerning the production and control of panic, with which the FCDA would be expected to grapple. What was the relation between public understanding of the effects of nuclear weapons and public morale? Would full information about the consequences of an atomic attack minimize the likelihood of panic? Or would knowledge of what the atomic bomb could do to them terrify its potential victims so completely that they would be unable to act intelligently? Would publications and broadcasts be sufficient to control public fears, or would civil defense drills also be necessary to prepare for a nuclear emergency? Employing an analogy that would reappear in confidential deliberations in the civil defense community, the consultants considered whether a physician should reveal to a cancer patient all the facts of his or her condition. The physician, who was presumed to possess both expertise and wisdom, was the federal government. The patient was the hapless and unwitting public. Cancer, a potentially fatal disease, was, of course, the prospect of an atomic attack.

The memorandum predicted that "social disorganization," including vandalism by criminals and the mentally disturbed, would occur in the aftermath of an attack. "Serious tensions" and "hostilities" among diverse ethnic, religious, and socioeconomic groups could also be expected. The consultants were particularly troubled by the effects of a nuclear attack on an ethnically complex city such as New York, Chicago, or Detroit. In the breakdown of authority that would follow an attack, the victims would be at one another's throats. The consultants anticipated interethnic violence, assaults by members of different religious groups on one another, and race riots: "It is awesome to reflect on what would happen in one of these cities if colored people and white people were forced into close association in shelters, in homes, and even evacuation reception centers."[11]

Worries about the emotional stability of the American people in the face of a nuclear attack were a central concern of the FCDA during both the Truman and the Eisenhower presidencies. On November 20, 1952, James J. Wadsworth, acting administrator of the FCDA during the transition to the new Eisenhower administration, reaffirmed the relation between the national will and national security in a speech in Chicago. The lesson of the two world wars, Wadsworth urged, was that American power is ultimately grounded in the will of its people to resist aggression and fight for freedom. This was why the aggressor in the next war would strike first at the American home front and the American people, the real source of the military and economic power of the United States. Because America's strength "lies first, last, and always in our people," an enemy unable to crush the American will to fight could not win a war against the United States. But suppose that dozens of American cities suffered simultaneous nuclear devastation. A remote possibility? Not according to Wadsworth, who warned that it could happen "any minute now." Not only would hundreds of thousands die. Even worse, in Wadsworth's estimation, the catastrophe might be so overwhelming that it would crush the determination of the American people to resist. In that case, "America, as we know it, would cease to exist.[12]

In April 1953, at the beginning of the Eisenhower presidency, the Public Affairs Office of the FCDA produced a thirty-four-page analysis of the relation between the national will and nuclear terror under the cumbersome title "Civil Defense Implications of the Psychological Impact and Morale Effect of Attacks on the People of the United States." The FCDA study began with the assumption that the success of a nu-

clear attack on the United States did not depend solely on the destruction of the American economy. It was equally important to "break our
will to resist and to fight back." Thus in preparing for nuclear war, a
major task of civil defense was to make sure that the conditions necessary to sustain American morale were in place. What was the most
likely psychological impact of a Soviet nuclear offensive? Would fear
of the bomb generate panic and destroy public morale? In order to
answer these questions, the FCDA study examined various reactions
that could be expected as a result of the extreme stress experienced in
a nuclear attack.

Some victims would behave like animals caught in a trap. Finding
no means of escape, they would act in an arbitrary and purely reflexive
fashion. Others would respond with uncontrolled acts of violence. Instead of venting their aggression against the enemy or channeling it
into constructive civil defense efforts, they would assault convenient
scapegoats. Likely candidates for attacks based on prejudice, fear, or
hate were members of religious and ethnic minorities. Once these assaults occurred, they would aggravate rather than diminish panic and
aggression, leading to what the FCDA study called "extraordinary
flights of inappropriate behavior." Finally, some survivors would attempt to isolate themselves from the terrifying consequences of nuclear
war by effecting a pseudo-escape into an interior psychological reality.
In creating a fantasy world in which the unrelieved horrors of nuclear
war were denied or displaced, these victims would become paralyzed
by apathy and fatalism.

The FCDA study contended that if the number of emotionally unstable victims in the first group were very large, postattack rehabilitation efforts would appear to be doomed, the casualty of a frenzy of
misinformation and the circulation of rumors of betrayal, sabotage, and
irredeemable catastrophe. If the number of attack victims who turned
their aggression against their fellow citizens were very large, the social
order might collapse. Nuclear war would strain American institutions
to the breaking point. Violence that under routine conditions would
remain suppressed or latent could no longer be contained. Because of
the breakdown of normal control mechanisms and the eruption of dangerous social conflicts, a nuclear war might ignite a Hobbesian civil war
on the home front. Social "explosions" would produce radical changes
in social organization. Old groups would disappear and new groups
would form. Emerging organizations would be locked in a merciless
struggle for dwindling survival resources. Attacking one another, they
would unwittingly tear apart American society. The result would be
"social chaos."

If the number of survivors who succumbed to their own escapist
fantasies were very large, it would be impossible to save whatever
might be left of American society. The political scene would be domi-

nated by mystical sects and cults, enthralled by the vision of an immeasurably happier future in an inner fantasy life or an extramundane kingdom of bliss that transcended the brutal empirical reality of nuclear destruction. The institutions and leaders of the preattack order would be replaced by charismatic mystics and sectarians promising salvation from nuclear terror in a new and unimaginably better world.

Faced with a nuclear emergency, the American people would also be an easy target for Soviet psychological warfare. In tandem with a nuclear offensive, the Soviets would do their best to weaken American morale by creating doubt and fear. The FCDA study credited the Soviets with a virtually omniscient grasp of American moral and psychological weaknesses as well as an impressive repertoire of subversive tactics: organized rumor-mongering; leaflets dropped from the air (whether from Soviet aircraft or American planes commandeered by fifth-column groups is not made clear); and "intruder radio" messages aired on regular commercial frequencies, the broadcasters cunningly representing themselves either as well-known commentators trusted by the public or as official government spokesmen. These methods could be expected to create a level of confusion that would disrupt civil defense efforts, increase the effectiveness of the Soviet military offensive, and delay the American recovery. In sum, the major concern of the FCDA study was that "the serious potentialities of panic, demoralization, and national paralysis may suddenly be converted into actualities."[13]

Certainly the most widely circulated statement of the FCDA position on nuclear terror was the article on panic by Frederick "Val" Peterson, Eisenhower's first administrator of the FCDA: "Panic: The Ultimate Weapon?" published in *Collier's* in 1953. On the whole, press coverage of civil defense in the 1950s exhibited the interests of both government and the media, which were acutely perceived and assiduously cultivated by both sides. Newspapers, magazines, radio, and television competed to gain government certification for their publications and broadcasts on civil defense as an official national security seal of approval. Both print and broadcast media submitted to the FCDA, for criticism and approval, prepublication and preproduction drafts of scripts and articles. Writers and editors solicited the FCDA for technical data and information concerning civil defense policy and also sought assurances that they had not compromised the national security. The FCDA Public Affairs Office took advantage of the press's interest in inside knowledge of what World War III would be like and how Americans could survive it. It also exploited the press's enthusiasm for informal self-censorship as well as official government oversight, using the media as marketing instruments to distribute its own version of nuclear reality under the guise of impartial reportage.

In his *Collier's* article, Peterson confronted readers with what he clearly regarded as a paradoxical fact: Although the American people were citizens of the most powerful nation on earth, they were also the most "panic-prone." This consideration led Peterson to pose a series of increasingly hysterical questions:

> What will you do if one day an atomic bomb blasts your town? Will you take calm emergency action—or will you dash screaming into the ruined streets, a victim of your own horror? In a war, the whole country's survival could depend upon your reaction to disaster . . . because mass panic may be far more devastating than the bomb itself . . . What will you do—not later, but right then and there?[14]

Like the atomic bomb, panic was fissionable: "It can produce a chain reaction more deeply destructive than any explosive known." This meant that "if there is an ultimate weapon, it may well be mass panic—not the A-bomb. Mass panic—not the A-bomb—may well be the easiest way to win a battle, the cheapest way to win a war." Peterson acknowledged that although a Soviet nuclear attack would produce appalling damage, the reaction of terror in the surviving population would create even more serious dangers. To illustrate this point, he asked readers to imagine the survivors of an atomic attack on Manhattan: "a hungry pillaging mob—disrupting disaster relief, overwhelming local police and spreading panic in a widening arc." Although New York might present distinctive problems of civil defense that other cities would not be forced to confront, Peterson cautioned readers that every American city exposed to atomic attack faced comparable perils.[15]

Accordingly, it is not surprising that government officials were hypersensitive about the potentially unintended and undesirable impact of their own public-information program on national morale. Could the mere mention of the bomb terrify the American people, creating the impression that their situation was hopeless? This question led officials to impression-manage their presentations of civil defense matters in order to minimize the likelihood of an overwrought public reaction. In this context, the June 19, 1953, memo of FCDA public-relations consultant Charles Ellsworth to Katherine Howard, FCDA deputy administrator, is illuminating. Commenting on Howard's television appearances on behalf of civil defense, Ellsworth advised some reflexive exercises in self-presentation:

> You have a reflex tendency to smile when you refer to the atom bomb, or to death and destruction—probably in an instinctive attempt to avoid scaring people to death. A little serious matter-of-factness might be better at such times; and in any case, I think that will wear off as you get over the shock that comes with full knowledge of the Civil Defense picture. I should have said, get *used* to it. We all suffer from it around here, and none of us ever really gets over it.[16]

The doctrine of nuclear terror hardly appears astonishing in light of the early press coverage of the atomic bomb—the first attempts to interpret the effects of nuclear war for the American public. In the main, the press characterized the atomic bomb as a weapon of virtually unimaginable force, a device of incalculable power from which no protection was possible.

Writing in 1956, Edward Shils noted that the initial "happy bewilderment" with which the American people responded to the atomic bombs that fell on Hiroshima and Nagasaki was quickly replaced by a "widespread horror over the prospect of atomic attack."[17] Just one day after the bombing of Hiroshima, Hanson Baldwin, military correspondent for the *New York Times*, wrote, "Yesterday man unleashed the atom to destroy man, and another chapter in human history opened, a chapter in which the weird, the strange, the horrible becomes the trite and obvious." Baldwin concluded his article with the speculation that atomic energy might produce a world in which "we shall become—beneath the bomb and rockets—a world of troglodytes."[18] On August 6, 1945, publicity about the atomic bomb was limited to the cryptic terms of President Truman's terse radio address officially announcing the Hiroshima bombing, a statement crafted to reveal as little as possible about the weapon and its effects.[19] On August 7, the atomic bomb was the major story of World War II. Baldwin's article marked the beginning of a torrent of news broadcasts, newspaper and magazine articles, editorials, essays, and books on what were described as the unique destructive powers of the bomb, the horrors of atomic attack, and the grave dangers of nuclear war for the human race.[20]

In the week following the Hiroshima and Nagasaki bombings, the Hearst Metrotone "News of the Day," which was played before the cartoon and the feature in movie theaters throughout the country, provided the first public footage of an atomic-bomb explosion under the headline "NOW IT CAN BE SHOWN! FIRST TEST FIRING OF AN ATOM BOMB!" Moviegoers were treated to pictures of the first atomic-bomb explosion at the Manhattan Project–testing area near Alamogordo, New Mexico. In the melodramatic voice-out-of-the-tomb style of broadcast favored in movie theater news programming of the 1940s and 1950s, the announcer portentously observed that "in this awesome spectacle, an era dies and a new age is born, the mysterious unchartered age of atomic power." Three such explosions, viewers were warned, could "wipe out" New York, Los Angeles, and San Francisco.[21]

In an influential *Saturday Review* essay with the worrisome title "Modern Man Is Obsolete," Norman Cousins argued that as a result of the atomic bomb, "time is running out." Writing in a mood of acute anxiety in the afterglow of the Hiroshima and Nagasaki blasts, Cousins told his readers that "every city in the world" could be annihilated in a matter of hours. As if this were not bad enough, even greater cataclysms might follow. In Cousins's vision of a nuclear *Götterdämmerung*, the earth is deflected from its axis and returned to its "original incandescent mass blazing at millions of degrees."[22]

By the end of 1945, many former Manhattan Project scientists had organized themselves as the Federation of Atomic Scientists, the so-called League of Frightened Men. Troubled by congressional and public indifference to the dangers of atomic weapons, they advocated the creation of an international commission to control the development and use of nuclear energy, a proposal that would require the United States to relinquish its monopoly over atomic bombs and the technology of their manufacture. Since there was virtually no public support for this proposal, the scientists attempted to terrify the public into action with blunt warnings about the frightful consequences of atomic warfare.[23]

Physicist James Franck, a senior member of the Manhattan Project and one of the earliest critics of the American atomic-weapons program, envisioned a "Pearl Harbor disaster repeated in thousand-fold magnification in every one of our major cities," introducing into public discourse the horrifying concept of a "nuclear Pearl Harbor": the United States again exposed and unprepared, but this time destroyed under a barrage of atomic bombs.[24] In his testimony before the Special Committee on Atomic Energy of the U.S. Senate, the physical chemist Irving Langmuir claimed that forty atomic bombs exploded over forty American cities would kill 40 million people and destroy the entire political structure of the nation. Langmuir also maintained that atomic bombs "a thousand times as powerful as those that now exist" could almost certainly be produced. With cheaper means of bomb manufacture, it would be possible to reduce every square mile of the United States to Hiroshima-like devastation and kill virtually the entire American population. In Langmuir's gloomy estimate, "there might be 2% of the people left."[25]

Perhaps the most widely publicized entry in the genre of popular scientific speculation and polemics about the bomb was the contribution by Harold Urey, the discover of the heavy isotope of hydrogen and an activist in the Federation of Atomic Scientists. On January 5, 1946, *Collier's* published Urey's open letter to the American public. "I write to frighten you," Urey declared. "I'm a frightened man myself. All the scientists I know are frightened—frightened for their lives—and frightened for **your** life." It was, of course, the prospect of nuclear war that frightened Urey and his colleagues. Urey attempted to shatter the illusions of readers who might be naive enough to believe in the possibility of protection against the bomb:

> In an [atomic] explosion, thousands die within a fraction of a second. In the immediate area, there is nothing left standing. There are no walls. They are vanished into dust and smoke. There are no wounded. There are not even bodies. At the center, a fire many times hotter than any fire we have known has pulverized buildings and human beings into nothingness.[26]

Certainly the most celebrated piece of journalism on the bomb was John Hersey's account of the bombing of Hiroshima, written from the perspective of six survivors. On August 31, 1946, for the first time in its history, the *New Yorker* devoted an entire issue to a single contribution, Hersey's "Hiroshima." The impact of the essay seems to have been electrifying. The issue quickly sold out, and copies became collector's items within a few days. The entire text of the essay was read over ABC radio in four thirty-minute broadcasts. When publication as a book followed, *Hiroshima* became an immediate bestseller and a Book-of-the-Month Club selection. Indeed, the Book-of-the-Month Club sent *Hiroshima* free to hundreds of thousands of subscribers, with the explanation that "we find it hard to conceive of anything being written that could be of more importance at this moment to the human race."[27]

Hersey depicted the atomic bombing of Hiroshima as an apocalypse produced by modern military technology. Most of the city was destroyed instantly, and the remainder was reduced to rubble and flame. The clear morning sky was unnaturally darkened by a cloud of dust and fission particles blown miles above the city. A conflagration caused by the innumerable fires ignited throughout the city generated blasts of hot air that propelled the flames from one neighborhood to another. Buildings crumbled, and power lines fell into streets strewn with household goods, smoldering corpses, and body parts. Survivors in shock and agony cried for help, their bodies crushed or disfigured by burns and lacerations. Masses of wounded filled the streets in an attempt to escape.

No measures of planning or preparation could protect potential victims. The mundane contingencies of life determined the fate of Hiroshima's inhabitants. Survival depended on whether one was at home or on the way to work, still in bed or at the kitchen window preparing breakfast, at the office or doing an errand in the center of the city.

Hersey's essay provided the first account of an atomic attack as experienced by its victims. At one point, readers accompany a survivor desperately searching for his family in the carnage and detritus of postattack Hiroshima.

> He was the only person making his way into the city; he met hundreds and hundreds who were fleeing, and every one of them seemed to be hurt in some way. The eyebrows of some were burned off and skin hung from their faces and hands. Others, because of pain, held their arms up as if carrying something in both hands. Some were vomiting as they walked. Many were naked or in shreds of clothing. On some undressed bodies, the burns had made patterns—of undershirt straps and suspenders and, on the skin of some women (since white repelled the heat from the bomb and dark clothes absorbed it and conducted it to the skin), the shapes of flowers they had on their kimonos.[28]

The qualities of Hersey's style placed in relief the horrors of his account. The ethnographic detachment and clinical restraint of his prose rendered the human experience of the attack all the more terrible: masses of people deposited in the streets bleeding, vomiting, burned, or crushed, with skin and pieces of flesh scorched off their bodies as if they had been flayed by a gigantic and supremely efficient engine of torture; "a woman with a whole breast sheared off and a man whose face was all raw from a burn"; victims "whose eye sockets were hollow, the fluid from their melted eyes had run down their cheeks"; survivors whose "mouths were mere swollen, pus-covered wounds, which they could not bear to stretch enough to admit the spout of a teapot."[29]

World War II erased the distinction between soldiers and civilians, the front lines and the home front. The destruction of Rotterdam by the Luftwaffe and its subsequent attacks on London and other British cities, the German policy of exterminating civilian populations in Eastern Europe, the partisan campaigns of resistance in the occupied countries, and the Allied bombing of every German and Japanese city within striking distance in 1944 and 1945 demonstrated that the line between the dangers of the front and the safety of home could no longer be drawn with confidence. Hersey's essay dramatized the impact of the atomic bomb on the collapse of the distinction between combatants and noncombatants. Although he identified his six informants, and other victims of the Hiroshima bombing as well, their names would convey no significance to Americans. The import of *Hiroshima*, written by an American journalist for an American readership, was clear. Here Americans learned for the first time the grim consequences they could expect should their cities share the fate of Hiroshima and Nagasaki.

A world of troglodytes, the pulverization of human beings into nothingness, the incredible but palpable hell of a nuclear attack, even the earth dislodged from its orbit and bursting into flames: Presented with this picture, national security planners, perhaps not unreasonably, were profoundly apprehensive about the ability of the American people to withstand the moral and emotional demands of nuclear war. Deterrence depended upon the American threat to use nuclear weapons in order to thwart Soviet ambitions. But nuclear terror would destroy the moral basis on which the credibility of this threat rested: the will of the American people to risk nuclear war.

The Cold War System of Emotion Management

In an attempt to address this problem and counter the desperate interpretation of the atomic bomb and its message of hopelessness and despair produced by the American press, civil defense theorists developed a comprehensive program of emotion management. Emotion management may be understood as a strategy for the mobilization, administration, and control of emotional life. The creation of those who aspire to the status of authorities and guardians of the soul, a system of emotion management represents the emotional life as framed by three basic parameters: cognitive standards, practical norms, and strategic controls. Emotion management defines standards that tell us what it is possible to feel, how far the horizon of emotional experience extends, and what our feelings mean. It also defines norms that tell us what is expected of us emotionally, what the limits of acceptable emotional expression are, what we ought to feel in specific circumstances, and how these feelings should be expressed. Finally, it defines a technology of emotional control that tells us what we can do with our emotions and how we can use them so that what we feel and the way we express our feelings can be deployed to our advantage.[30]

A system of emotion management regards emotions not so much as private or inner states and the inaccessible objects that may be felt in these states, but as cultural artifacts—products of our knowledge, intelligent planning, and practical endeavors.[31] The practices that form our culture tell us not only what can be done and what we should do, but also what can be felt and what we should feel, what feelings can be expressed and how we should express them. If emotions are cultural artifacts, they can be intentionally, even self-consciously, formed, molded, manipulated, worked at, and worked upon.

The purpose of the Cold War system of emotion management was to solve the problem of national will by confronting what was regarded as the most serious obstacle to American resolve in the face of nuclear attack: nuclear terror. Emotion managers would control nuclear terror by promoting civil defense to the American people. Civil defense would teach Americans what they needed to know about nuclear weapons. It would also spell out norms specifying appropriate responses to a nuclear attack. Finally, it would elaborate the techniques that Americans could use to control their emotions regarding nuclear war.

Project East River

The main lines of the Cold War system of emotion management were first sketched in Project East River, a study of civil defense commissioned during the Truman administration. The results of this study were quickly acknowledged as the canonical text of Cold War emotion management and "the Bible of civil defense."[32]

Project East River was undertaken by Associated Universities, Inc., at the request of the FCDA, the NSRB, and the Department of Defense. Associated Universities was an early Cold War think tank sponsored by several Ivy League universities—Cornell, Columbia, Harvard, the University of Pennsylvania, and Yale—as well as Johns Hopkins, MIT, and the University of Rochester. Negotiations for a contract with Associated Universities for the purpose of civil defense research were initiated by

the Army Signal Corps on June 27, 1951 The first meeting to plan
Project East River was held on August 1, 1951, at the office of Associated Universities in New York. The recruitment of research personnel—
including physicists, chemists, engineers, economists, political scientists, sociologists, and psychologists—began on August 15. Participants
were recruited from member and other universities as well as from
government, business, and industry. All Project East River personnel
met for the first time in New York for a three-day planning session
from November 26 to 28, 1951.[33]

The objective of Project East River was to develop proposals that
would enable the federal government to prepare the American home
front for nuclear war. The contract between Associated Universities and
the Signal Corps stipulated that Project East River would produce research tailored to the needs of three agencies: the FCDA, which was
responsible for planning how to protect the public from nuclear attack;
the NSRB, which was responsible for advising the president on maintaining the federal government's continuous functioning during a
nuclear attack and the strategic relocation of industries essential to national security; and the Department of Defense, which was responsible
for assisting the FCDA and the NSRB in discharging their obligations.

The *Report of the Project East River* consists of ten parts, each printed
under a separate cover. Part I is a general survey of the principles,
objectives, organization, operation, and findings of the project. Parts II
through IX are the reports of various research panels, each covering a
specific area of civil defense. Part X is a bibliography. Each panel worked
under the direction of a chairman, who was also responsible for writing
the panel report.

Project East River concluded that the United States had seriously
underestimated the gravity of the Soviet nuclear threat: "An attack
with modern weapons would be much more damaging to our population, our property, our way of life, and to our democratic institutions
generally than is realized by the public or even by many responsible
government officials."[34] The novel dangers of nuclear weapons were
not due exclusively to their destructive capacity. Unlike earlier weapons, their "most lucrative use" was not against military assets. Instead,
the most profitable targets of an atomic bomb were the industry, agri-
culture, and civilian population of an adversary. This meant that in
World War III, Americans homes would be a primary target of the
Soviet nuclear strike force.

Therefore, the American victory in World War II did not promise
a generation of peace and prosperity. On the contrary, it marked the
beginning of the most dangerous period in American history. The world
had entered a "perilous atomic era." Those who rested their hopes for
a better world on a early end to the Cold War labored under an illusion.
The Cold War was only beginning. The United States did not face a

transitory emergency that would pass with the resolution of specific international tensions. For the current generation of Americans, the anxieties of the Cold War would become permanent features of life. The loss of the American nuclear monopoly obviously reduced the relative military advantage that the atomic bomb had given the United States. Nuclear weapons as a means of deterring Soviet aggression could no longer be counted on with confidence. In the near future, increases in the Soviet nuclear stockpile would reach a critical mass, at which point the Soviet Union would be in a position to launch "a knockout, saturation attack against the United States." Although the absolute size of the American nuclear retaliatory force might still be larger than its Soviet counterpart, this factor alone would not deter the Soviets' aggressive policies. The prospect of a Soviet nuclear offensive was so staggering that it produced a feeling of futility. Both the intellect and the imagination were overwhelmed by the "sheer magnitude of problem so large, so complex, and so seemingly impossible of adequate and practical solution."[35]

The situation was far from hopeless, however. The problem of protecting the United States from nuclear attack could be solved, but only by transforming American life through the construction of "a permanent civil defense system." Because the national security crisis was permanent, it called for a permanent civil defense apparatus: "Like the Army, the Navy, and the Air Force, civil defense must function as long as a national security program is required."[36]

In confidential planning papers drafted in the winter of 1952, the Project East River staff argued that the fundamental objective of civil defense was to sustain public morale not only in the face of an imminent nuclear attack and during the perilous interval in which the United States might be subjected to attack, but also over the indefinite but protracted duration of the Cold War. Because national security depended on the morale of the home front, the moral and psychological resilience of the American people was the principal desideratum for a civil defense program that would protect "the way of life which we are determined to defend." This objective posed major problems of emotion management. The United States had no experience in confronting challenges of indefinite duration. Americans were at their best responding to immediate and evident dangers or reacting swiftly in the aftermath of a disaster. But the Cold War called for virtues with which history had not favored the American people: patience, persistence, and perseverance. How could these qualities be acquired? How could Americans learn to stand firm against long-term threats to their national survival? The Project East River staff maintained that it was necessary to train Americans to avoid the emotional extremes of panic and a false sense of security. Unless the American propensity to panic were brought under control, public morale would collapse. Unless the illu-

sion of security and a misplaced national overconfidence and complacency were broken, the public would become apathetic, in which case
the moral energies required for the prosecution of the Cold War could
not be sustained. Thus the ethical requirements of the Cold War depended on a specific emotional regime.

In the thinking of the Project East River staff, certain practical consequences concerning the organization of civil defense followed from
these general considerations. In the main, the responsibility for protecting the American people from nuclear attack would rest with the
people themselves, not with the state. Civil defense was based on the
principle of self-help. Americans would become well informed about
the nuclear threat and what they could do to protect themselves against
it. Given the proper information and the requisite training, the danger
of panic could be reduced, perhaps even to a point at which it would
no longer imperil the national security. The problem of national will
would be solved, albeit somewhat paradoxically, by the American people themselves, who were said to lack the moral qualities needed to
prevail in the Cold War.[37]

In framing its emotion management program, the Project East
River staff attempted to enlist the Psychological Strategy Board to provide advice and expertise. Established on April 4, 1951, by a secret
presidential directive, the Psychological Strategy Board was responsible
for planning and coordinating the "psychological operations" of the
Cold War. This was a usefully amorphous objective, which could be
understood to embrace both psychological warfare and the entire pan-
oply of Cold War propaganda. During the Truman presidency, the Psychological Strategy Board was one of many agencies engaged in the
effort to define the Cold War and promote its own vision of the struggle
with world Communism. These organizations battled against the common enemy and in some cases even more ardently against one another
in a competition to conceptualize and organize the Cold War, control
the resources for managing it, and dominate the growing national security bureaucracy.[38]

The Project East River staff endeavored to convince the Psychological Strategy Board to collaborate in investigating the psychological
problems posed by a nuclear attack as well as the difficulties of recruiting the general public into a national civil defense program. Joseph E.
McLean, a professor in the Woodrow Wilson School of Public and International Affairs at Princeton and a staff member of Project East River,
contacted the Psychological Strategy Board on January 8, 1952, in order to invite its director, Raymond Allen, to attend a briefing in Washington on these issues. McLean was reminded that the Psychological
Strategy Board was legally restricted to "psychological affairs outside
the United States," and so it could not officially take part in any effort
to subject the American people to psychological controls. McLean re-

sponded by pointing out that Project East River could profit from the expertise the board had developed in running its overseas propaganda programs. He mentioned two matters on which it could be especially helpful: the relation between the perceived urgency of threats to American security and the timing of civil defense operations, and the problem of managing both official statements and rumors about nuclear war.

Although Allen declined this particular invitation on the grounds that it would be inappropriate for the Psychological Strategy Board to engage in a discussion of these issues, his rejection of McLean's request for help was not unconditional. As an alternative, he proposed a more general briefing for the Project East River staff that would cover the origin and mission of the Psychological Strategy Board. McLean interpreted Allen's compliance along the lines of his original and more specific request for help on questions of emotion management. As a result of these exchanges, he wrote Allen on January 12, 1952, expressing appreciation for the latter's "willingness to cooperate" and confirming Allen's stipulation, made in their telephone conversation that same morning, that the collaboration between the two agencies "should best be kept on an informal basis." In other words, the links between the Psychological Strategy Board and Project East River would remain unofficial and secret. McLean stressed that Project East River was interested neither in Allen's views concerning psychological warfare generally nor in an account of the official policies of the Psychological Strategy Board. Allen would be useful to Project East River as a consultant who would assist in developing the emotion management strategies essential to a national civil defense program.

Project East River undertook to domesticate the psychological warfare tactics that were employed against America's enemies abroad. The propaganda instrumentarium used against the Communists would be retooled as emotion management techniques for psychologically manipulating the American people. The weapons devised to protect the United States from its enemies would now be turned against its own citizens, but, of course, in their own interest. The rationale for the use of psychological warfare techniques abroad and the justification for their incorporation into domestic civil defense were the same: national security.[39]

Conventionalization

The first phase of the Cold War system of emotion management was to develop new cognitive standards governing the conception of nuclear weapons. These standards were designed to suppress nuclear terror by reconceptualizing nuclear arms as "normal" instruments of military policy, by portraying the atomic bomb as a very powerful conventional weapon. Although atomic bombs might be quantitatively more destructive than the conventional bombs used in World War II, qualitatively they achieved essentially the same results. This was the conventionalization argument.[40]

As noted earlier, the initial American press coverage of the atomic bomb depicted nuclear war in sensational terms calculated to terrify the public. The early reportage on Hiroshima and Nagasaki left no doubt that an atomic attack on American cities would be a catastrophe too horrible to contemplate. Although attempts were made to quantify the impact of nuclear war on the United States, the public was left with the impression that the destruction would be virtually unimaginable. Civil defense theorists attempted to replace this apocalyptic view of nuclear war with a very different conception designed to check American anxiety about the bomb.

In January 1951, shortly before the FCDA became operational, the Office of Civil Defense in the NSRB produced a remarkable little booklet, *Survival Under Atomic Attack*. Although its original printing was limited to 225,000 copies, within a year more than 20 million copies were in circulation.[41] The booklet's main contention was that the dangers of nuclear attack had been wildly exaggerated; actually they could be survived without difficulty. Except for radioactivity—"the only way besides size in which atomic bombs differ from ordinary ones"—nuclear weapons were not fundamentally different from conventional arms. On the opening page, readers were apprised of the following surprising fact: "You can live through an atomic bomb raid and you won't have to have a Geiger counter, protective clothing, or special training in order to do it. The secrets of survival are: KNOW THE BOMB'S TRUE DANGERS. KNOW THE STEPS YOU CAN TAKE TO ESCAPE THEM."[42] The explosion of atomic bombs over America would not mean the end of the world. It would not be the ultimate catastrophe against which all protective measures were useless and illusory. In fact, an atomic bomb was "just another way of causing an explosion." Although the atomic bomb might be immensely destructive, its power, like that of any other bomb, was limited. This meant that "your chances of living through an atomic attack are much better than you may have thought."

Survival Under Atomic Attack reduced the phenomenon of nuclear attack to three general problems: blast, heat, and radiation. It developed a strategy to deal with each and outlined measures of self-protection dictated by these strategies. For example, in its instructions on protection from an atomic blast, the booklet noted that the specific steps Americans should take to diminish their chances of injury hinged on where they were at the moment the bomb exploded. If caught without warning in the open, they should fall flat and face down, ideally picking a spot protected from shattering glass and flying projectiles. The best move was to drop alongside the foundation of a "good substantial building," taking care to eschew poorly built wooden structures that would probably collapse. Or if there were no buildings in the vicinity, they should "jump in any handy ditch or gutter"—the "duck and cover" maneuver.[43]

Those with better luck, who found themselves inside a building when the bomb exploded, were advised to dash to the basement as quickly as possible and lie flat along an outer wall or underneath a heavy table. Or if the building had no basement or there was no time to reach it, they should pick an outside wall for protection or crawl under a bed or a table, taking care to stay as far as possible from windows. Because the blast would produce a blinding flash of light, it would be a mistake to look up in order to see what might be coming. Injury from the flash, flying glass, and other small projectiles that might damage the eyes could be prevented by burying the face in the arms and maintaining this position for ten or twelve seconds after the blast.

In an effort to blunt the distinction between nuclear and conventional weapons, *Survival Under Atomic Attack* also attempted to diminish the dangers of radioactivity. Although the booklet claimed that heat and blast would be the main causes of death and injury in an atomic attack, it devoted much more space to radioactivity, presumably because the public was believed to regard this danger as novel, uncanny, and perhaps irresistible. Readers were reminded that the phenomenon of radioactivity was neither new nor mysterious; indeed, everyone had inhaled and ingested very small amounts of radioactive materials without knowing it. And because science and medicine had experimented with X-rays for more than a half-century; more was actually known about radioactivity and its effects on humans than about infantile paralysis or even the common cold. Moreover, even if Americans were exposed to injurious radioactivity, they were not "doomed to die an early death." The hazards of radioactivity were trivialized by comparing them with a midsummer sunburn. The chances for a complete recovery from exposure were "much the same as for everyday accidents."[44]

In order to avoid contamination, readers were told to remain in their homes, where "there is little or nothing to fear" from this danger. Or as an alternative, they might seek refuge in their cars, taking care to roll up the windows. Those caught in the open at the moment of the explosion were advised to choreograph their technique of self-protection so that they could grasp something with which to cover themselves as they fell to the ground. A piece of board was recommended or perhaps some sheets of newspaper or a raincoat. Then "when it is safe to get up, throw away your covering."[45]

If, in spite of all their efforts, readers were exposed to radioactivity—perhaps by walking through contaminated rubble or getting wet in a rainfall—the procedure for self-decontamination turned out to be astonishingly simple. First, remove the contaminated clothing and bury it. Then take a shower or a bath, paying special attention to hair, hands, and fingernails. Special decontaminants were unnecessary. Warm water and soap were said to be ideal cleansers for this purpose. In short, an ordinary bath or shower would do the trick. "You can get rid of all the radioactive dirt you've picked up if you keep scrubbing."[46]

Survival Under Atomic Attack was the first of many media—government publications and films, newspaper and magazine articles, radio and television scripts, interviews and speeches, and even novels—that employed the conventionalization argument in order to diminish the horrifying aspects of nuclear weapons. The argument was that damage to life and property in a nuclear attack would not be more extensive than the destruction produced by the conventional air raids of World War II, in which Allied air forces delivered a mix of incendiary and high-explosive bombs that created huge firestorms and reduced hundreds of German and Japanese cities to rubble. Moreover, if the victims of a nuclear attack survived the initial blast, their injuries would not be more dangerous or debilitating than those suffered in the air raids of World War II.

This argument made inferences from the defensive measures that enabled civilian populations to survive large-scale conventional attacks to determine what would be needed to survive an atomic attack. These inferences were based on assumptions drawn from the United States Strategic Bombing Survey. This influential investigation documented the conditions under which Germany and Japan were able to sustain political coordination and maintain economic production despite the Allied bombing campaigns of 1944 and 1945. President Franklin D. Roosevelt established the survey on November 3, 1944, in order to study the impact of the Allied bombing of Germany. On August 15, 1945, President Truman extended its scope to include an analysis of the bombing of Japan, including the nuclear attacks on Hiroshima and Nagasaki. The survey staff was made up of 300 civilians, mainly scientists and engineers; 350 officers; and 500 enlisted men. Among the studies issued by the survey during 1945 and 1946, those most relevant to postwar American civil defense were the report on the Hiroshima and Nagasaki bombings and the summary report on the role of strategic bombing in the Pacific theater.[47] Since Hiroshima and Nagasaki were the only cities thus far subjected to atomic attack, the survey was the most important source of data for the conventionalization argument.

The survey held that the damage and casualties left by the Hiroshima bomb could have been reproduced by 220 B-29s. Only 125 B-29s would have been needed to duplicate the effects of the Nagasaki bomb. These considerations suggested that atomic bombs were nothing more than extraordinarily destructive conventional weapons. Indeed, the most devastating air attack of the war had not been the Hiroshima bombing, but the spectacular incendiary raid on Tokyo on the night of

March 9/10, 1945, a mission that had employed 334 B-29s carrying a total of 2,000 tons of ordinance. Sixteen square miles of the most heavily built-up and populated parts of the city had been consumed in flames, killing 83,793, wounding 40,918, and leaving more than 1 million homeless. All together, more than 2.5 million buildings had been destroyed, including 81 percent of the industrial district of Tokyo, 63 percent of its commercial establishments, and many of its residential districts. The survey also diminished the importance of radioactivity, arguing that it was responsible for no more than 20 percent of the casualties at Hiroshima and Nagasaki.

Although the survey estimated that the Hiroshima and Nagasaki bombs had increased the destructive power of a single bomber by a factor ranging from 50 to 250, based on the character and size of the target, this did not mean that the atomic bomb had invalidated all the principles of preatomic air war. Despite the horrors of nuclear war, specific steps could be taken to limit the loss of life and property. The survey maintained that in fact the civilian casualties in the conventional air raids of both the European and Pacific theaters could have been reduced by 95 percent if the victims had been protected by civil defense measures such as air-raid warnings, shelters, evacuation, and postattack assistance. The experience of Hiroshima and Nagasaki indicated that civil defense would be even more important in the era of atomic weapons. Anticipating arguments that would appear in the Bull Report, the Hopley Report, the Blue Book, and Project East River, the survey applied the implications of the conventionalization argument to American civil defense planning: "If we recognize in advance the possible danger and act to forestall it, we shall, at worst, suffer minimum casualties and disruption."[48]

Because of the mysteries associated in the public mind with the atomic bomb—a new superweapon with miraculous powers that unleashed the forces of nature—it is not surprising that theoreticians of conventionalization devoted most of their attention to the ghastly medical effects of nuclear weapons. For example, Ralph Lapp—atomic physicist, alumnus of the Manhattan Project, and early advocate of civil defense—attempted to demystify the phenomenon of radiation and neutralize the "numbing effect" that the mere mention of radioactivity had on the lay person. According to Lapp, radioactivity was just another of the innumerable hazards of contemporary life. Troubled Americans, nervous about their fate in a nuclear war, were reassured that the perils of radiation sickness had been wildly exaggerated. In fact, they were no more serious than the injuries inflicted by many other modern weapons. Although Lapp admitted that the damage to the human organism produced by the absorption of radiation could be quite appalling, this did not mean that Americans should be petrified by fear of atomic weapons. On the contrary, the dangers of radiation simply marked one more entry in the catalog of risks produced by modern technology, comparable to the risks of automobile driving. The attainment of what Lapp called a "rational perspective on radiation" required nothing more than an intelligent program of public information.[49] Lapp also discounted the seriousness of the grotesque burns suffered by the victims at Hiroshima and Nagasaki. Widely publicized in American newspaper and magazine photographs, these burns were caused by the initial flash of radiation created by the atomic explosion. The more hideous burns resulted in the formation of horribly disfiguring masses of keloid, or scar tissue. Cause for worry? Not according to Lapp, who claimed that "burns from an atomic blast are no worse than those resulting from other forms of modern weapons."[50]

One of the chief theoreticians of the Cold War system of emotion management was Yale University psychologist Irving L. Janis. In his Rand Corporation study of the psychological impact of World War II's bombing raids and their implications for American civil defense, Janis claimed that survivors of the atomic-bomb attacks on Japan presented essentially the same symptoms observed in survivors of other bombing disasters. Drawing on interview data collected from survivors of the Hiroshima and Nagasaki bombings by the United States Strategic Bombing Survey, Janis contended that the psychological disorders suffered as a result of atomic attack—from psychosis, sociopathic behavior, panic, depression, anxiety, persistent phobias, and posttraumatic psychiatric dysfunctions to "the more transient symptoms of emotional shock"—did not seem to differ from the psychological effects produced by intensive conventional bombing. As a result of these considerations, he concluded that "a single atomic bomb disaster is not likely to produce any different kinds of effects on morale than those produced by other types of heavy air attacks."[51]

The conventionalization argument was not confined to civil defense booklets, government pronouncements, and studies by members of the civil defense community. On the contrary, the mass media were perhaps even more active in promulgating this position. Popular magazines took the lead in publishing stories about nuclear attack and postattack recovery in which nuclear war was depicted as a technologically more sophisticated version of World War II. The most dramatic example of this sort of imaginative reportage appeared in *Collier's*, which devoted its entire October 27, 1951, issue to a fictional account of World War III. The editors noted that this conflict could start tomorrow, bringing "the most terrible calamity that has ever befallen the human race."[52] Although the issue was entitled "Preview of the War We Do Not Want," the editors left no doubt that its real purpose was to show how the United States could win a nuclear war. In the *Collier's* scenario, the war begins when the Red Army invades Yugoslavia and the United States responds with a three-month saturation atomic-bombing campaign against military and industrial targets in the Soviet Union. The air war escalates with Soviet nuclear attacks on New York, Washington, Philadelphia, Chicago, and Detroit. As was de rigueur in American Cold War ideology, Moscow was responsible for initiating the atomic bombing of civilian populations. Maps of American cities, with the now-famous series of concentric circles marking levels of destruction from the center of the bomb's detonation, charted the results of these attacks.

The story of World War III was narrated in the hyperrealism of the superpatriotic "You Are There" journalism familiar to Americans from the reportage on World War II. Legendary Associated Press war correspondent Hal Boyle filed a breathless account of the atomic bombing of Washington. The accompanying two-page color picture depicted the city in flames, the Washington Monument snapped in half, the Capitol dome decapitated, and the White House gutted. In Boyle's melodramatic prose: "The American capital is missing in action: Washington is burning to death."[53] Edward R. Murrow was recruited to relive the experience of his thrilling B-17 raids on Germany. In the World War III reincarnation of the fearless and laconic war correspondent, Murrow accompanied the crew responsible for the atomic bombing of Moscow. In an article entitled "A-Bomb Mission to Moscow," Murrow described how the B-36 bomber crew professionally delivered two atomic bombs over its designated target and flew home, as if this were a 1944 mission over Berlin.

The editors of *Collier's* stressed that the catastrophic levels of destruction were due largely to public indifference to civil defense. The problem was not flawed federal civil defense planning, but the general apathy of the American people, who had failed to grasp that "civil defense involves the active instantaneous participation of every able-bodied man, woman, and child."[54] However, the result of the nuclear devastation of American cities was hardly what might be expected: the breakdown of the state, the collapse of the economy, and the disintegration of the American war-fighting capacity. On the contrary, the mutual destruction of American and Soviet cities in nuclear thrust and counterthrust transpired as an atomic Battle of Britain. The state and the economy remained intact, and the population survived in spite of terrible ruin and hardship.

Consistent with *Collier's* commitment to the conventionalization argument, the American public reordered its civil defense priorities, and the American military gained control of the nuclear exchange. In an operation called Task Force Victory, American forces destroyed the remaining Soviet nuclear stockpile, following the Hollywood format of how America had won World War II. The enemy was unconditionally defeated, presumably demonstrating to *Collier's* readers that even "if The War We Do Not Want is forced upon us, we will win."[55] In the end, Philip Wylie provided a romanticized account of the postattack reconstruction of Philadelphia. Although the two-page layout accompanying Wylie's article pictured a cityscape of total desolation, the reader surveyed the debris in the company of a clean-shaven American army officer—trousers perfectly creased and shoes shined—and a female locomotive engineer in overalls, in the unlikely guise of a fetching Veronica Lake–blonde. The pair seemed to contemplate a glowing future together, suggesting that although war may be hell and nuclear war even worse, an atomic attack leaves all things essentially the same in American life.

On October 30, 1953, the NSC systematized the strategic doctrine of the Eisenhower presidency in NSC 162/2 and embraced the conventionalization argument as the official policy of the United States government. A Soviet challenge to vital American interests would be countered by a crushing nuclear response, executed under circumstances best calculated to serve American objectives. NSC 162/2 proposed to minimize the risk of Soviet aggression by means of an "adequate offensive retaliatory strength" based on "massive atomic capability."[56] The historiography of NSC 162/2 has stressed its endorsement of "massive retaliation," an expression not used in the document. However, NSC 162/2 is also important for its commitment to the conventionalization argument, which is treated as a self-evident axiom of military strategy requiring no justification or even discussion. Nuclear weapons are tacitly understood as routine instruments of warfare, to be employed as opportunities dictate: In the event of war, "the United States will consider nuclear weapons to be as available for use as other munitions."[57]

This position was not altered by the advent of the hydrogen bomb, which exceeded the destructive power of the first atomic bomb by more than a thousand times and introduced the troubling and indeterminate danger of "radioactive fallout": by-products of the detonation that are blown into the stratosphere and fall back to the earth as radioactive rainfall or ash. Depending on the prevailing winds, fallout from a single hydrogen bomb could be dispersed over hundreds or even thousands of square miles, poisoning the earth and indiscriminately killing crops, animals, and human beings.

On November 1, 1952, the United States secretly detonated its first thermonuclear weapon as part of a series of tests code-named OPERATION IVY and performed at the AEC testing area in the Marshall Islands. Information about the hydrogen-bomb test was not released until April 1954. The FCDA summary of the test results noted that had the explosion occurred in Washington, it would have produced "complete annihilation" from the Capitol as ground zero to Arlington National Cemetery. The OPERATION IVY detonation created the largest nuclear fireball ever produced: three and one-half miles in diameter, or large enough to engulf about 25 percent of Manhattan, roughly from Washington Square Park to Central Park.

In performing the delicate task of informing Americans about this weapon and the fact that it might be used against the United States, the FCDA and the AEC collaborated in producing a highly sanitized twenty-eight-minute black-and-white documentary film entitled *Operation Ivy*, which recorded the scientific preparations for the test, the explosion, and its immediate effects. In the press information kit on OPERATION IVY prepared by the FCDA—much of it designed as copy for both print and broadcast media—the magnitude of the blast and its sensational visual effects were highlighted. Neither the film nor the FCDA media package, however, mentioned the fallout produced by the test.

In its discussion of the significance of the hydrogen bomb for civil defense planning, the FCDA maintained that it would be "unrealistic" to draw a sharp distinction between the "conventional atomic bomb"— now categorized as just another instrument of warfare, so that the distinction between conventional and nuclear weapons seemed to disappear—and the new hydrogen bomb. The two weapons differed only in the amount of damage each produced. The type of damage— in both cases, blast, heat, and radiation—remained the same. It followed that there were only incremental differences between the two bombs, the same kinds of differences that allegedly differentiated the atomic bomb from conventional World War II bombs. By stressing the differences in levels of destruction and ignoring the phenomenon of fallout, the FCDA encouraged journalists to interpret the new weapon within the conceptual apparatus of the conventionalization argument. If the hydrogen bomb were simply a larger atomic bomb, a thermonuclear attack on the United States would require no changes in its civil defense policy. The hydrogen bomb would merely create larger areas of destruction, which would call for more civil defense workers and equipment. The new weapon might create disasters of greater magnitude, but it would not produce a new kind of disaster.[58]

In the press release announcing the forthcoming film, FCDA chief Val Peterson reiterated this point. The individual preparedness and community organization required to protect the American people in an atomic attack would also prove serviceable against the hydrogen bomb. A thermonuclear attack would be manageable by tried-and-true American self-reliance. Even in the thermonuclear age, Peterson insisted, "home front preparedness is and will be a manageable problem if we recognize the dangers fully, face them calmly and prepare our defense intelligently. That is our American tradition."[59]

At the beginning of the same month in which the United States prepared to release the film of its first thermonuclear test, it also conducted what proved to be its largest and most controversial hydrogen-bomb detonation. This test demonstrated that although the existence and potentially fatal dangers of fallout could not be concealed, they could be accommodated by the rhetoric of the conventionalization argument.

On the morning of March 1, 1954, the AEC carried out its test, code-named BRAVO, at the Bikini Atoll in the Marshall Islands. Due to unanticipated changes in wind direction following the explosion, 28 Americans working at a weather and observation station as well as 236 Marshall Islanders were exposed to dangerous levels of radiation produced by fallout from the blast. Some eighty-five miles east of Bikini, the crew of the Japanese fishing boat *Lucky Dragon* was even less fortunate. By the time the vessel reached its port on March 14, most of its crew presented symptoms of radiation poisoning. The *Lucky Dragon* had entered the history of the nuclear age.[60]

These events were quickly picked up by the American media, which pressed the White House for an explanation. Accordingly, when AEC Chairman Lewis Strauss returned to Washington from the Marshall Islands, he appeared at President Eisenhower's press conference on March 31. Both this press conference and the subsequent news coverage of BRAVO focused not on the phenomenon of fallout and the new dangers it posed, but on the magnitude of the thermonuclear blast and its destructiveness. When Richard Wilson of Cowles Publications pressed Strauss on the question of exactly how extensive the damage produced by a thermonuclear explosion could be, his response shocked the Washington press corps:

> A: Well, the nature of an H-bomb, Mr. Wilson, is that, in effect, it can be made as large as you wish, as large as the military requirement demands, that is to say, an H-bomb can be made as—large enough to take out a city.
> CHORUS: What?
> MR. SMITH [Merriman Smith of United Press]: How big a city?
> A: Any city.
> Q: Any city, New York?
> A: The metropolitan area, yes.

The next day, the *New York Times* reported the Strauss statement and press conference under the headline "H-BOMB CAN WIPE OUT ANY CITY." A map of the New York area indicating incendiary damage from a thermonuclear attack on Manhattan covered a twenty-five-mile radius that extended to Scarsdale and Tarrytown in Westchester County, Hicksville on Long Island, and perilously close to Greenwich in Connecticut and Morristown and Plainfield in New Jersey.[61]

Throughout 1954, the extent and danger of the fallout produced by the BRAVO test remained a bureaucratic secret closely held by the

AEC.[62] The secret report on BRAVO prepared by the AEC found that the blast had produced radioactive debris that covered an elliptically shaped area of 8,800 square miles, some 220 miles long and 40 miles wide. Within a distance of 160 miles downwind of ground zero, anyone exposed to the blast would have been killed. After the Eisenhower national security apparatus spent some ten months debating how to handle the public relations of the AEC report—what to tell and how and when to tell it—a public version was finally released on February 15, 1955, but not before Ralph Lapp preempted the government's public-relations efforts by publishing articles in both the *Bulletin of the Atomic Scientists* and the *New Republic* that accurately summarized the AEC findings. Lapp estimated that if the BRAVO bomb were dropped on Washington, it would create a cloud of radioactive particles large enough to cover the entire state of Maryland. The fallout from the blast would cause more deaths than the explosion itself.[63]

Val Peterson was informed of the unexpectedly extensive fallout from the BRAVO test on July 8, 1954. Yet in his speech in December to the Washington Conference of Mayors on National Security, he maintained that the hydrogen bomb had no important implications for civil defense. Peterson reminded the mayors that current American civil defense doctrine was based on the British and German experience of World War II, when both countries organized their cities for protection against air raids. Had the hydrogen bomb invalidated this doctrine? Was the civil defense program developed in the early 1950s obsolete? Not according to Peterson, who contended that there was not "a single thing that has been developed in civil defense that is not just as pertinent today as it has been at any time."

Although the syntax was somewhat tortured, the substance of Peterson's position was clear: The training, techniques, and equipment developed by the British in the early 1940s for protection against the Luftwaffe and modified by the United States in the early 1950s for protection against the atomic bomb would prove equally effective in a thermonuclear attack. New Yorkers could survive a hydrogen-bomb attack by doing essentially the same things that Londoners had done to survive the blitz. Americans anxious about poisoning, disease, or death from fallout were offered the soothing reassurance that radioactive material decays rapidly, frequently in a matter of hours. Even under "very bad conditions," shelter from fallout would not be required for more than four or five days. What kind of shelter would be needed? The cellars used by American farmers to preserve vegetables in the cold months and milk and cream in the summer were, suitably modified, the best protection from radioactivity that the former governor of Nebraska could recommend. If Americans applied Peterson's homespun methods, they would be "perfectly safe against radioactivity." In order to emerge unscathed and uncontaminated from such a shelter, American families would require nothing more than "a jug of water, some cheese and crackers, or the equivalent thereof, and some kind of sanitary facility."[64]

In sum, the hydrogen bomb, like the atomic bomb, was a standard piece of military hardware, whose uses and effects were not fundamentally different from those of the bombs employed in World War II. In preparing the home front for World War III, the civil defense community assured the public that the advent of thermonuclear weapons marked no essential difference in the possibilities of survival and the means of achieving it.

From Nuclear Terror to Nuclear Fear

The purpose of the Cold War system of emotion management was to solve the problem of national will. This was held to be possible only by developing a method for handling its most extreme expression: the phenomenon of nuclear terror. The way to attack nuclear terror was to dispel this dangerous emotion by means of a restrained and prudent nuclear fear that could be controlled by civil defense in accordance with the demands of national security. Americans needed to be convinced that the decisive weapon in the Soviet arsenal was not the atomic bomb, but their own terror of atomic attack: Nuclear terror, not the bomb, was the absolute weapon. They also needed to be persuaded that the real object of their deepest anxieties should not be the possibility of nuclear war, but their own extravagant response to such a possibility: Nuclear terror also displaced the bomb as the primary object of anxiety.

It followed that a key maneuver in the turn from nuclear terror to nuclear fear was the subjectification of the nuclear threat. This process of internalization—transposing the nuclear threat from the domain of politics to that of psychology—consisted of shifting the main Communist menace from the Soviet nuclear arsenal to the emotional weaknesses of the American people. The ultimate obstacle to victory over Communism lay within the soul of the individual American. In the final analysis, the inadequacy of the American response to Soviet expansion could be traced not to errors of policy, the bad judgment of politicians, or the questionable loyalties of bureaucrats. Rather, defects in the American character were at fault. From the standpoint of civil defense planners, the advantages of this tactic were obvious. The forbidding technological, political, and economic problem of devising plausible strategies for surviving a nuclear attack was translated into a much more tractable personal, psychological, and therapeutic problem for which the individual was finally responsible: How do I make sure that I do not become a Communist dupe, a danger to American security, and the principal weapon in the Soviet project of world domination? This was a question of emotional self-knowledge and self-control. The chief issue it raised was not how to manage survival in a nuclear war, but how Americans should manage themselves in preparation for such a war. How should they control their excessive fears so that nuclear terror did not break the self-discipline and paralyze the moral energies required for the struggle against Communism?

By psychologizing and depoliticizing the problem of survival, civil defense planners attempted to effect a fundamental displacement in the public consciousness. Two steps were involved.

First, the public learned new norms for emotion management that specified how nuclear weapons should be experienced. Americans were told that they must scrutinize their own psychology. Anxieties about nuclear attack were thus transformed into worries about the reasonableness of these very anxieties. An irrational terror of nuclear weapons now became the main danger. As a result, the American people would lose sight of the crucial role of nuclear weapons in American national security policy and the atomic bomb as the major threat to survival. Their primary concern would not be the possibility of nuclear war, but the possibility that in the event of such a war, their own performance might be badly compromised by panic. The only responsible attitude to take toward the bomb was a healthy and measured fear. In the social psychology of Cold War emotion management, nuclear terror produced panic, apathy, or stupefaction. However, a robust and prudent fear would serve as a useful inducement in motivating the public to protect itself. Most important, a belief in self-protection would encourage the public to participate in civil defense. Civil defense would, in turn, provide the domestic support essential to the policy of containment. If the American people, motivated by a rational fear of nuclear attack, were convinced that they could survive by means of careful planning, sound training, and firm moral discipline, then the problem of national will would be solved.

Second, Americans learned new strategies for controlling their emotions in preparing for a nuclear war. Nuclear fear could be controlled only through civil defense training. This position supplied a powerful rationale for civil defense as the politically and psychologically correct response to the bomb. Civil defense would function as a social technology of emotion control that taught the public how to manage its newfound anxieties about nuclear terror and how to channel its fear of nuclear attack to its own best advantage and, most important, in ways that would support the policy of containment. As a result, civil defense became the therapy of choice in "beating" panic. In negotiating this passage from nuclear terror to nuclear fear, Americans would learn, in the parlance of the 1950s, to live with the bomb.

Project East River clearly articulated the logic and pragmatics of the shift from nuclear terror to nuclear fear. Part IX of the *Report of the Project East River*, entitled *Information and Training for Civil Defense*, included an appendix, "Panic Prevention and Control," that emphasized the differences between panic and fear. Panic is "highly excited behavior" characterized by "aimless, unorganized, unreasoning, nonconstructive activity." It results from anxieties that are sudden, desperate, frequently groundless, and impervious to reason and evidence. The same conditions that produce panic can also lead to apathy, a "mass paralysis" that may weaken capacities for self-protection as seriously as can panic itself. Fear, on the contrary, is a useful reaction to danger because it sets in motion the effort required for a satisfactory response.[65]

"Panic Prevention and Control" treated the possibility of panic in a nuclear attack as a "working assumption." In a subsection, "The Special Problems of Mob Aggression, Rioting, Scape-Goating, Looting, Etc.," the American public is characterized as a xenophobic, emotionally unstable, and violence-prone mass. "What is the likelihood during a raid upon our cities that mob aggression would seek and find scapegoats to destroy instead of the real enemy?" In answering this troubling question, "Panic Prevention and Control" noted that the recent history of American society—with its record of lynchings, race riots, and the indiscriminate seizure and incarceration of Japanese-Americans during World War II—was not reassuring. The domestic political culture of the Cold War, which condoned "aggression toward merely unorthodox persons as symbols of communism," was also disturbing.[66] Would the public respond to a nuclear attack by undertaking productive civil defense work or by hunting down scapegoats? "Panic Prevention and Control" concluded its discussion of this issue on a decidedly pessimistic note: "The very real possibility exists that in the event of sudden attack, mob action could readily break out. There are convenient scapegoats, and the nature of the world situation has made inevitable a long accumulation of anxiety and frustration toward Russia which could easily be translated into senseless aggression.[67]

In light of these considerations, "Panic Prevention and Control" outlined a program of emotional reeducation designed to instruct the public in the proper response to a nuclear attack:

> Civil defense education must make people aware that a considerable degree of fear under attack is normal and inevitable. As with the development of healthy attitudes among combat troops, civil defense must, in effect, tell people: "You will feel afraid when the first attack comes. So will everyone else, for attack is dangerous. There is no abnormality and no cowardliness in such justified fear. It is not whether you feel afraid, but what you do when you are afraid that counts. The fear you experience will make you more alert, stronger, and more tireless for the things that you and your neighbors can do to protect yourselves."[68]

The pragmatic fear advocated by Project East River is "healthy" for three reasons. It is a normal, indeed an inevitable, response to the dangers of nuclear war. But unlike nuclear terror, it can motivate appropriately trained citizens to take positive steps to protect themselves from these dangers. Finally, the instrumentally rational behavior motivated by fear can be "channeled." If people are properly trained, their fears will prompt them to react in conformity with this training. Like soldiers who have been disciplined to exploit their fear of death in order to execute military assignments despite the hazards of combat—the "we've got a job to do" work ethic of warfare—Americans can be trained to take advantage of their fears of nuclear attack in order to perform useful civil defense work. Therefore, the lesson the public must learn is clear and simple: Nuclear terror is abnormal and uncontrollable. Nuclear fear is a normal and manageable response to the bomb.

It followed that Americans could be expected to respond to a threat of nuclear attack in an organized and disciplined fashion only if they had been trained to do so. In the social psychology of Project East River, training was "the surest simple preventive measure against panic." In the same way that combat troops were rigorously trained to estimate dangers quickly and react unreflectively with the most appropriate measures, so the objective of civil defense was the "intensive training of the public to recognize the main sources of danger in foreseeable emergencies and practice in effective actions to combat these dangers."[69] Following the model of combat training, the realism of civil defense exercises was regarded as crucial. Insofar as possible, it was important to reproduce the dangers that would actually be encountered in a nuclear attack. By drilling and rehearsing the proper response to these dangers, Americans would acquire a panic-resistant moral and emotional self-discipline.

Although the best safeguard against panic was a program of thorough drills in which the correct responses to expected dangers were mastered, the experience of a nuclear attack could not be reproduced in civil defense exercises. Therefore, it was unlikely that a real attack would be followed by the organized and constructive responses called for by civil defense emotion managers. An actual attack would create disorganization and panic. This meant that during a nuclear emergency, civil defense education should be reinforced by what Project East River called "authoritative instructions" that connected prior training with the impending attack and specified precisely what attack victims should do. In the postattack environment, survivors would suffer acute anxiety. Exactly what had happened? What was the extent of the damage? What perils did the survivors face? What was the fate of their families? How long would the danger last, and what measures were being taken to eliminate it? If timely and credible answers to these questions were not forthcoming, "rumor and imagination" would take over, "with consequent danger of paralysis, panic, and senseless reaction."[70]

Spontaneous rumors were an inevitable consequence of a nuclear crisis. And rumors were likely to be magnified and exploited by enemy agents distributed throughout the United States to spread false information calculated to panic the victims of the attack. Project East River envisioned a postattack America riven by anxiety, panic, and the proliferation of false information and invaded by networks of Communist agents, invisible and hard at work recycling existing rumors and placing new misinformation in circulation in order to aggravate the emotion management problems of civil defense authorities.

As a means of countering postattack Communist subversion, Project East River proposed an intensive propaganda effort that would achieve state control of mass psychology by penetrating the relations of private life. In the section of Part IX of the *Report of the Project East River* entitled "Rumor and Dangerous Public Reactions," this endeavor is innocuously characterized as a program of public information designed to enlighten Americans about common concerns of national security. As Project East River conceived of the program, it would generate a continual stream of information that Americans would need to carry out the civil defense tasks for which they had been trained. Total continuity and consistency in propaganda were essential, since any unexplained break in the flow of information might lead to disorganization and panic.

In setting up a postattack communications network, the management of misinformation and disinformation would present a major challenge for civil defense planners. In order to limit the proliferation of harmful rumors and reduce their damage, Project East River proposed a two-channel system of communication. Over one channel, civil defense control centers would communicate reliable information to neighborhood and block wardens. Wardens would organize a system of local surveillance by recruiting informants to report on rumors circulating through the neighborhood.

Over the other channel, these rumors would be reported back to the civil defense control centers: "To detect and counteract dangerous public reactions during attack the communication system requires a circuit leading back from wardens' areas to control centers. Over this return channel, appropriate civil defense personnel should report rumor and dangerous public conditions so that these may be countered by authoritative information and instructions."[71] On this second channel, "public misunderstanding, dangerous rumors, and need for further information or special instructions" would be relayed to civil defense control centers from "public shelters and other places where the public gathers."[72] Sites for monitoring the public would be linked to control centers by telephone or courier:

> Every broadcast center for public information should designate a member of its staff (preferably one trained in the techniques of rumor-control) to

assess incoming reports of public reaction, and to devise and initiate rapid countermeasures for dangerous rumors. This running assessment of public morale and reaction should bear continuously on the information program which is put on the air.[73]

In this manner, officials would be able to manage the public reaction to the attack and minimize the possibility of dysfunctional emotional responses and inappropriate conduct based on local misreadings of the postattack situation.

Project East River seems to have contemplated the following scenario: The United States is hit by a Soviet nuclear offensive, creating immense physical and human destruction and social disorganization. American society is infiltrated by Communist agents working to destroy the morale of the home front. Under attack, the American people prove to be morally weak and intellectually irresponsible. Credulous, impressionable, ready to accept what they hear and pass it on despite the obvious hazards of this conduct, their behavior hardly satisfies the highest standards of civil defense discipline. In addition, if things go badly, as Project East River warns is likely to be the case, Americans will also react badly. They will panic, create obstacles to civil defense rescue and rehabilitation efforts, and blame real or imagined threats on fellow citizens who are less fortunate or less well integrated into American life than they are—scapegoats who are likely to become innocent victims of irrational aggression and violence.

In spite of these unpromising assumptions, civil defense wardens—presumed to be alive and well in the wake of the attack—will be in place to operate a network of informants, recruited and trained in the preattack phase of the nuclear crisis and also alive and on their feet. These neighborhood intelligence agents will gather rumors germane to the effective management of the postattack community and report to their controllers. The latter will dispatch this information through the fire and rubble of nuclear destruction or telephone it through the chaos of postattack electronic breakdown to a civil defense control center, also presumed to have survived the attack. Emotion management specialists at this center will identify the information as false or, should it be true but damaging to the postattack recovery program, as inappropriate or inoperative. At that point, instructions for squelching the rumors will be transmitted back to the local wardens, who will arrange for the authoritative communication of the "correct information" to their neighborhoods. In this manner, rumors, misinformation, and disinformation will be labeled as such and condemned as foolish, unpatriotic, and dangerous.

Project East River stressed that the performance of this communications network depended on a relatively unfettered and comprehensive distribution of knowledge. Maximum publicity of information about the effects of nuclear weapons and the real conditions of nuclear

war in the preattack phase of the nuclear crisis and a continual feed of
current news at the time of the attack were crucial. It must be "plain
to people that the whole story can be calmly told and that the situation,
as bad as it may be, is not wholly disastrous and is being dealt with as
effectively as possible by the orderly machinery of civil defense."[74] The
Cold War system of emotion management required a free flow of information to and from the public. In a nuclear war, the home-front
morale could not be sustained by employing the doctrine of military
secrecy derived from World War II.

According to World War II rules, all military information was subject to strict censorship. Battle plans, the disposition of forces, and even
the results of engagements had to be held as closely as possible in order
to protect forces in the field. Project East River argued that these axioms
of military secrecy were based on "obsolescent ideas of warfare." In a
nuclear war, "the citizen in his home or shop is in the battle scene. It
is as essential that he be apprised of the situation as the engineer in the
boiler room of a carrier or the combat team dug in for the night on
some lonely hill." The collapse of the distinction between battlefield
and home front and the importance of a full distribution of war information in maintaining public morale meant that the new exigencies of
propaganda and emotion management outweighed the old argument
for military secrecy.[75]

In his *Collier's* article on panic, Val Peterson provided a simplified,
mass-market version of civil defense as emotion management. Because
panic was the ultimate weapon in the Cold War, Peterson examined
the failures of individual emotional self-control that were alleged to be
responsible for the American predisposition to panic. His purpose was
to persuade *Collier's* readers that they were typically panic-prone Americans. Readers' anxieties about the dangers posed by their own panic—
Peterson discussed in some detail and with accompanying photographs
some recent disasters in American life said to have been caused largely
by panic—would lead them to the question of how they could manage
their emotions. By employing techniques of emotional self-control,
they could learn how to defeat panic and thereby foil any Soviet attempt to dominate the United States by exploiting the emotional weaknesses of its citizens.[76]

Accordingly, Peterson stressed the importance of becoming "panic
proof." His article even provided a simple self-administered psychological test by means of which readers could measure their susceptibility
to panic: "Test Yourself: How Panic Proof Are You?" Peterson's test
included ten questions on mathematical and logical relations to be answered within ten minutes, requiring the performance of unfamiliar
quantitative operations under artificially imposed conditions of stress.
It also included a brief psychological self-evaluation. How did readers
feel when they saw a spider dart across their pillow or when they ex-

amined a picture of the victims of a fatal accident? How did they react when they were alone and stranded in an automatic elevator stalled between floors? Not worried at all? Tense? Badly jarred? Worse?[77]

Peterson claimed that 83 percent of American men and 55 percent of American women could be made "reasonably panic resistant." How could this condition be achieved? It was necessary to "make fear work for you." Readers were urged not to be ashamed of being afraid. "When you're under attack, fear is natural—even healthy." The key, Peterson advised, was to use your fear to your best advantage instead of allowing it to use you. In the latter case, victims of fear would quickly find themselves in the grip of panic. In the former case, trained citizens, like trained soldiers, would employ their fear as a means of becoming both more alert and emotionally more resilient, even under conditions of ultimate stress. Peterson insisted, however, that these results could be expected only on the basis of civil defense training that would teach people what to expect in a nuclear attack, what measures to take, and how to develop the determination and self-control necessary to perform the measures required.

Civil defense training was represented mainly as a means of achieving emotional self-mastery. Along these lines, Peterson provided readers with a list of "panic stoppers": techniques of emotion self-management drawn from FCDA public-information booklets that told householders how to prepare for a nuclear crisis. The performance of civil defense exercises—practicing drills at home, building a home shelter, taking a first-aid course, learning "fireproof housekeeping," storing emergency supplies—would provide "insulation" against panic. It would also enable family members to discharge their civil defense obligations "like trained soldiers under fire."[78] Thus civil defense would teach Americans how to control their emotions so they did not become victims of their own terror. In the final analysis, the mastery of a nuclear crisis would be achieved by self-mastery conceived as emotion management.

The theoretical basis of the Cold War system of emotion management elaborated by Project East River and popularized by the FCDA was first outlined by Irving L. Janis in his studies on the psychological problems of civil defense. Janis argued that the solution to the problem of panic required a national program with two components: a public-information campaign regarding the effects of nuclear weapons, and civil defense training that would prepare the American people for a nuclear attack. Full and accurate information would enable Americans to develop "realistic expectations" about their prospects for survival and also combat "feelings of helplessness." Janis regarded civil defense as a way of "channelizing" apprehensions about nuclear attack in order to minimize "disruptive fear reactions." Civil defense should stress "emotional-training techniques" that "build up a tolerance for insecurity." In the final analysis, training should result in an "emotional inoculation" against panic.[79] Of course, feelings of insecurity could not be eliminated altogether, but from the standpoint of emotion management, this was not a disadvantage: "A slight dose of insecurity often serves as a powerful motivation for participating in group activities which are designed to ward off the danger."[80] Or less obliquely, fear would motivate Americans to enlist in civil defense training programs as the most effective way to protect themselves.

Janis recommended a private, voluntary bomb-shelter program as an effective means of channeling nuclear fear. With the advent of Soviet nuclear weapons, the strategy of deterrence placed new demands on the American economy. In order to develop a credible deterrent, it was necessary to allocate funds, material, and manpower to build weapons systems as well as installations to protect them from attack. It also was imperative to protect economic production essential to national security and the command and control centers of the American polity. At a minimum, this would require underground shelters for key political, military, and industrial personnel and facilities to safeguard the apparatus on which the operation of the state and the economy depended. Because of the immense fiscal requirements of deterrence, what could realistically be expected in the way of a public-shelter program? At best, underground dormitories reserved for workers in critical industries. The construction of public shelters for most Americans, including the inhabitants of those cities judged to be most vulnerable to attack, was out of the question. City dwellers, left exposed to the hazards of nuclear attack, would be expected to look after themselves.

The American urban population could hardly be expected to ignore the plain facts of the preattack world. Ambitious plans would be set in motion to protect favored strata of the society. These plans would require the acquiescence of the public in general as well as the active participation of the urban work force. Should a nuclear war become imminent, these circumstances might produce a social crisis. They could even precipitate a civil war between the haves—those who enjoyed privileged access to protection from attack—and the have-nots—those left to fend for themselves. Janis envisioned urban populations resisting, rioting, or otherwise struggling to gain access to resources for survival, instead of submissively executing the tasks that strategists had assigned them in the national security program. What to do? How could the cooperation and docility of the cities be guaranteed under these wrenching conditions? How could the fears of urban dwellers be "channelized" in ways that supported national security?

Janis answered these questions by proposing that Americans be encouraged to build their own private or neighborhood shelters. The project of constructing a domestic shelter was not unduly complex. And even if homemade structures did not provide ideal protection, they still might save tens of thousands of lives. Janis also suggested that urbanites would be willing to devote their leisure hours—and presumably their savings as well—to construct shelters for their families. Standardized specifications adaptable to a variety of locales, terrains, and housing conditions could be made available, and interested parties could receive detailed instructions on how to build the shelter best tailored to their needs. Janis acknowledged that the unequal distribution of wealth and access to building materials and labor, especially during a national emergency, might cause "acute social resentments among those classes of the population which are not in a position to acquire or build expensive private shelters." However, this problem could be handled by rationing building materials and subsidizing those unable to meet construction costs.[81]

What would a program of do-it-yourself shelter construction achieve? Protection from nuclear attack? Hardly. In Janis's analysis, the real objective of the program was not security, but the illusion of security. This is clear in his explanation of the rationale for the program, which was based on three considerations. First, shelter construction would give citizens the feeling that they were making an important contribution to their own safety. In addition, if Americans assumed personal responsibility for their security, this would minimize the obligations of the state, reduce the perception of government neglect, and make it less likely that the public would resist a policy of selective human resource protection. Finally, "nonrational factors," such as the pride of ownership and self-esteem enjoyed by those who had built their own shelters, might endow domestic shelters with what Janis called "considerable symbolic value" in reducing anxiety: "Even though surprise attacks may preclude their usefulness for some people, shelters will probably be psychologically advantageous."[82] The purpose of voluntary shelter construction was not to safeguard the lives of shelter builders, but to give them reassurance. The real aim of the program was not survival, but emotion management.

The Social Psychology of Emotion Management: American Society in World War III

In 1954, Philip Wylie published *Tomorrow!* a novel about a Soviet atomic attack in the mid-1950s on the fictional midwestern twin cities of Green Prairie and River City.[83] Wylie was a prolific novelist and magazine writer, popularizer of Jung and Freud, and the author of *The Generation of Vipers*, a vituperative indictment of what he took to be fundamental hypocrisies and illusions of American life. In the late 1940s, he had served as a self-appointed adviser to Senator Brian McMahon, chairman of the U.S. Senate Special Committee on Atomic Energy, and during the early 1950s, Wylie had worked as a special

Civil defense exhibit, 1953: the mobilization of nuclear fear. (Courtesy of
Dwight D. Eisenhower Library)

consultant to the FCDA. In *Tomorrow!* the Soviet Union launches a nuclear strike against the United States on the Saturday afternoon before
Christmas. Major cities are obliterated, millions are killed, the surviving
population is reduced to panic, and the social and political order of the
American nation threatens to break down.

As Wylie documents in lurid and fatiguing detail, surviving a nuclear attack depends on civil defense planning and training. What happens to those who fail to master the disciplines of civil defense? Wylie
sees three possibilities. They are killed, they become casualties, or they
panic. One woman, untrained in civil defense procedures and contemptuous of the civil defense program, is "sliced to red meat" as she
gazes out a window of her house at the moment of the explosion. A
working-class family that failed to prepare its leaking basement as a
shelter is badly injured in the blast. In an effort to escape their collapsing
house, most of its members are trampled to death by mobs stampeding
through the city. When the "red alert" siren announcing the air raid
is sounded in the center of the city, unprepared motorists create vast
traffic jams. Pedestrians fill the sidewalks and overflow into the streets,
trampling over abandoned vehicles and their hapless drivers. Yuletide
shoppers in heedless flight crack ribs, break legs, and crush their fellow
citizens to death in a futile effort to save themselves. Survivors of the

CIVIL DEFENDER

40 CENTS   DECEMBER, 1956

Elaine Stewart, forgotten starlet of the 1950s, admonishes Americans that
they must be alert today in order to stay alive tomorrow. The corollary,
of course, is that if they are not, they will be dead tomorrow. (*Civil Defender*)

attack, driven to a frenzy by the bomb blast and the firestorm it creates,
assault one another as well as the police and military units summoned
for their protection. Police are forced to fire on crowds of rioting civilians in order to protect themselves and reestablish order. Drunken
members of the underclass loot homes in outlying suburbs, murder the
owners, and rape their daughters. Waves of refugees from the city rav-
age the midwestern countryside, burning barns and houses for warmth
and looting shops for food and jewelry. Urban masses sack and burn

villages and strip them of their resources for survival, only to abandon
them and move on to other villages where the pillage is repeated. Control of the marauding civilian population becomes the new military
front in World War III. In Wylie's Hieronymus Bosch–like vision of
Middle America in the 1950s, only the threat of force backed by the
power of the police stands in the way of moral chaos. When the police
lose control of the public, nuclear terror overwhelms the institutional
order. The result is political and social breakdown, a post-Hobbesian
world deprived of a calculating and instrumental rationality and governed by uncontrolled and violent passions.[84]

Not all the citizens of Wylie's twin cities become victims of atomic
blast, radiation, fire, panic, riot, murder, or rape. At the beginning of
the novel, the reader is introduced to the Conner family of Green Prairie. The Conners live the American pastoral as pictured by Norman
Rockwell on the covers of the *Saturday Evening Post*, in a two-story,
white frame house on Walnut Street with front and back porches, a
large lawn with ample flower beds, and a vegetable garden in the rear.
The Conners are sitting down to Sunday dinner—a cholesterol-laden
feast of roast beef with mashed potatoes and gravy, fresh rolls with
wild-strawberry jam, and pumpkin pie with whipped cream—when
their repast is interrupted by the wailing of a siren summoning the civil
defense organization of Green Prairie to an air-raid drill.

The father, Henry, is a district warden, responsible for coordinating
civil defense in a neighborhood of some 3,000 homes, where he exercises authority over a thousand volunteers and supervises a team of
block wardens. At the siren, he dutifully interrupts his dinner and
equips himself with his crimson civil defense armband, whistle, and
helmet. The mother, Beth, is a member of the first-aid group. Proud of
her set of copper-bottomed cookware, she is responsible for preparing
sandwiches and serving refreshments for the civil defense–planning
meetings held in the Conner house. The younger son, Ted, is a high-
school student of sixteen and a ham-radio buff. As a member of the
civil defense communications division, he operates out of his attic bed-
room. When the alert sounds, he rushes to his post and tunes in the
local civil defense headquarters for information about a possible attack.
The older son, Charles, currently serving as an intelligence officer in
the air force, is enjoying a leave at home. Perhaps it is not surprising
that there is also a girl next door: Charles's sweetheart, Leonore, who
lives just across the privet hedge. Leonore is the local beauty queen
and, somewhat implausibly, a "Geigerman" outfitted in yellow plastic
"fire-resistant and chemical-proof" overalls and an anticontamination
suit with a hood and visor that, we learn, provides protection from
radioactivity. Armed with her Geiger counter, she monitors simulated
blast sites for dangerous radioactivity. The siren is a summons for the
Conners and other public-spirited citizens of Green Prairie to gather for

a surprise drill at the local high-school yard, where hundreds of volunteers train themselves to survive a Soviet nuclear attack by practicing fire-fighting and rescue techniques under conditions of simulated disaster.

On the Saturday afternoon before Christmas, the Green Prairie civil defense organization receives a warning that waves of Soviet bombers have penetrated North American airspace. The Conners respond quickly, their fears controlled by civil defense training. Henry rushes from a pre-Christmas dinner to his district headquarters at the high school, where the volunteers in his unit have assembled in accordance with preestablished plans. Grimly determined, they go about their assigned tasks quietly and efficiently. Rescue squads recheck their equipment a final time. Bulldozer and crane engines are tested. Radiation safety volunteers monitor their gauges. Patients are moved from the community hospital to nearby homes in order to make space for the casualties of the impending attack. Ambulances, fire trucks, and police cars are poised and ready. Ted speeds to the empty family house and waits alone at his radio set, patiently collecting information on the nuclear destruction of San Francisco, Los Angeles, and Dallas. When Leonore receives the coded telephone instruction informing her of the "red alert," she is having her hair done at the smartest hairdresser in the city in preparation for a chic Christmas party. Without hesitating, she rips herself untimely from the hair dryer and dashes from the salon. Maintaining icy self-control, she conceals news of the attack from the patrons and employees of the salon and even from neighbors who offer to drive her home.

When the bomb explodes, the citizens of Green Prairie who have learned correct civil defense procedures not only survive, but even manage to negotiate the hazards of the postattack environment without undue hardship. At the flash of the atomic blast, Henry Conner dives under a desk at his command post on the top floor of the high school. Within a few moments, he emerges unscathed and brushes off a few bits of dust. Ted takes refuge under his radio-equipment table and escapes with nothing more than a bruise and a cut leg. The Conner house, battered and scorched, still stands. Ted dutifully checks the gas and electricity, calmly puts on his coat, and makes his way through the nuclear debris to submit his report at civil defense headquarters. At the final alert signal, Beth packs a suitcase of civil defense equipment and walks to the neighborhood Presbyterian church, now designated as an emergency hospital, where she will begin her work as a volunteer nurse. When the attack catches her under way, she immediately drops to the ground at the foot of a neighbor's front lawn, picks herself up after the blast, and continues purposefully on her way to the church, not forgetting the suitcase.

As a result of sound civil defense measures taken in the Conners' district, mobile kitchens are in operation with volunteers preparing hot meals. Kerosene stoves, coats, and sweaters are distributed to those without heat. Housewives, "having nothing better to do," arm themselves with brooms and dustpans and begin to clean up plaster and loose debris. Boys on motorcycles and bicycles gather disaster information from the city. The well-trained civil defense organization brings fires under control, clears rubble from the main thoroughfares, patrols the streets for looters, commandeers the inventory of damaged food and clothing stores, organizes a systematic program of relief for homeless victims, identifies lost children with identification tags, performs rescue missions and emergency medical services, and assists doctors and nurses in caring for the overload of patients at makeshift hospitals. Civil defense workers move through the neighborhood, checking houses and marking them with "inspected" signs, indicating whether levels of radiation are "acceptable" and the houses are safe for occupancy.

In short, within hours after an atomic attack, life returns to the routines of the preattack world, demonstrating that for those who have undertaken the requisite preparations, nuclear war is not such a bad thing. Henry can relax from his responsibilities as district warden and sit down to a hot corned-beef sandwich with baked beans and coffee. The plucky Leonore, dressed in her yellow plastic outfit, tests a huge slag heap for radioactivity, judges it to be contaminated but "safe," lights a cigarette, inhales deeply, and takes a break to engage in shop-talk with a police lieutenant—insouciant, nonplussed, and self-possessed. The Conner home has, of course, been equipped with a basement shelter: canned goods labeled on shelves, a portable stove, and bottles of distilled water. Because of these careful preparations, Beth, despite a long night of first-aid service, is back at home making herself a cup of instant coffee with a spoonful of sugar in the first light of the first postattack dawn.

Two and one-half years after the attack on a sunny afternoon in late June, Ted Conner is mowing the lawn. His mother is planning a dinner for more than twenty guests. Henry is back at his job as an accountant, driving home with a keg of cold beer in the same family Oldsmobile that survived World War III. Charles, of course, has married Leonore, who remains a radiant exemplar of white middle-class feminine beauty, in spite of the radiation she has absorbed. Indeed, she has even managed to become pregnant, gamely facing the prospects of genetically transmitted birth defects with witticisms—they might have to have four babies for every three they keep—and the determination to produce what America now needs most from her: children.

The moral of Wylie's story is obvious. Americans who fail to exercise self-discipline can expect to suffer a terrible fate in a nuclear attack. If they are not killed instantly, they will die of injuries, bleed to death, succumb to exposure, go mad, or be murdered or raped. But if they acquire the necessary civil defense skills, they will be able to survive a nuclear disaster by gaining control over their moral and psychological weaknesses. Although Wylie's novel is a nuclear fantasy, it reproduces without significant exaggeration the basic assumptions of Cold War emotion management. An intelligent fear of nuclear attack motivates the public to take the steps recommended by the civil defense public-education program. Civil defense training involves the acquisition of technical skills for self-protection as well as the moral discipline required to exercise these skills coolly and efficiently under conditions of maximum stress. Technical skill and moral discipline lead to emotional self-control. As the American people are repeatedly admonished, they must respond like soldiers in battle—good soldiers, naturally, who follow instructions competently, automatically, and unflinchingly so that the objectives of their commanders can be achieved. Civil defense militarizes life by nonmilitary means, using techniques of emotion management in order to train Americans to manage themselves. As a result, they will solve the problem of nuclear terror and thereby fulfill the moral requirements of American national security policy.

3

The Cold War Conception of Nuclear Reality

The Construction of Nuclear Reality

What would it really be like to experience a nuclear attack? More important, what could Americans be persuaded to believe about their prospects for survival? How should the theater of World War III—the United States under nuclear bombardment—be conceived?

In the 1950s, civil defense planners addressed these questions by developing a conception of American society in a nuclear crisis. The assumption that Americans would be able to protect themselves in a nuclear attack presupposed an account of nuclear war that showed how survival by means of self-protection could be achieved. Civil defense planners provided what was needed: the Cold War conception of nuclear reality, an interpretation of American society under nuclear attack designed to sustain the view that the American people could make the best of the worst. Its purpose was to define the public perception of nuclear war by writing the future as history and telling the story of what would happen when Soviet nuclear weapons struck their ultimate target, the American home front. The story was intended not as an accurate picture of what the United States devastated by nuclear bombs would look like, but as a representation of an "ideal" nuclear world, a highly selective and stylized account designed to legitimate the strategy of deterrence. Deterrence was defended not on the grounds that it would actually work, but by showing that even if it failed, the consequences would still be tolerable.

The Cold War conception of nuclear reality represented an attempt to think about the unthinkable, to conceptualize an unintelligible event and rationalize a world that seemed to be irrational, by reducing the apparently unimaginable experience of nuclear war to a set of routines. The world of nuclear attack imagined by civil defense theorists was an ensemble of technical problems, intimidating but thoroughly manageable by local communities and individual households trained in civil defense procedures. Nuclear crisis management would produce no significant changes on the American scene. American institutions and practices would remain in place. After the nuclear crisis was successfully negotiated, everyday life would be resumed as if nothing had happened. This was the doctrine of nuclear crisis mastery.

Crisis Mastery

National security strategists represented the Soviet nuclear threat as a crisis in American life, the first time in modern military history that the American people would be directly exposed to the dangers of warfare. The primary target of a Soviet nuclear offensive would be not the armed forces of the United States but its people, on whom the responsibility for responding to the attack, waging World War III, and rebuilding the country ultimately rested. What was the character of this crisis?

In answer to this question, the architects of the Cold War conception of nuclear reality developed an interpretation of a nuclear attack as an event that could be controlled by careful planning and good management. A nuclear crisis was not regarded as a technologically produced national disaster to be suffered and, if fate decreed, endured, or as a catastrophe incommensurable with the conceptual apparatus of American culture and irresistible to a resolution within the limits of its stock procedures and strategies. True, millions of people would die. Millions more would be injured, their property would be destroyed, and they would be left homeless. The levels of death and destruction would be especially high in the large cities and centers of industry and communications. But regardless of how terrible the consequences might be, they would not mean the end of the American nation. The crisis was conceived by reference to the conditions of its mastery, instead of by reference to the potential destruction it could have on American life. It was an event over which Americans could exercise substantial control by making the requisite preparations. Therefore, survival was not an occurrence, something that would or would not happen, but an artifact, something to be organized and produced by intelligent endeavor. A nuclear attack would be mastered by producing a plan to ensure the survival of the American people and preserve intact the structure and values of American society.

This plan depended on technique, in the sense that there was a method for managing a nuclear crisis. Civil defense would identify the procedures essential to survival and teach the American people how to perform them. As a result, they would learn how to manage their own survival. The methodology of nuclear crisis management was understood as a protocol: a set of rules that, if correctly followed, would produce the desired result. This meant that survival was a product of training. Only those who learned the requisite skills would survive, although, obviously, survival could not be guaranteed. As *Survival Under Atomic Attack* pointedly observed, no civil defense measures could spare those unlucky enough to be unprotected and within ten miles of the blast. Given this qualification, however, Americans who followed the proper procedures would survive. Those who ignored them or failed to execute them correctly would not. Therefore, survival was reduced to the performance of routines.

Because the rules for nuclear crisis mastery would be carried out by the American public at large and not by a small cadre of professional experts, their execution was regarded as a matter of simple pragmatics. Mastering a nuclear crisis was not based on an arcane body of knowledge, nor did it require complicated skills beyond the reach of the ordinary citizen. On the contrary, the techniques needed to survive a nuclear attack were elementary operations that anyone could learn by participating in civil defense training.

The American people would not be asked to make choices about the appropriate methods to follow in a nuclear emergency. Instead, they would receive prefabricated packages of information on the proper civil defense measures to take and instructions on how to employ them. In this project of mastering a nuclear crisis, both ends and means were given, already settled by the national security establishment and its civil defense specialists. Americans were told that civil defense was indispensable to both national security and personal survival, that civil defense meant self-protection, and that they would be trained in the procedures required to protect themselves. The ideal response to a nuclear crisis was an unreflective, swift, and automatic execution of recommended civil defense techniques. Policy deliberations would only confuse the American people and weaken their resolve. Strategic deliberations would bewilder and mystify them. It followed that Americans under nuclear attack were conceived as morally resolute, psychologically resilient, and intellectually stunted members of the species *Homo faber* who would master survival skills and apply them to their own circumstances.

Mastering a nuclear crisis was not an attempt to escape the experience of nuclear attack. On the contrary, it was an effort to reduce the overpowering and anomalous features of this experience by integrating them into the mundane reality of American life. As a result, the basic character of American society would remain unchanged even under the conditions of a nuclear emergency. In this fantasy, nuclear reality was neither evaded, denied, or nullified. It was incorporated into everyday life by means of strategies regarded as among the most deeply institutionalized practices of American culture: planning for the future and executing these plans by means of do-it-yourself techniques. As a result, the project of managing a nuclear crisis guaranteed the realization of core American values even under exceptional conditions that were barely imaginable before the advent of nuclear weapons.

Manageability was the fundamental methodological assumption of the Project East River program of nuclear crisis resolution. Surviving a nuclear attack was possible, but only by using the concepts and tools of management. A nuclear crisis was defined as a problem whose various facets were subdivided and reformulated as practical tasks. Following this definition, manageable solutions were designed for each task. A nuclear attack was a system of phases that could be exhaustively analyzed into their component parts. Each part could be subjected to further analysis and broken down into its component elements until the level of analysis arrived at tasks for which workable solutions could be formulated. When that stage of planning was reached, the problem of nuclear crisis management was solved: "When civil defense is broken down into small parts, it is then possible to do something effective about each part within practical limits of time and economy. When each of the individual accomplishments has been added to the total picture, the results are impressive."[1]

This strategy of management by reductive analysis was one of the basic premises of the Cold War conception of nuclear reality. In this method, the first step was to break down the nuclear crisis into what were regarded as its three elemental phases: the preattack phase, the attack phase, and the postattack phase. A phase was defined by a single objective and the operations that were expected to achieve it. On the basis of this analysis, specific plans would be drawn up to solve the distinctive problems of each phase.

The objective of the preattack phase was preparedness. This called for public education that would teach Americans what they needed to know in order to live through a nuclear attack. It also required a national recruitment program to enroll citizens in training courses for the services that would be needed in the later phases of the crisis. In 1950 and 1951, plans were made to recruit 15 million people to perform volunteer civil defense work. The police service would assist regular law enforcement organizations in patrolling the streets, protecting persons and their property, and arresting or shooting down survivors whose self-control had snapped under the stresses of a nuclear crisis, compelling them to panic, loot, or riot. The fire service would assist regular fire departments in combating what was expected to be the main source of destruction. The welfare service would organize housing, clothing, and feeding for the millions of refugees created by the attack. The warden service would organize the mobilization of neighborhoods so that every household would be ready. The rescue service would be responsible for emergency operations to extract survivors from the rubble created by the attack, and the health service would provide emergency medical care. The engineering service would clear away debris so that main thoroughfares would be open for the transportation service to deliver assistance and supplies to survivors. The communications service would operate the media required to coordinate all these functions in a national network. The responsible political authorities on federal, state, and local levels would be linked to civil defense organizations on these same levels. Naturally, staff services would be required to provide bureaucratic support.

In June 1951, the FCDA initiated Alert America, its first national marketing effort. The general aim of Alert America was to promote the program of nuclear crisis management by dramatizing the danger of the Soviet threat and convincing Americans that civil defense was necessary for their survival. Its specific objectives were twofold: to provide to the entire population comprehensive information on civil defense as self-protection, and to persuade some 15 million people to volunteer for training in one of the specialized civil defense services. In 1951 and 1952, the FCDA produced or sponsored pamphlets, posters, comics, newspaper inserts, radio and television programming, and traveling exhibits designed to achieve these objectives.

The most heavily promoted project in the campaign was the Alert America Convoy: three caravans of ten large motor trucks and trailers painted in bold colors. Each caravan carried an exhibition made up of posters, blown-up photographs, movies, three-dimensional mock-ups, and dioramas. The exhibits were intended to depict as vividly as possible the effects of an atomic attack on the United States and show Americans how they could "beat the bomb." In 1952, the Alert America Convoy toured the country for nine months. Visiting armories and civic centers in some seventy cities, it was seen by 1.1 million people.

The advertising designed for the convoy by the Advertising Council theatricalized civil defense public information in a format that was characterized as "hard-hitting and dramatic": "The Alert America Convoy is Coming to Town! To show you what atomic warfare is really like . . . to show you how you can protect yourself and your family . . . to show you how Civil Defense can save your life. Don't miss it . . . it's the show that may save your life!" The convoy was touted as "the most unforgettable show you'll ever see!" and "a 'must' for every American." According to the Advertising Council, Alert America was "the most far-reaching public-education project of its kind ever undertaken." It promised to "spearhead a campaign which will alert the citizens of your community to the menace of modern warfare—to show them what they can do about it through Civil defense."[2]

The objective of the attack phase of the crisis was to survive. Survival would depend on the mobilization of millions of civil defense volunteers, efforts at self-protection on the part of the public at large, the appropriation by the state of private property required in the interest of national security, the emergency evacuation of threatened urban populations, and the relocation of officials, organizations, and services judged to be essential to national survival.

The national security establishment regarded the survival of the American state and its continuous operation throughout the nuclear crisis as necessary to the survival of the country. In order to maintain the continuity of government, plans were made to protect critical federal agencies. As a result of these endeavors, the state would be able to enforce civil order during the attack, carry the war to the enemy and bring it to a satisfactory conclusion, and undertake the postattack reconstruction. Plans to guarantee the continuity of government were not based on the same principles that governed the civil defense program for protecting the public. Instead, plans for the continuity of government held that certain officers and agencies of the federal government should be protected by the state, which meant that the state would tax the American people to protect itself. The basic assumption of the national civil defense program was self-protection. Because the state was not prepared to spend substantial federal revenues in order to ensure the survival of the public, ultimately, every family was responsible for its own survival.

The command and control of the polity and the economy would be secured by establishing a system of leadership and management succession. In every organization designated as essential to national security, officials would be identified to assume executive responsibilities in case those ahead of them in the order of succession were eliminated. Because every organization in every major city was expected to lose its headquarters, alternative operational sites would be selected and equipped, and key personnel would be transported to these sites so that crucial functions would not be interrupted.[3]

The objective of the postattack phase of the crisis was to recover. Recovery would require a national reconstruction program that enlisted the active cooperation of all survivors to rebuild America. In the early 1950s, civil defense planners seemed to regard a Soviet nuclear attack not as a remote possibility, but as an imminent reality. In the autumn of 1951, the NSRB organized an interagency planning group in the federal government to solve the problems of postattack rehabilitation. This group proposed the formation of mobile cadres of specially selected skilled workers, who would be recruited and indoctrinated in

the preattack phase. After the attack, they would be shuttled from city
to city, repairing transportation and communication links, restoring industrial capacity, and rebuilding housing and community facilities.
Such an operation would be mandatory, since in the euphemistic language of the NSRB planners, "the normal patterns of employment may
be severely disturbed or damaged." The planners also considered
whether the recruitment of these mobile units should rely on volunteers or whether "compulsion" would be necessary.[4]

Detailed proposals were also drawn up to rebuild private housing
in the postattack period. Nuclear war was expected to result in severe
shortages of material and labor, the depletion of private funding for
housing construction, and the collapse of the private housing market.
But it was assumed that private construction companies, together with
their equipment and labor forces and a state apparatus with the bureaucracy and the funds needed to reshelter America, all would survive
and work together to rebuild homes according to preattack standards.
Postattack housing-reconstruction plans were based on the premise
that huge tracts of residential real estate would be destroyed in the first
strike. There was also a strong probability of subsequent strikes. Thus
postattack construction sites were contemplated on which workers
anxiously scanned the skies for the characteristic flash of a nuclear
explosion as they went about building new homes for surviving con-
sumers whose dwellings had been destroyed.[5]

The objectives of the attack and postattack phases of a nuclear crisis
could be achieved only if careful planning for their execution had been
completed in the preattack phase. Therefore, preattack planning was
the key to resolving the crisis. It was obvious that plans for survival
could not be made as late as the weeks and days before the bombs
began to fall. If preparations for preattack readiness were completed in
a timely fashion, then the attack—the exact particulars of which need
not be delineated with graphic precision for the public—could be managed without excessive hardship. But if preattack planning was incom-
plete or careless, then the nation would not survive, in which case plans
for reconstruction would be pointless. In order to explore the Cold War
conception of nuclear reality more closely, we will consider in some
detail the plans for the first phase of the nuclear crisis.

Operation Alert

Beginning in 1954, the federal government initiated a series of annual
rehearsals for World War III. Christened Operation Alert, these yearly
rituals enacted simulations of a nuclear attack in an elaborate national
sociodrama that combined elements of mobilization for war, disaster
relief, the church social, summer camp, and the county fair.

The purpose of Operation Alert was to test preattack plans for survival by fabricating an imaginary nuclear reality that approximated, within the limits of feasibility, the actual conditions of a nuclear attack. Each Operation Alert was designed as a play, in the sense of both an exercise and a drama. The drama was framed as a grand national epic, in the style of the MGM movie epics so popular in the 1950s. Following the logic of nuclear crisis mastery, the plot of the drama moved from threat to crisis to resolution. Naturally, the American people emerged from the radioactive mists of nuclear war essentially unchanged, if not altogether unscathed. The outcome of the exercise and the resolution of the dramatic ordeal were a foregone conclusion, preordained by the constraints of nuclear crisis mastery as well as the public-relations requirements of the FCDA.

By 1955, the FCDA had secured comprehensive national media coverage of Operation Alert. Perhaps more important, publishers and broadcasters collaborated with the FCDA in defining Operation Alert and interpreting its results for the public in conformity with the Cold War conception of nuclear reality. By 1956, participants in Operation Alert included many agencies of the federal government, with the president and the cabinet playing leading and highly visible roles; scores of cities that had been marked for "destruction"; businesses that had developed their own civil defense plans; organized labor; and thousands of small towns across the country that did not want to be left out of an event that appealed to the passions of patriotism as well as the interests of civic pride and the competitiveness of community spirit.

The protocol of each Operation Alert was worked out months in advance of the exercise. The main strategic premise was invariably a well-coordinated nuclear attack on 50 to 100 American cities. Participants were expected to test their survival plans by following the scenario of the protocol. Generally a date in the summer was reserved, usually including a weekend so that maximum participation would not be compromised by workday responsibilities. The simulated attack occurred on Friday. Over the weekend, the American people and their leaders demonstrated their ability to master the attack by putting into practice their civil defense training and survival skills.

The protocol often employed the fiction of telescoping: concentrating into days or hours of simulation the performance of tasks that might require weeks or even months in an actual nuclear war. For example, the first Operation Alert, which postulated an assault on forty important industrial targets and a large number of Strategic Air Command bases, was planned as a two-day exercise in June. Its purpose was to test the civil defense organization that the federal government had formed during the previous three and one-half years. How effectively would the local civil defense units perform in a nuclear emergency? What efforts by the federal government would be required? Because Operation Alert 1954 was designed to evaluate the response of civil defense organizations, general public participation was not contemplated.[6]

Operation Alert 1955 was a much more ambitious enterprise. Not only the more carefully planned simulation and the increased scope of the exercise, but also the more sophisticated and elaborate public-relations apparatus set in motion to define the event for the American people marked Operation Alert 1955 as a national political event, a public ritual, and a symbolic moment of major importance. Operation Alert 1955 was held on June 15 through 17. The protocol was based on a list of ninety-two "critical target cities." Before the exercise, fifty were designated for simulated attack. At its beginning, seven more were marked for surprise attack. This meant that the remaining critical target cities were expected to ready themselves for surprise nuclear bombing or, if that did not occur, participate in efforts to assist other areas that had been bombed. Estimated casualties were 8.2 million killed, 6.5 million injured, and 24 million left homeless.

The highlight of the test and its most widely publicized feature was the transfer of critical functions of the federal government from Washington, based on the assumption that the capital would be destroyed. Accordingly, some 15,000 federal employees, including the president, the cabinet, and agencies declared to be indispensable to the continuity of government, were evacuated to thirty-one undisclosed sites outside the city. Here, under the direction of an emergency White House situated in the comparative wilderness of the mountains of Virginia some six hours by car from the capital, the operations of the American state continued uninterrupted by a simulated nuclear holocaust.

The official purpose of the exercise was twofold: to assess current levels of civil defense preparedness in the country at large, and to test plans to maintain the continuity of the state in a nuclear attack. By demonstrating that the relevant agencies of the federal government and the ninety-two cities chosen for participation were able to carry out the protocol of the exercise, Operation Alert would confirm a basic premise of the Cold War conception of nuclear reality: Given careful planning and proper management, the American people could sustain a nuclear strike and survive without the imposition of draconian measures that violated their political traditions.

This demonstration depended on whether the civil defense community was able to produce a credible interpretation of Operation Alert that conformed to the premises of nuclear crisis mastery. The operation would succeed only if it were perceived as a success. This effort to interpret Operation Alert for the American people was the purpose of a concerted press and public-relations campaign initiated some six weeks before the exercise.

Instructions concerning the management of public information at government-relocation sites were distributed to the relocation officers of each participating government agency. In order to guarantee a realistic simulation, agencies were advised not to allow visits from families of employees during the operation. In order to establish a seamless consistency in the public relations of the event, participating federal employees were given basic guidance on how to handle the press. A briefing on the public-relations strategy of Operation Alert was held for the public-information officers of the principal agencies taking part. This meeting was followed by more detailed conferences on public relations with individual government officials.

Given the planning assumptions of the exercise, the capital would be destroyed, and so all the participating federal agencies would obviously be unable to release information from their offices in Washington. In addition, the real conditions of a nuclear attack would preclude press coverage at relocation sites. The government wanted to encourage maximum press coverage of Operation Alert and at the same time subject this coverage to strict but unobjectionable controls. For this purpose, NEWPOINT was established, a media center with the sole function of releasing government-generated news on Operation Alert. Located in an office building in Richmond, Virginia, NEWPOINT provided the concentration of resources and personnel needed to control the media effectively. By outfitting NEWPOINT with elaborate communications technology and providing ample staffing, the government simplified the task of reporting on Operation Alert. Plans were made to install basic communications equipment for print and broadcast media as well as additional telephone and telegraph facilities for the many reporters who, it was hoped, would use the new press facilities. A preoperation press briefing was held to determine in advance the number of journalists who would be on hand at NEWPOINT. This meeting would lay the groundwork for solving potential media problems before the exercise was actually under way. Operation Alert planners wanted to make sure that the appropriate facilities would be in place to enable reporters to file their stories directly from NEWPOINT. For this purpose, the NEWPOINT press room remained open around the clock from the beginning of the exercise to its conclusion. In anticipation of the large number of journalists expected at NEWPOINT, backup government information officers were brought in from the United States Information Agency and the Department of Defense to serve on the Operation Alert press staff.

NEWPOINT was an artifact of the White House, set up and operated by the Office of the Press Secretary to the President. All information emanating from the relocation sites and all contact between the press and participating government officials were managed directly by the White House. By guaranteeing the participation of the president, cabinet officers, and press officers of the executive branch, all of whom were regular sources of information for Washington journalists, the government made sure that Operation Alert would be an important

news item. By situating the journalists in a single office building, iso-
lating them from the relocation sites, and feeding them appropriately
timed releases and pool radio and television coverage generated by the
White House public-relations apparatus, the government attempted to
make sure that press coverage would follow, and ideally reproduce, its
own conception of Operation Alert as mastery of a nuclear crisis.[7]

An advance meeting with media executives was held to establish
the ground rules for covering Operation Alert, to work out the specific
plans for its coverage, and to identify and resolve any problems the
executives might have. By including media executives in planning the
coverage of the operation, the White House and the FCDA were able
to use editors, publishers, and broadcasters to frame and streamline the
official interpretation of the exercise. In the collaboration between media executives and government officials, an interesting modus vivendi
emerged. The interest of the government in promoting a specific interpretation of Operation Alert was linked with the interest of the press
in producing commercially viable news articles and broadcasts. As a
result of these joint efforts, the government enjoyed considerable success in using the media to refine and then distribute its own conception
of Operation Alert as a demonstration of managing a nuclear crisis.

Media executives made suggestions for radio and television coverage that were much more comprehensive than the government's
original plans. In considering the most effective use of the president,
they proposed live radio and television reporting from Eisenhower's
headquarters. This would make possible live broadcasts by the networks from the emergency White House and tapes that could be
inserted into regularly scheduled programming. Following the government's conception of Operation Alert as a confirmation of the Cold War
conception of nuclear reality, media executives urged that the president
deliver a live radio and television address from his headquarters early
in the exercise. Such a broadcast would achieve one of the main objectives of the operation: to show that "the president is alive and working and that the government is in operation." The media chiefs also
recommended that the closed-circuit-television communications between the president and the various government-relocation centers be
made available to network representatives at NEWPOINT, arguing that a
controlled demonstration on commercial television of the government's ability to function in a nuclear emergency would be "most
newsworthy" as well as "most reassuring to the American people."[8]

The public-relations managers of Operation Alert recognized that
the decision requiring all information about the exercise to originate
from NEWPOINT might needlessly frustrate the press and create undesirable restrictions in coverage. In order to avoid these difficulties, radio
interviews with participating government officials were arranged by
establishing telephone lines between their secret locations and NEW-

POINT. Plans were also made to supply journalists at NEWPOINT with timely reports by holding special press conferences with Operation Alert participants on the outskirts of Richmond. Officials would be flown in by helicopter from their operational relocation sites. Since only government photographers were allowed at these sites, arrangements were made to develop their pictures and have them flown to NEWPOINT, where they would receive the widest possible distribution.[9]

Some of these photographs document the effort to define Operation Alert within the framework of the Cold War conception of nuclear reality. The government did in fact adopt the suggestion of a live broadcast by the president. In one photograph, Eisenhower delivers his television speech, dressed in a tan double-breasted summer suit and seated in a tent in front of three microphones, serious of mien but inspiring confidence. Demonstrating that government business was being conducted as usual, even though Washington had been flattened by a hydrogen bomb, the president proclaims a simulated civil defense emergency, summarizes the nationwide progress of Operation Alert, and reassures the American people that the country still exists.[10]

In another photograph, Eisenhower is flanked by his two chief civil defense advisers, Val Peterson and Arthur Flemming. The latter was head of the Office of Defense Mobilization (ODM), which was primarily concerned with nonmilitary defense planning for the government, especially the question of maintaining the federal government's continuous operation in the event of a nuclear attack. All three are immaculately suited, pressed, and creased, proving that the nuclear crisis required no compromises in the cosmetics of executive self-presentation. Appearing relaxed but appropriately grave, Eisenhower demonstrates that he remains in control of the country. This event also represents Val Peterson at the apex of his glory, receiving his apotheosis at the left hand of the president and presiding over the nuclear apocalypse.

A third photograph pictures the Eisenhower cabinet convening in a large tent furnished with rough-hewn tables, neon lights, and television cameras and monitors. Standing and smiling into a camera is Eisenhower's hunting and fishing companion and economic adviser, the multimillionaire Secretary of the Treasury, George Humphrey, who seems to be in remarkably good spirits in spite of the devastation that Soviet nuclear forces have visited on the American economy. The lights are on, and the television cameras are whirring. Even though Washington and every other major city in the country has been destroyed, there seem to be no communications difficulties or energy deficiencies. There is also plenty of fresh water, despite the fallout that would be produced by a massive thermonuclear assault. In short, everything is in order as the nation conducts its business in the wake of the attack.

A final photograph of the government in action during Opera-

Operation Alert 1955: President Eisenhower, speaking in a live television broadcast from his emergency headquarters, reassures the American people that the country still exists. (Courtesy of AP)

Operation Alert 1955: President Eisenhower and his two chief civil defense advisers, Val Peterson and Arthur Flemming, demonstrate the confidence and gravity required by experts in emotion management. (Courtesy of UP)

Operation Alert 1955: At the secret White House, the cabinet conducts the business of the country in the aftermath of a simulated nuclear attack. (Courtesy of Dwight D. Eisenhower Library)

Operation Alert 1955: Nelson Rockefeller (back to camera), White House assistant; Allen Dulles, director of the CIA; Max Rabb, White House assistant and secretary to the cabinet; and Arthur Larson, undersecretary of labor, relaxing from the rigors of nuclear crisis management. (Courtesy of AP)

Alert 1955 is worth noting. It is an incongruous snapshot of four men in suits in what appears to be a Boy Scout camp. The four are Allen Dulles, director of the CIA; Max Rabb, White House assistant and Secretary to the Cabinet; Arthur Larson, Undersecretary of Labor; and Nelson Rockefeller, then a presidential assistant on national security matters. Relaxing on folding chairs at the president's emergency headquarters, they take a break from the grueling task of managing the national security state in the midst of World War III. No one seems worried about radioactive contamination or the possibility of further bombings. The sky is clear and cloudless, and there is not a rubber suit or gas mask in sight. In fact, Dulles even has time to smoke a pipe.

Following the plan of Operation Alert 1955, the objectives of Operation Alert 1956 also were articulated within the framework of the Cold War conception of nuclear reality. The exercise would acquaint government officials, civil defense workers, and the public at large with the problems that were likely to arise in a nuclear war. It would also "test the national readiness" to respond to these problems. By identifying deficiencies in the current level of civil defense readiness, this test would provide a basis for more sophisticated training and improved plans and programs.

In Operation Alert 1956, the production of a ritualized national simulation of a nuclear emergency became more systematic and highly rationalized. By approximating more closely the conditions of a real attack, Operation Alert would demonstrate the American capacity for mastering a nuclear crisis. As a result, or so civil defense planners hoped, the interpretation of the exercise promoted by the government would be validated. A number of refinements not present in earlier plans were introduced to tighten the correspondence between simulation and actual attack. In Operation Alert 1956, ninety-seven thermonuclear bombs were exploded over fifty-two cities. An unspecified number of additional bombs were exploded over air bases, AEC installations, and eleven smaller cities. Other enemy actions expected to be coordinated with a major nuclear offensive—such as submarine attacks against coastal shipping and missile attacks launched from submarines, commando raids, and internal sabotage—were also included in the attack protocol. The attack pattern outlined in the protocol stipulated the number and yield of enemy nuclear weapons, the types of explosive bursts—on the surface or in the air or water—and approximate ground zeros as well as times of detonation. In order to retain an element of surprise, the exact locations of each explosion were not distributed to state and local civil defense organizations until the beginning of the exercise. Operation Alert 1956 assumed no strategic warning, no weeks or months of political tensions that would produce evidence of Soviet preparations for a nuclear offensive. There was a minimum tactical warning of 100 minutes, the expected time that would elapse between the launching of the first enemy forces and the explosion of the first bombs.[11]

Operation Alert 1956 scheduled a seven-day exercise, beginning on Friday, July 20, and ending on Thursday, July 26. This represented an attempt to reduce the artificial telescoping of time, events, and operations that had been responsible for an important discrepancy between simulation and reality in the exercises of 1954 and 1955. To the extent practicable, the sequence of actions planned for the exercise reproduced the sequence of actions that would be called for in a well-designed national civil defense effort during the first seven days following an actual attack.

Another innovation of Operation Alert 1956 was the development of more realistic casualty and damage estimates. These new figures were arrived at through two modifications: by introducing the variable of casualties produced by expected patterns of radioactive fallout, and by assessing casualties and damage during the exercise itself, using only those instruments and methods of measurement presumed to be available after the attack. Civil defense planners also developed criteria for evaluating the quality of nuclear crisis management during the operation. These standards, which were used to assess government agencies participating in the exercise, would provide a benchmark for further improvements in preparedness. In order to arrive at a systematic assessment of performance during the event, each participating federal agency was required to form an inspection team to work with inspectors assigned by the ODM. Finally, a higher level of civil defense readiness and more comprehensive nationwide participation were encouraged by a new program of incentives and awards, including a "Presidential Unit Commendation for meritorious performance."

Like the architects of Operation Alert 1955, the planners of Operation Alert 1956 attempted to frame a public interpretation of the exercise that conformed to the requirements of mastering a nuclear crisis. The seriousness with which Operation Alert was taken outside the government and the success of civil defense strategists in promoting an interpretation of nuclear attack within the framework of the Cold War conception of nuclear reality are nicely illustrated by a telegram sent on the first day of the exercise by AFL-CIO President George Meany to President Eisenhower. "In this dark hour of our nation's history," Meany gravely announced, "I want to pledge to you the fullest support of American workers. All America must work together to repel attacks of the enemy, to restore damage, and to mount an offensive that will carry us to victory." Following the logic of nuclear crisis mastery, Meany envisioned a nuclear attack as a managerial problem that could be solved by the proper organization and deployment of skilled labor power. After personally promising Eisenhower that no AFL-CIO member unions would engage in strikes or work stoppages that would interfere with civil defense, he emphasized that the unions were ready to provide the manpower needed for reconstruction and rehabilitation. "Throughout the nation," Meany assured the president, "groups of skilled union workers are ready to serve on special assignments to meet the needs of bombed-out areas."[12]

Local civil defense organizations throughout the country did their part to ensure that the objectives of Operation Alert 1956 would be met. In Canton, Ohio, Mercy Hospital evacuated patients, personnel, and supplies to a special field hospital twenty miles from the city. According to the Operation Alert protocol for Canton, the hydrogen bomb designated for explosion over the city would destroy Mercy Hospital and leave the city's other two hospitals badly damaged or contaminated by radioactivity. Although the original plans allotted two hours for Mercy Hospital's evacuation, the entire operation was performed in less than ninety minutes, to the immense satisfaction of hospital administrators and civil defense officials. The five-floor building was cleared of 270 patients, personnel, and critical supplies in only forty-five minutes. Boy Scouts, Girl Scouts, and members of B'nai B'rith volunteered to take the role of patients. In order to make the exercise more realistic, Operation Alert patients were tagged to duplicate the actual patients in the hospital and were classified and evacuated as litter, chair, or ambulatory cases. Ninety percent of the hospital personnel responsible for conducting the evacuation were women, assisted by local civil defense organizations and law enforcement agencies. At the field hospital, a reception area for bombing victims was set up. Radiological monitoring teams and decontamination units tested survivors for radioactive contamination and provided emergency treatment. Mass feeding for the 1,000 participants in the exercise was also organized. The County Restaurant Association prepared sandwiches, soups, and beverages, which were served by the local chapter of the American Red Cross. Local officials attributed the success of the evacuation to thorough planning, careful organization, and close cooperation.[13]

In Wright City, Missouri, forty-four miles west of St. Louis on U.S. Highway 40, the local civil defense organization managed the reception and care of evacuees from the hydrogen-bomb attack on St. Louis. On the second day of Operation Alert, Wright City was fully prepared for the exodus from St. Louis. Large signs directing evacuees to the Wright City public park were posted at all strategic locations. The civil defense auxiliary police service, "smart in their crisp uniforms," were stationed on U.S. 40 to direct incoming traffic. Families from St. Louis County playing the role of evacuees were registered by a team of five women.

Each registrant was assigned an identification number in order to systematize feeding, housing, and medical care. Supervised by the director of the Wright City school lunch program, members of six local women's service organizations prepared and served a meal of stew, "hot corn flakes," and coffee. A first-aid station was set up in a tent, where evacuees were given emergency medical treatment by trained personnel using equipment transported from St. Louis. As in Canton, local officials praised the efficiency of the operation and the planning, training, and teamwork that made it possible.[14]

Subsequent installments of Operation Alert attempted to refine further the conception of the simulated attack world so that the exercise would conform more close to the doctrine of nuclear crisis mastery. Plans became more precise and systematic, introducing more variables and developing strategies for handling them. Operation Alert 1957 was divided into three phases. The first, which ran from June through mid-July, postulated an international crisis to which the United States would respond with a graduated mobilization for war and a partial activation of emergency relocation sites. The second, scheduled for July 12 to 14, assumed a hypothetical nuclear attack on the United States and a three-day national civil defense exercise. In order to deprive the cities of advance warning, targets were not announced before the exercise. All data concerning casualties and damage were gathered by community organizations, which would presumably survive and have access to information about the local effects of bombardments. Situation reports generated by municipal organizations would then be forwarded to the national civil defense headquarters. In the third phase, July 15 to 19, reconstruction operations began. In response to worries of emotion managers about the levels of stress and the range and difficulty of tasks that could actually be accommodated in a nuclear war, steps were taken to simplify the organization of civil defense work.[15]

Operation Alert 1958 attempted to confront more directly the problem of nuclear fallout. Its planners worked on the premise that civil defense operations would be impossible for the period immediately following the attack, during which time "human activity might be reduced to a minimum due to fallout hazards." Proceeding on this assumption, planners drew up a "blueprint of actions" that should be taken as rapidly as the decay of fallout permitted. Instruction was also given in emotional self-management so that civil defense workers would not snap under the extreme psychological pressures of the attack. Accordingly, Operation Alert 1958 included efforts to train personnel in what were called, in the meretricious language characteristic of the Cold War conception of nuclear reality, "habits of thinking needed to cope with emergency conditions."[16]

Operation Alert: The Movie

An essential objective of Operation Alert was to achieve what strategists characterized as "the maximum release of information to the public media."[17] The success of the annual exercises required not only mass participation and public exhibitions of civil defense readiness. It was also critical that the American people understood what they were doing. For this reason, it was important to make sure that Americans experienced Operation Alert not as a summer festival, a national holiday, or a community-service drive, but as a full-scale test of national resolve and local preparedness. In order to see that the popular understanding of Operation Alert conformed to the official interpretation, the FCDA commissioned films of the exercises. The American people would see themselves on movie and television screens responding to a nuclear attack in accordance with the requirements of the Cold War conception of nuclear reality. Edited to demonstrate an exact correspondence between the performance of the public and the assumptions of nuclear crisis management, the Operation Alert movies were accompanied by didactic commentaries that made fully transparent the relation between the conduct of the exercises and the demands of an actual nuclear emergency.

The FCDA film *Operation Alert* presents a buoyant and confident picture of the nation during Operation Alert 1956, an exercise that was said to constitute "a realistic rehearsal for survival" in the thermonuclear age.[18] In the protocol of Operation Alert 1956, the United States received 124 nuclear strikes, with 5 hydrogen bombs hitting New York City alone. *Operation Alert* offers a stirring account of the national program of nuclear crisis management and its execution in selected cities. The film's main theme is the chief premise of the Cold War conception of nuclear reality: Although unprecedented in its horrors, a nuclear attack can be reduced to routine problems that can be solved by the exercise of managerial rationality.

The America of *Operation Alert* is a strikingly homogeneous society. Government officials, community leaders, civil defense volunteers, and even the population at large are represented as white, middle class, and of northwest European ethnicity. Americans seem to be differentiated only by gender, age, and occupation, with stereotypically different modes of dress worn by professionals, white-collar, and blue-collar workers. The middle class of *Operation Alert* is also fastidious to the point of compulsiveness in its hygienic and cosmetic habits. From sea to shining sea, from the largest cities to the smaller towns, from the highest levels of the federal government to the local elementary school, everyone is clean, carefully coiffed, and neatly laundered. The well pressed bodies also seem to encase equally well-fashioned minds. Americans preparing for nuclear war appear to possess remarkable resources of self-control. Despite of the conditions of ultimate crisis, they respond in an energetic and purposeful fashion. At the same time, their manner is quiet and reassuring, as if their conduct were but the visible expression of an inner calm and conviction. Their voices are well modulated, expressing no fear, compulsion, or even worry.

The actions and passions of Americans negotiating the wrenching transition from the mundane reality of everyday life to the hyperreality of a nuclear crisis produce a curiously surreal and dreamlike effect. The denizens of the 1950s captured on film in *Operation Alert* recall another cross section of the American people in a more familiar film from the same year: the characters in *Invasion of the Body Snatchers*, Don Siegel's unforgettable reflection on American Cold War anxieties of internal security. Like the Americans of *Operation Alert*, Siegel's characters are determined and fearless, but also robotlike and uncomfortably inhuman, as if their behavior were the product of an elaborate internalized program. The profile of the American people presented in *Operation Alert* reflects a larger sociological picture of American society as totally planned and engineered for a single contingency. All the preparations for a nuclear attack have been laid well in advance. The personnel are at hand, and the equipment is in place. Both have been thoroughly tested to determine that they are in perfect working order and will function according to plan.

As the colorless voice of the announcer informs viewers, America has a master plan or "blueprint for survival," and throughout the country—from Olympia to Minneapolis and Manhattan—Americans put this blueprint into action. In Manhattan, a traffic officer directs a seemingly endless flow of vehicles out of the Times Square area and into the Lincoln Tunnel. The flight from New York is relentless, but also orderly and uneventful. New Yorkers, legendary for their volatility and mercurial tempers, carry out a faultless evacuation of the city. There are no breakdowns or accidents on the highway. Perhaps even more astonishing to New Jersey commuters, there is no congestion at the entrance to the Lincoln Tunnel. Nor have the suburbanites on the other side of the Hudson River, facing a presumed invasion of millions of evacuees attempting to escape thermonuclear incineration in New York, sealed the New Jersey side of the tunnel.[19]

In Minneapolis, the execution of emergency survival plans also proceeds admirably. As in New York, both people and machinery function smoothly. At a hospital, nurses load patients into waiting station wagons ready to be driven to safe destinations. Public altruism and community spirit have been mobilized and carefully coordinated. The imminence of the attack has obviously not led to social breakdown, moral collapse, and Hobbesian disorder in Minneapolis, where all station-wagon owners appear to have placed themselves and their vehicles at the disposal of civil defense authorities.[20] While hundreds of hospital patients are transported into the countryside, condemned buildings are set on fire "to add a realistic touch" to the alert and provide practice for the civil defense fire-fighting service. Boy Scouts are pressed into service as stretcher bearers, carrying the injured to first-aid stations and demonstrating that "volunteers are never too young in time of emergency."

The evacuation of the commercial and industrial area of St. Albans, West Virginia, is also featured in *Operation Alert*. Banks, stores, and other businesses assist police and fire department officials, closing their doors and evacuating their employees from the city. There is a totalization of effort and a seemingly mechanized and automatic uniformity of response. "Everyone takes part." Comprehensive planning extends to postattack arrangements for the resumption of business as usual. Post office workers open a field station where volunteers are hard at work, literally in the middle of a field in the countryside, sorting mail from a truck onto a portable mail rack. The Bank of St. Albans is reestablished on crates and card tables loaded off a truck onto a field outside the city. Here bank employees practice what the film calls a "postattack plan for business," although exactly what this plan calls for is left to the viewer's imagination. In any case, the weather is marvelous, and no one is dressed in anticipation of radioactive contamination. There is no mention of the likelihood of multiple nuclear assaults. No one seems to be worried about the breakdown of communication, transportation, and commerce, much less the collapse of the social order. On the contrary, in *Operation Alert*, inertia, both social and mechanical, has disappeared. In the fantasy of nuclear crisis mastery, after the dust of more than 100 nuclear explosions has cleared, letters will be written and delivered; checks will be drafted and cashed; debts will be incurred and settled; employees will show up for work, and the technological, social, and economic conditions for their labor will remain in place. In sum, the business of everyday life will return to normal.

In the meantime, *Operation Alert* captures the eerie vistas of ghost-like American towns of the 1950s, emptied and silenced by the mobilization of the population in the service of national security. What does all this mean? *Operation Alert* has the answer: "The nation is ready." As reports of terrible damage are compiled and digested, volunteers respond dispassionately and laconically. Enemy bombs have obviously spared the civil defense emergency centers featured in *Operation Alert* as well as the entire technological, political, and economic apparatus on which they depend. Electrical, plumbing, communications, rescue, and fire-fighting equipment all operate according to plan. Indeed, despite of the massive nuclear assault, everyone seems to have showered, shaved, shampooed, and changed into fresh clothes, for *Operation Alert* betrays no evidence of dirt, sweat, torn or wrinkled garments, or even extraordinary exertion.

The large volume of requests from bombed-out areas for emergency assistance and supplies produces neither distress nor surprise. A call for 5,000 to 10,000 pints of blood per day is handled by expressionless civil defense volunteers with a bland insouciance. "Mobile emergency hospitals" are ferried from city to city—how this would be possible immediately after a large-scale nuclear bombing is not revealed—with medical personnel, equipment, and supplies to care for victims in badly stricken areas. In the frictionless world of nuclear crisis mastery where nothing malfunctions and no one misperforms, everything works according to the master plan for survival. Everyone does his or her job, and no one seems to be affected by fear, anxiety, nervousness, impatience, or even a headache or a bad mood.

Officials act "quickly, decisively, effectively," making sure that the "knockdown blow" struck against America does not become a "knockout blow." Preparing for a nuclear attack, it seems, is comparable to preparing for an athletic contest, perhaps a boxing match. America is the "clean" fighter, who refuses to throw the first punch. In this contest, what will happen to areas that are devastated and knocked down? By effort of will, they will "pick themselves up and go on." A scene at the emergency White House illustrates what is intended by this muscular rhetoric. Although Washington may have disappeared in the haze of a thermonuclear blast, the nation still has a capital, even though no one knows exactly where it is. The emergency White House press center operates at full throttle. A government press secretary provides news of the attack to a room filled with reporters, all of whom seem to have survived in admirable physical, cosmetic, and sartorial condition. Val Peterson, in a suit, dazzling white shirt, and tie, is cool and amiable as he ambles through the press office and chats with teletype operators.

Meanwhile, the announcer warns that "all America lives under an ominous cloud"—the danger of radioactive fallout. A serious problem for nuclear crisis management? Not really. In California, civil defense volunteers perform radiation-monitoring operations on an empty stretch of highway. They confirm that the roadway is "hot" and send the appropriate signal to a nearby radiation-detection van. From there, this information is transmitted to communications centers that plot safe routes for the transport of disaster relief and emergency supplies. The radioactive contamination of the United States produced by the explosion of 124 hydrogen bombs proves to be just another routine problem of nuclear crisis control, amenable to the application of appropriate technology, effective training, and good organization. Nor does nuclear crisis management seem to call for highly sophisticated techniques, arcane devices, or elaborate measures of protection. The civil defense volunteers on the dangerously contaminated California highway have the appearance of suburbanites on a Sunday afternoon. Dressed in chinos and short sleeves, they tackle the threat of deadly radiation as if they were checking for crabgrass on the front lawn.

Operation Alert also features radiologists and meteorologists plotting the formation and likely course of radioactive clouds that, viewers are told, may extend for hundreds of miles. However, contamination by airborne radioactivity portends no serious danger. Citizens in what are described as "contaminated areas" line up in an orderly manner and cheerfully wait to be tested by a monitor with a Geiger counter. The contaminated victims are in astonishingly good spirits. A young man stands with arms outstretched as volunteers give his clothes a vigorous sweeping with an ordinary household broom. Procedures for radioactive decontamination, it seems, do not exceed the demands of everyday housecleaning. "Youngsters happily take their showers in stride," the announcer comments, as three small boys in swimming shorts frolic under a portable shower administered by three men in army uniforms and helmets. Treatment for radioactive contamination is not only painless and routine. It can even be fun. Furthermore, the demands of waging World War III have obviously created no manpower shortages for the armed forces. One soldier is available to shower each contaminated child.

Operation Alert sheds no additional light on the dangers of fallout or the details of exactly what Americans can expect in the aftermath of a nuclear attack. Are further attacks likely? If so, how would self-protection during a continual thermonuclear assault be practicable, or even possible? Will large tracts of the country be contaminated for weeks, months, or perhaps even years? Will parts of the United States, even substantial areas that were entirely untouched in the nuclear bombing, become uninhabitable for the indefinite future? Will animals and crops die? Will food supplies dwindle and disappear? Will those Americans who survived the bombing and also escaped death by radioactive poisoning starve to death? No answers to these obvious, eminently practical, and pressing existential questions are forthcoming. Instead, viewers are simply told that "America comes back to life as Operation Alert ends." Empty towns and cities refill. Their inhabitants return to pick up their lives in the postattack world, which seems to be indistinguishable from the preattack world. As the film ends, Times Square is back in business. America is as it was, and appropriately inspirational music swells as Operation Alert 1956 fades to black.

The interpretation of the American home front under nuclear attack presented in *Operation Alert* articulates the main themes of the Cold War conception of nuclear reality. Survival is achieved through sound planning, training, and organization, all of which leave intact the fundamental institutions and values of American society. These themes are reinforced in a later thirty-minute film made by CBS television in cooperation with the FCDA and narrated by the movie actor Glenn Ford:

The Day Called X.[21] "X" is the hypothetical day on which a hydrogen bomb will obliterate Portland, Oregon, which, the film notes, is about the size of Hiroshima. In the film, Portlanders enact the evacuation of their city following the attack warning.

Like their fellow citizens in *Operation Alert*, Portlanders seem to be unexceptionably white and middle class. All municipal officials and civil defense workers are impeccably dressed in anticipation of the thermonuclear destruction of the city. Fire department officers are impressively outfitted in double-breasted uniforms as they await their assignments. The mayor of Portland appears in a perfectly fitted suit and crisply starched shirt. Nor has he forgotten to insert a flower in his lapel for his formal announcement of the impending attack, an astonishingly deadpan and matter-of-fact performance that generates no more emotion than a speech announcing local highway repairs.

The essence of the Portland evacuation is comprehensive and detailed planning. The responsibilities of every citizen have been carefully and repeatedly rehearsed. Since nuclear preparedness has been incorporated into the city's normal functioning, civil defense measures seem to be indistinguishable from the routines of the workday world. The continuity between normality and crisis suggests that the nuclear crisis has been reconceptualized as an aspect of normality. Because the nuclear crisis falls within the conceptual space of routine existence, on the day called X there is no discernible difference between the civil defense measures required for preattack readiness and the circumstances of everyday life. The conditions of nuclear emergency have themselves become routine.

The collapse of the distinction between crisis and normality is a definitive feature of the Cold War conception of nuclear reality. It means that when the nuclear emergency occurs, nothing extraordinary or unexpected can happen. A nuclear attack is not a horrible and barely conceivable anomaly, but a problem, immensely challenging, of course, although still amenable to solution by means of standard methods and strategies indigenous to American culture. The attack alert or the CO-NELRAD broadcast keys up familiar plans that are executed without incident. "When the siren sounds," Ford assures his audience, "each man knows his responsibility." Because the logic of a nuclear crisis has been translated into the logic of everyday life, the people of Portland "follow a pattern well learned and practiced."

Although Ford observes portentously that the day called X is no ordinary day, this observation is belied by the demeanor of the Portlanders themselves. Conditions of life in extremis produce no corresponding extremes in conduct. With the exception of their artless expressions of gravitas—an awkward concession to the emotional rhetoric appropriate to a crisis of civilization—the people of Portland maintain an utterly flat affect, betraying no emotions that would indicate they are engaged in the final preparations for World War III. Under the nuclear gun, they behave in an emotionally colorless and quasi-mechanical fashion, as if wound up and programmed to act without reflection. The more general civic plans for nuclear emergency seem to have been internalized by each citizen and incorporated into consciousness and conscience as a plan of inner regimentation.

The Day Called X contains numerous scenes that exhibit this phenomenon of internal self-management. As the siren sounds, firemen file down a staircase in military fashion, manning their posts as if they were automatons. A fleet of police cars emerges from an underground garage, one after the other as if expelled by a clever machine. Drivers bring their vehicles to a simultaneous halt and abandon them in the streets. Monitored by civil defense volunteers, they follow pedestrians into conveniently located underground shelters. Clerical workers quit their offices with blank expressions and a purposeful gait. Schoolchildren instantly rise from their desks. Without further urging, they flock behind their teachers and march out of their classrooms. When the CONELRAD alert interrupts a morning radio program, patrons in a café enjoying their morning coffee break respond immediately without comment or surprise.

Routes for the evacuation of all sections of the city to areas beyond blast and radiation danger are clearly marked. Drivers follow the green traffic lights of the evacuation path. As in *Operation Alert*, all traffic moves as planned. Evacuation instructions are broadcast continuously on the radio. Naturally, all drivers have their radios on and tuned to the proper channel. Everyone understands the instructions and follows them precisely and unreflectively. When traffic becomes congested in certain areas, alternative directives specified in the plan automatically go into effect. Specially trained traffic engineers are at their posts, directing the evacuation by means of a communications network set up specifically for this purpose.

The Portland plan for survival is self-correcting and works according to built-in negative-feedback mechanisms. All the problems that might arise in a nuclear emergency as well as the means for their solution have been anticipated. There are no malfunctions, human or mechanical. No engines misfire; no vehicles break down; no one panics or even fails to perform the assigned tasks up to the expected standard. There are no blunders, anger, distress, or even excitement. Despite the extreme conditions of nuclear emergency, both individual conduct and collective action approximate virtually inconceivable standards of rigor and efficiency. The Portlanders work together like the parts of an immense, complex, and beautifully designed machine that is constructed for a single purpose and performs perfectly. None of the lapses, miscalculations, and disagreements that characterize the mundane world of human organizations are visible on the day called X. On the contrary, the human mechanism of civil defense operates as if these sources of friction did not exist.

The Portland evacuation plan is represented as a set of simple, unambiguous, and self-applying rules. There is no evidence of the commonplace need to interpret instructions in order to understand them. The plan has been designed so precisely and operates so faultlessly that there is no logical space between the rule and the behavior that constitutes its correct application. The place for interpretations has disappeared. Since civil defense instructions do not require interpretation, the conflicts that typically result from incompatible interpretations do not arise. Because no interpretation can intervene between a rule and its application, the friction produced by the process of interpretation and the possibility of conflicting interpretations also disappears. It follows that the Portland civil defense plan is virtually godlike in its perfection.

Comparable powers and virtues are ascribed to those who carry out this plan. *The Day Called X* repeatedly insists that all responsibilities for civil defense in Portland, strategic as well as operational, fall on the shoulders of the Portlanders themselves. The rhetoric of local self-sufficiency and community spirit has an important political implication. Ambitious and expensive federal programs to protect the people of Portland—which neither the White House nor Congress was willing to support—are unnecessary. Playing on the myth of American local autonomy, *The Day Called X* maintains that even though a nuclear attack represents the most extravagant threat to life and property imaginable, in the final analysis it remains a local issue. Like any other community problem, it can be handled by native pragmatism, quiet courage, and selfless devotion to the common good.

The principle of grass-roots self-sufficiency also implies that any American community can achieve what Portland has done. The Portland plan demands no heroics or uncommon feats of valor. Civil defense does not impose unusually strenuous tests of individual or collective courage, nor are its requirements extraordinarily exacting in other respects. On the contrary, civil defense is represented as routine planning carried to an astonishing degree of perfection through incremental and unspectacular efforts on the part of each citizen. Because the division of labor for civil defense is elaborate and precisely articulated, prodigious efforts are not expected from any individual participant. It is essential only that everyone do his or her part and adhere rigorously to the plan. Given the requisite energy and will, the Portland blueprint for survival can be reproduced throughout America.

The preparations of the Portlanders are so complete that at the conclusion of the evacuation, two lone motorcycle policemen patrol the empty streets of the city, confirming the full compliance of the public with the attack alert. Some twenty minutes before the nuclear strike, all evacuees are comfortably housed in relocation centers. The resettled Portlanders even have time to relax and take a break for coffee and a cigarette before their city disintegrates in a thermonuclear blast. Behind the gleaming stainless-steel counters of a cafeteria, uniformed waitresses in matching aprons and caps cheerily serve the citizens of Portland a hot lunch in the last few minutes before the attack. Life on the edge of the nuclear abyss, it seems, is not so bad. City officials and civil defense workers await the event with remarkable serenity and dispassion: smoking, watching the clock, and exhibiting no signs of emotion or even reflection. The Cold War conception of nuclear reality apparently includes no space for the experience of the bombing itself. "What happens after that moment," Ford concludes, "we leave you to contemplate."

The yearly performance of Operation Alert and its reproductions on film constituted an attempt to produce the future as the past. The critical event in the future of the American nation—the day called X—was represented as if it had already happened. The future, seemingly unknown, was already written and determined. The story of World War III, enacted in Operation Alert and reenacted in *Operation Alert* and *The Day Called X*, was not an ominous hint at the uncertainties of things to come, but a record of the future conceived as an extension of contemporary middle-class American culture. This vision of the future reduced the unthinkable terrors of a nuclear holocaust to a technical problem. Daunting but manageable, it could be solved by relying on strengths and deploying strategies that were institutionalized in the preattack world of American life. As a result, the terrors of an open and undetermined future were dissolved. The future held no dreadful secrets and opened up no new possibilities of ultimate disaster. Nuclear war was envisioned as won even before it had begun.

4

The Nuclear Family

The American Family Under Nuclear Attack

In a speech during his first year in office, President Eisenhower declared that an effective civil defense program required sober training and self-discipline. In the final analysis, the American response to a nuclear attack depended on a moral regime to which the American people would subject themselves.[1] The main training site where civil defense discipline would be cultivated was the home.

The decisive role assigned to the household in Cold War national security planning was a consequence of the fundamental premise of civil defense: In World War III, the American people would be responsible for protecting themselves. Because the federal government had ruled out a publicly financed program of civil defense, survival would largely be a do-it-yourself enterprise. The state would provide a central organization, a national plan, education and training, modest financial assistance, and the consolidation and standardization of operations across the country. But in the end, civil defense was essentially self-help, which meant that its success depended on the traditional American virtues of self-determination, personal responsibility, and voluntary cooperation. These virtues were believed to be anchored in the family, the primary locus of their inculcation and practice. Therefore, civil defense rested on moral foundations that were situated in the home. As Eisenhower observed, civil defense was grounded in the "moral structure" of the family and the "spiritual strength" of Amer-

ican home life.[2] National security was tied to the character of family
life, and civil defense was linked to family values. In the shrill rhetoric
of the FCDA film *Frontlines of Freedom,* the front lines of the Cold War
were drawn at the front door of the American household. The mobilization of the family behind civil defense would determine whether
the American people would confront preattack panic effectively, develop the skills necessary for survival, and participate enthusiastically
in postattack reconstruction.

During the early months of the Eisenhower presidency, plans were
made to incorporate the home into national security policy. In a February 27, 1953 letter to Allan Wilson of the Advertising Council, FCDA
Executive Assistant Administrator J. M. Chambers outlined the objectives of civil defense in the new administration and underscored the
importance of advertising in their realization. Nuclear weapons and the
crisis in international relations created by the Cold War had changed
the concept of national security. National security now meant "total
security," which required both a strong military establishment and civil
defense.

In an era of permanent international crisis, however, civil defense
planning could not succeed by attempting to persuade the public to
accept a constant state of alert. On the contrary, it was necessary to
"sell civil defense" on what Chambers characterized as "a calm, long-
range, common sense basis." Because total security demanded the in-
tegration of civil defense into everyday life, it was crucial to develop a
marketing plan that would make civil defense "a permanent part of
our way of life in an atomic age." Such a plan would work only if the
American people could be convinced that civil defense was indispensable to their personal security. According to Chambers, "not enough
people as yet visualize civil defense as something which intimately af-
fects them as individuals, and in their families and communities."

Chambers regarded this problem as a practical issue of mass psychology. In order to muster public support, it was necessary to reorient
the public relations of civil defense. Although the FCDA would not
abandon the recruitment of volunteers to work in specialized cadres—
the Alert America program of the Truman administration—its future
efforts would be increasingly devoted to an "action program" for local
communities designed to stress the importance of civil defense preparedness in the home itself. At least one member of every family would
be trained in first aid. In addition, each family would learn what Chambers called the "principles of fire-safe housekeeping" and the techniques of household fire fighting. "The list could go on," Chambers
explained to Wilson, "but I am sure you get the pitch."[3]

Val Peterson made the same pitch at much greater length in an
address delivered shortly after his appointment as FCDA administrator.
Speaking on the relation between home safety and national security,

Peterson warned that household hazards were no longer limited to the mundane dangers of faulty wiring and leaking gas pipes. Families now faced a new and unique peril: nuclear attack. In a standard résumé of current Soviet–American relations, Peterson characterized the Soviet Union as a "cold, calculating enemy" with a growing stockpile of atomic weapons and the means to deliver them at any time and on any target. Even worse, "the soundest military defenses yet devised cannot prevent this enemy from getting through to his targets in the event of a determined mass attack."

In such an attack, the chief Soviet target would not be military installations or material assets but *"our people—our human resources at home."* A radical "depletion" of these resources—or, less obliquely, the death of millions—could lead to the collapse of the home front and "the end of our nation as we know it." This was why the home front in the Cold War "actually exists in our homes, right in our living rooms." It was also why national security desperately required a civil defense program for the family. Indeed, Peterson argued that failure to incorporate civil defense into the household would be unpatriotic in the extreme, even disloyal and tantamount to a "'fifth column' action which undermines our national defense."[4]

Accordingly, Peterson urged the conversion of every household into a domestic civil defense unit. All family members—fathers, mothers, and children—had to be "fortified with every possible training and plenty of practice, prepared to do everything [they] can to protect [themselves] in an emergency with assurance and without panic." A civil defense program centered in the home would achieve dramatic results. It would neutralize the Soviet nuclear war machine by denying the Communists their immediate objective: the collapse of American morale that would paralyze the home front. Following the official government position on civil defense as a deterrent, Peterson argued that a home-protection program would also convince the Soviets that a nuclear offensive was simply not worth the risk: "No enemy is likely to attempt an attack foredoomed to failure."[5] Family civil defense would not only protect America's most cherished resource, but also preserve the peace by making a nuclear war less likely.

Even if deterrence failed and the American home front became the battleground of World War III, it was possible to survive a nuclear bombardment in virtually any domicile. Regardless of whether home was "a cottage, a mansion, an apartment, a hotel, or a trailer," the American family would be able to take care of itself, but only if it had been thoroughly trained in "civil defense housekeeping." In order to sustain the fighting spirit of the armed forces and maintain confidence at home, Americans needed assurance that they could prevent panic, care for survivors, and rebuild the economy—even if the Soviets did their worst. How could this assurance be achieved? Again, Peterson's answer

was to strengthen morale in the home by providing families with training. Household civil defense would give Americans the confidence that
even in the face of the enemy's most ambitious efforts, they would be
able to take the appropriate steps to protect themselves.[6]

In the end, Peterson exhorted Americans to examine their con-
sciences. Using an appeal repeated thousands of times in the Cold War
propaganda of home-front mobilization, he asked his audience to
consider what they had done to prepare their own families for World
War III:

> Have you *actually* seen to it that they know what to do in an atomic emer-
> gency? Have you prepared a shelter or pointed out to them the safest
> refuge in the house? Have you drilled them thoroughly in getting there in
> a hurry and staying there until it is safe to come out? Have you assembled
> for them a few necessary emergency supplies? Have you seen to it that
> they are trained and drilled in first aid and home fire fighting? Have you
> explained to them what to do if caught out in the open in the back yard?[7]

The FCDA's home-protection program of the 1950s envisioned the
American family under nuclear attack within the framework of the
Cold War conception of nuclear reality. The FCDA's home-protection
manuals taught nuclear crisis mastery by means of family initiatives
grounded in patriotism, enlightened self-interest, and a rationally controlled fear of nuclear war. By planning and practicing at home, families
would acquire the requisite skills and develop the self-control necessary
to survive a nuclear attack. Home-protection exercises were marketed
to the public as the basic tools of self-protection and the ultimate line
of defense against nuclear attack. Strategists held that if civil defense
could be effectively institutionalized on the microlevel of the family,
then the problem of social disintegration and disorder on the macro-
level would be solved.

In the home-protection literature, one imperative of survival was
emphasized above all others: the reorientation of the family as a civil
defense work unit. In the Cold War conception of nuclear reality, all
the interests and values of American life were subordinated to the end-
less quest for national security. Citizens were reduced to the skills and
disciplines needed to mold them into serviceable tools of civil defense.
Everyday life in the permanent national security crisis was patterned
on an interminable round of alerts, drills, tests, and rehearsals, all devoted to the development and refinement of civil defense technique.
By means of continual training and retraining and the exercise of civil
defense procedures according to increasingly sophisticated standards of
efficiency and precision, the American people would reconstruct their
lives around the ultimate value of national security.

The aim of the home-protection program was to enlist every family
in civil defense and hold the family responsible for its own survival.

Although the rhetoric of the home-protection program embraced all families, its actual objectives were limited by three factors: a view of the Soviet's targeting strategy in a prospective nuclear war, the domestic politics of financing civil defense, and post–World War II demographic and residence patterns. The primary target of a Soviet attack and the crucial American asset in World War III would be the American public, the human resource required to prosecute the war and rebuild the country. This meant that it was necessary to convince both Soviet leaders and the American people that the home front could be protected. But Truman, Eisenhower, and Congress were unwilling to support a publicly funded program of protection, which meant that civil defense was inevitably understood as home-front self-defense. Finally, in the 1950s, the suburbs accounted for 64 percent of American population growth. By the end of the 1950s, as many people lived in suburbs as in cities. The main dwelling of the American suburb is, of course, the detached house, which in the 1950s increasingly represented home for newlyweds and young couples of twenty-five to thirty-five and their children. By the end of the 1950s, 31 million of the 44 million families in the United States owned their own homes. Between 1948 and 1958, 13 million new houses were built in the United States, 11 million of them in the suburbs.[8] Because the most likely targets for Soviet nuclear bombs would be cities, the FCDA had written off the possibility of protecting urban populations. Unless they could be evacuated before an attack, the residents of cities would be sacrificed to the larger requirements of American national security. These considerations entailed a distinctive conception of home preparedness: Civil defense would teach suburbanites how to survive by learning how to protect their houses.

With this end in view, the family would be restructured to conform with the imperatives of civil defense. Civil defense would coordinate domestic life as a set of purely instrumental tasks, whose timely and proficient performance was necessary and sufficient to guarantee surviving a nuclear attack. These tasks required the consensus and participation of all family members and the reorganization of the family in accordance with the objectives of civil defense home protection.

In 1953, the FCDA began distributing a new home-protection manual, *Home Protection Exercises: A Family Action Program*. By 1956, it had gone through three revisions in an effort to keep abreast of the development of the hydrogen bomb, the publication of the dangers of fallout, and shifts in federal civil defense policy. Each exercise in the manual was divided into two parts. The first, "Procedure," provided a brief and semitechnical explanation of the facts germane to the exercise, followed by "Practice," which instructed the family in performing the exercise. Families were expected to make periodic self-evaluations and progress reports in order to assess their performance. The progressive acquisition of skills was measured by report cards, to be completed four times a year. By practicing at home scenarios of simulated nuclear attack, the family would forge itself into an accomplished civil defense team. And as the family achieved higher levels of competence and self-confidence, it became less likely that its members would blunder, vacillate, or break down at the moment of maximum crisis.[9]

The first edition of *Home Protection Exercises* outlined seven tasks that were said to be essential to family survival under nuclear bombardment. First, the home must be prepared as a shelter: a bomb or blast shelter if it was located within ten miles of an expected target, such as a military installation, an industrial complex, or the center of a large city; a fallout shelter if it was situated more than ten miles from a key target. Second, families must be prepared for emergency action as soon as the warning alert sounded, for by that time bombs might fall within minutes. Third, the home must be subjected to a systematic regimen of "fireproof housekeeping." Since most of the destruction of a nuclear explosion would be caused by fire, all home fire hazards should be eliminated. Fourth, it followed that the family must be organized as a domestic fire-fighting force. Because local fire departments would be unable to respond to most fires, "fighting fires in your home or neighborhood will be up to you."[10] Fifth, the family should be prepared to perform basic first-aid procedures. Every family member should be capable of treating bleeding, burns, shock, broken bones, and suffocation—the injuries most likely to occur in an nuclear attack. Sixth, the family should be capable of carrying out emergency rescue operations before trained rescue workers arrived: locating missing family members and aiding victims trapped in wreckage and in danger of succumbing to fire, electric shock, or asphyxiation. Finally, public utilities and services such as water and sewage systems and garbage collection could not be taken for granted in the period immediately following a nuclear attack, nor could routine commercial services such as the distribution of food. Accordingly, the family would have to manage its own food, water, and sanitation needs, at least during the first three postattack days, after which time "it is expected that Civil Defense health and welfare measures would be in operation."[11] The second edition of *Home Protection Exercises*, published in 1954, added an eighth task to this list: home nursing, which required that every "homemaker" be trained to care for bedridden, sick, or injured family members during a nuclear emergency.

The production of its own survival obviously represented an ambitious undertaking for the family. In order to achieve this objective, it was necessary to impose a new division of labor on the home, creating specialized domestic civil defense functions that would require each family member to master a specific ensemble of survival assignments. The routine practice of these assignments would prepare the family for a nuclear crisis. Their competent and coordinated performance in a nuclear attack would ensure the family's survival. In the construction of domestic civil defense elaborated in *Home Protection Exercises*, each of these eight tasks called for the selection of a manager, a family member whose primary responsibility was monitoring and supervising other members of the family so that they would be prepared to carry out their assignments up to the standards that would guarantee survival. Managers would have alternates at their disposal who would assist in making sure that all jobs relevant to the task were performed in a proficient and timely fashion.

For example, in planning family action during a nuclear emergency, one family member would be responsible for giving orders when the alert sounded. The job of the emergency manager was to gather the family and see to it that all members performed their previously assigned emergency tasks swiftly and effectively. Immediately before the attack, utilities had to be turned off and appliances disconnected, fire buckets filled with water and placed at their proper locations, the house secured, and last-minute supplies and equipment transferred to the shelter. After infants and infirm family members were safely situated, all other family members, after completing their emergency tasks, would also repair to the shelter, tune the portable radio to a CONELRAD channel, and calmly await the nuclear attack. The emergency manager would distribute these tasks, making sure that a given job was assigned to only one person so that there would be no uncertainty concerning the precise definition of roles and responsibilities. The manager also would name alternates for each task in case the person primarily responsible was unable to perform.

In planning home fire protection, a family fire marshal would be selected to supervise the family in fireproof housekeeping—the identification and elimination of all household fire hazards. Here as well, a division of functions was crucial. The fire marshall would appoint one member and an alternate to secure quick access to the attic and clear it of flammable debris. Other members of the family and their alternates would clean out closets and storage lockers, the cellar and the garage, and rubbish in and around the yard. Finally, someone would be assigned to outfit the home with fire-fighting equipment and maintain it for emergency use.

Because of the danger of fire in a nuclear attack and the importance of domestic fire fighting to the survival of the family, it also would be necessary to appoint a family fire chief, who would assign fire-fighting duties, conduct drills, and train the family to work as an efficient fire-fighting unit. Because any family member might be confronted with a variety of fire-fighting tasks, the fire chief needed to make sure that everyone had a minimum working knowledge of every fire-fighting job. The fire chief also would be responsible for training the family in rescue and escape techniques. Everyone needed to know how to get out of a smoke-filled room, escape from the upper floors of a burning house, and search for missing persons in a house that was burning and badly damaged. A fire inspector and an assistant would also be appointed. After the attack, they would leave the safety of the shelter and conduct a swift and thorough examination of the house in order to determine whether any fires had been started.

During a nuclear emergency, the management of food and water consumption as well as hygienic and sanitary needs called for a survey of food and water requirements, the storage and maintenance of a three-day supply of both—including special foods to meet the dietary specifications of infants, the ill, and the injured—the improvisation of temporary toilet facilities, and the supervision of waste disposal after the attack. A family first-aid director and an alternate should complete a first-aid course and instruct other family members in the delivery of emergency first-aid. The household first aid unit would have the services of a family pharmacist, who would acquire the first-aid supplies needed in a nuclear emergency and store them in a safe and easily accessible place.

Finally, since doctors and nurses would be overworked, injured, trapped, killed, or otherwise unavailable after a nuclear attack, the family would have to meet its own medical needs. According to *Home Protection Exercises*, postattack domestic medical services would require preparations more demanding than elementary first-aid training. One person should complete an American Red Cross home-nursing course and train others in caring for patients confined to bed. Another family member would be responsible for maintaining a supply of clean linens. Still another would see to it that adequate stores of nursing supplies were available for the emergency.

In this manner, the family would be reorganized with a view to maximizing technically flawless performance, efficiency, and the smooth functioning of collective domestic action, all the utilitarian virtues, according to the FCDA, essential to family survival. As a result, the American family of the 1950s would be converted into a household putting-out system for the production of nuclear survival. More often than not, civil defense training would take place elsewhere—in schools, hospitals, or fire stations, where families would receive instruction in the various survival skills. Since the ultimate payoff of these skills was to be the redirection of family life in the interest of national security, they would be practiced and exercised and their benefits would be realized in the home.

By reorganizing the family as a labor force for the production of nuclear survival, domestic civil defense undertook to change the structure of the family itself. When the family became a civil defense work unit, the differentia for identifying and characterizing family members would shift from their roles, rights, and responsibilities as spouses, parents, children, and siblings to their job requirements as members of this unit. Because the objectives of the family as a civil defense workforce superseded other domestic interests, the ethos of family life would center on a new set of values. Production for nuclear survival and the importance of the efficient performance of civil defense tasks outweighed other household activities. When the state appropriated the home as an instrument of national security policy, spouses and parents would become managers and supervisors of the work units required by the domestic civil defense organization. The younger members of the family would become alternates and assistants in these units. The result would be a new domestic regime based on utilitarian and functional criteria.

The reorganization of the family would also politicize the household in a specific sense. In the Cold War conception of nuclear reality, the family would serve as a tactical unit trained and coordinated to carry out the mission assigned to it by the civil defense program: the achievement of national security objectives in the home. Civil defense home protection would recast the family as an agency of the state. When the state entered the home, patriotism, which now included nuclear housekeeping, would become a family value. Housework and household management, which had been purely domestic responsibilities, would become civic obligations. These results, as Max Weber might have said, would rationalize the family in a certain direction.

Civil Defense and the Regimentation of Family Life

The Cold War conception of nuclear reality imported historically unprecedented modes of production into the household that imposed new demands on the family: new problems, chores, and projects and new standards for their execution. In turn, these new standards entailed more exacting criteria of technical refinement and higher levels of precision in the performance of tasks.[12]

Obviously, new assignments in nuclear housekeeping meant more work for everyone. New domestic jobs called for new skills and training. As a result, the concept of routine household work was redefined. More time would be needed for domestic chores. Because of the proliferation of tasks necessary for nuclear survival, the job description of each family worker would become much more complex, and so family time would have to be used more efficiently. The focal point of home life would now be the acquisition of competence for the performance of survival tasks. Although some of these tasks—such as first aid and home nursing—were hardly new, they had not been the responsibility of all capable family members. Others, such as the positions of domestic fire chief and fire marshal, had not been regarded as essential to proper household management. And some tasks, such as the jobs required by a nuclear emergency alert, had not existed at all.

New tasks also necessitated stricter standards of housekeeping that would alter the character of household work. Crisis management would become routine. Since the nuclear crisis was, in principle, end-less—the attack that could occur at any moment: today, next week, or next year—housework would no longer be a casual chore that could be done or not as circumstances allowed. Instead, the home would be chained to the implacable conditions of survival in the nuclear age. Since the survival of the family was tied to its performance as a civil defense team, domestic life would assume a new and deadly serious-ness. Because of the grim consequences that could follow from house-hold mismanagement, the quality of housework would become a matter of life or death.

Following Max Weber, these changes can be understood as a ra-tionalization of domesticity: a process in which family life is increasingly systematized, more intensively managed, and more thoroughly regu-lated on the basis of standards that become progres-sively more demanding and rigorous.[13] The Cold War conception of nuclear reality envisioned a rationalization of domestic life by means of two key socialization processes: the acquisition of civil defense skills in training and testing, and the refinement of criteria for assessing these skills through surveillance over every area of domestic life. *Home Pro-tection Exercises* required the family to train for a nuclear attack by sched-uling regular practice sessions in which the execution of civil defense procedures would be rehearsed and tested. In order to determine where improvements were needed, the tests themselves would be assessed by subjecting the conduct of every family member to close scrutiny.

Home Protection Exercises emphasized that in preparing the family to act decisively when the emergency alert sounded, everyone should be "trained to act instantly and automatically.[14] After the emergency alert manager assigned the various emergency alert jobs, family members would be expected to practice their assigned tasks so that both they and the manager could verify that the individual jobs and their relation to the total project of emergency preparedness were thoroughly under-stood. Because the expeditious execution of tasks was crucial, the man-ager would time everyone. Other team members would be expected to observe their fellows at their respective tasks so that the role of every job in emergency planning would be clear to the entire family. Emer-gency alert practice would be made as realistic as circumstances per-mitted, in part by distributing family members throughout the home, indoors and out, before the sessions began. Because interdependence and integrated execution were indispensable to domestic civil defense, it was especially important to drill lagging members of the team whose performance did not measure up to the requisite standard. After every member rehearsed his or her job to the satisfaction of the emergency alert manager, a general practice session would be scheduled in which all team members carried out their tasks together. As a realistic goal, *Home Protection Exercises* suggested that the family practice completing the entire emergency alert routine in two or three minutes. Once the family had been thoroughly trained and tested in the conduct of emergency alerts, the manager would periodically schedule sessions to polish skills and reassess team discipline. These sessions would ensure that the commitment of each member to the overall performance of the domestic nuclear workforce was maintained at the highest level of readiness.

In securing the home against damage by fire, each family member would also be assigned a task and a time limit for completing it. When that limit expired, the family fire marshal would call a meeting to check the work of all participants. Team members experiencing difficulties in completing their assignments would receive new deadlines and additional helpers. When the team demonstrated its ability to perform the routine satisfactorily, weekly or monthly reinspections would be scheduled so that all members could maintain their skills and periodically check their equipment. Family fire fighting would be handled in the same way. Here as well, precise timing was crucial to execution. The inspector and a helper would be tested to determine how much time they required to reach the attic from the shelter and conduct a thorough search for fires as they worked their way down. The fire-fighting team would be allotted two minutes to complete all its maneuvers: putting hoses in place, connecting them to sources of water, getting water to attic fires, and carrying hand extinguishers or buckets of water and sand in the event that the public water system was shut down.

In order to improve the household emergency alert response and determine how each task in the routine could be carried out more quickly and effectively, the family was encouraged to assess its own performance according to more rigorous standards. *Home Protection Exercises* stressed the importance of postpractice family discussions in which the conduct of each member would be evaluated and suggestions made for further improvement.

In its recommendations on training the family in fire fighting, *Home Protection Exercises* also emphasized postrehearsal discussions of the best techniques for executing various maneuvers, such as confining and extinguishing fires in different parts of the house and treating various types of flammable material. The purpose of these discussions was, of course, to develop more effective fire-fighting techniques and thereby raise the standards and expectations of the domestic fire department.

The constant refinement of standards was crucial to every aspect of family civil defense. Because advances in weapons technology and delivery systems imposed an endless and increasingly strenuous sequence of demands on domestic civil defense, *Home Protection Exercises* reminded Americans that standards of readiness would have to keep pace with these changes. In the nuclear age, the price of survival was not only constant vigilance, but also an unremitting regimentation of life designed to achieve a continual enhancement of civil defense skills. Because the rationalization of domestic life in the interest of national security was a consequence of the arms race and the inexorable logic of weapons technology, it was interminable. Therefore, the formation of civil defense skills by means of training, testing, and assessment could never be concluded, nor could it be suspended or even relaxed.

From the standpoint of rationalization as the acquisition and assessment of skills, the strategy of *Home Protection Exercises* was based on the assumption that the family learned by doing. That is, the mastery of survival techniques was a product of reiteration: Family members would acquire civil defense skills by repeatedly performing certain stereotypical actions in the appropriate situations. Learning was regarded as habituation, a matter of changing old habits and acquiring new dispositions. The result would be a permanent change in behavior. Survival skills had to be practiced repeatedly, both individually and in concert with the entire family workforce. It was necessary to rehearse each operation until it could be performed with an unstudied and effortless ease, even under conditions of ultimate stress. In a nuclear emergency, timing and timeliness could decide the family's fate. Therefore, the exercise of civil defense skills had to approximate an automatic and reflexive response, executed without deliberation or consultation. *Home Protection Exercises* required the family to exercise systematic control over the conduct of domestic life as a whole and all its details. Nuclear survival was a product of strict self-management and regulation. In order to survive a nuclear attack, the family had to see its entire way of life—and not merely specific episodes and activities—as an object of methodical training, testing, and correction. This reconfiguration of life as an unending exercise in total cognitive, emotional, and moral self-control would produce a new family, prepared for the risks and uncertainties of the nuclear age.

From the standpoint of rationalization as the refinement of criteria for assessment, civil defense would reduce each family member to an ensemble of faculties subjected to continual oversight. In the early phases of training, oversight would be exercised by the family as a collectivity that scrutinized the performance of each member. Eventually this oversight would become self-assessment, in which every family member would examine his or her own performance in order to discover ways to make a more effective contribution to the family's civil defense effort. As *Home Protection Exercises* made clear, two aspects of control over the training process were especially important: the intensive mode of surveillance and the minute scale of its operation, in which all aspects of family life would be carefully examined and reduced to their smallest manipulable parts; and the uninterrupted and unrelenting quality of surveillance, which required a ruthless search for weakness and disloyalty within the family. Constant vigilance required of Americans both a constant self-examination and an unceasing and merciless scrutiny of their own husbands and wives, brothers and sisters, and parents. This new vigilance over the details of everyday life was imperative in order to make sure that when World War III began, American families would be ready.

Considered in this light, survival was determined by a mechanism of social selection that could operate for or against a family. It worked in favor of the family that disciplined and regimented itself according to increasingly demanding standards of preparedness. It worked against the family that fell behind in the rationalization process and failed to measure up to more rigorous criteria for performance. In order to motivate the family to face these hard truths, *Home Protection Exercises* provided a score card on which the family was encouraged to keep a record of its progress in every area of domestic nuclear crisis management. The essential household civil defense tasks were listed in a column, with blanks to be filled in for each practice session. For each task, the family would record preparations completed and progress made over a period of months or even years. "Keep practicing," families were admonished, "until you can conscientiously score the family performance as 'excellent.' "[15]

In the end, the systematic regulation of domestic life by means of civil defense would inculcate imperatives that functioned as positive and negative sanctions. Positive sanctions—the satisfaction of a job well done, the knowledge that one was doing his or her part for the family team, the belief that the competent performance of civil defense skills would actually achieve the objective of survival—would motivate and validate the conduct required by the home-protection program. Negative sanctions—the fear of panic or the breakdown of family discipline, the fear of the consequences of failure, the opprobrium that attached to the laggard or the bumbler, the importance of not letting the family down—would proscribe behavior that jeopardized home protection. In the end, civil defense for the home articulated a strategy for survival, and it also defined a way of life, an ethos that formed the character of the family.

Radioactive Fallout and Nuclear Housekeeping

What was the impact of the hydrogen bomb on family civil defense planning? In its official statements, the Eisenhower national security establishment maintained that despite the tremendous increases in destructive power achieved by the hydrogen bomb and the new menace of fallout it introduced, the basic principles of civil defense enunciated in the early 1950s remained unchanged. The hydrogen bomb was simply a new weapon in the American arsenal, another entry in the expanding inventory of modern military technology. Civil defense strategists stressed its limitations and discussed its novel hazards only in the context of recommending measures that would render them harmless. The hydrogen bomb did not demand conceptual or qualitative changes in civil defense, only incremental adjustments. It was not the occasion for a new policy, only for minor revisions in existing policy, which was declared to be fundamentally sound. Thermonuclear weapons called for more exacting standards of preparedness and a more elaborate battery of techniques for household protection. But the basic assumption of civil defense for the home remained unchanged: By organizing as a battle-ready civil defense unit, the family would be able to survive a nuclear attack.

This benign interpretation of the hydrogen bomb notwithstanding, radioactive fallout meant that populations located hundreds of miles from an explosion might become unwitting victims of a nuclear attack, weeks, months, or even years after the bombs were dropped. Since the distribution of fallout would be determined by wind patterns in the upper atmosphere shortly after the detonation, it seemed that no place in the United States could be considered safe, regardless of its remoteness or insignificance as a target. Following the publicity about the danger of fallout in the spring of 1955, the civil defense home-protection program focused on this new problem of nuclear housekeeping. Information that trickled from the AEC and the FCDA to the public treated fallout as a new household germ. Appropriate technologies of prevention and control were produced and marketed for homemakers. Revelations about this uncommonly potent form of household dirt—invisible, insidious, apparently uniquely dangerous, but still manageable by means of simple housekeeping techniques—generated new anxieties about the cleanliness of the home, its personnel, and their impedimenta. These concerns called for higher standards of housekeeping, more rigorous measures and determinants of personal hygiene, and a new level of order and purity.[16]

Following established civil defense–marketing strategy, the new rules for housekeeping in the thermonuclear era were promulgated in a variety of media. The task of selling these new rules to the public was the job of the FCDA and its successor, the Office of Civil and Defense Mobilization (OCDM), which was created in 1958 when the FCDA and the ODM were integrated in an attempt to save money and coordinate civil defense policy more effectively. The FCDA produced two new booklets on family fallout protection[17] and new editions of *Home Pro-*

tection Exercises, which were revised to take account of the problems posed by the hydrogen bomb.

The 1953 and 1954 editions instructed families to rotate three-day supplies of food and water in their shelters. Three days after the attack, it was confidently asserted, health and welfare organizations would be in operation, delivering relief to the stricken population. By the third edition, published in 1955, families were told to lay in supplies sufficient to sustain them for seven days, reflecting the new doctrine that in the week following the attack, the entire country might be blanketed with fallout. In that event, relief efforts would have to be delayed until radiation levels were safe enough for civil defense personnel to do their work without exposing themselves to unacceptable risks.

Although the third edition, in 1955, was printed after the revelations of the BRAVO test, its discussion of home-shelter construction remained astonishingly insubstantial. The important differences between a blast shelter, designed to protect the family from the local effects of a nuclear explosion, and a fallout shelter, designed for protection from fallout that could be present anywhere in the United States in the aftermath of a large-scale nuclear attack, were ignored. This lapse was not corrected until the fourth edition, published in 1956, which distinguished the two types of shelter and provided more detail on the specifications of building a shelter.

In 1956, readers were warned for the first time that blast shelters should be insulated with shielding material such as concrete, sandbags, or earth. This precaution was necessary in order to reduce radiation inside the shelter to what were characterized as "safe levels," a concept that was not defined more precisely.[18] Therefore, concerned and patriotic Americans who had heeded the warnings of the original FCDA home-protection literature and constructed a home shelter in accordance with the criteria set out in the earlier editions of *Home Protection Exercises* were now told that their efforts might not meet the challenges of the thermonuclear age.

Readers learned, also for the first time, that regardless of where they lived, they needed protection against fallout. The amounts of drinking water that should be stored increased: up from one gallon for each adult in the family and two gallons for each child younger than three years, to two gallons for adults and three gallons for children. However, later editions retained the earlier cursory warnings concerning the radioactive contamination of food. Readers of all editions were told that although food contaminated by fallout could cause illness, protecting food from contamination was easy. Food stored in a refrigerator, freezer, or cupboard or wrapped in cellophane was declared safe to eat. Although uncovered food might not be, it could be rendered safe by washing or wiping clean the food itself or its container. The same instructions applied to cooking or eating utensils, which should be washed following a nuclear attack.[19]

The recurrent promulgation of new rules for home protection and their periodic revision in the face of new threats to survival demonstrated that the permanent national security crisis called for tireless attention to the minutiae of domestic life. Although the basic principles of civil defense were said to be unaffected by the hydrogen bomb, Americans were also told that they needed to master new techniques for self-protection. The progressive revision of standards for preparedness demanded more careful family planning, more exact attention to the precise execution of plans, and more rigorous adherence to rules of nuclear hygiene—in short, a scrupulous regard for all household civil defense procedures, as the neglect of any could make the difference between life and death.

With the advent of television as the principal medium for gaining access to the home, television programs and films made for television became the preferred means of publicizing the new rules of nuclear household care. In the film *This Is Your Civil Defense*, OCDM Director Leo Hoegh, flanked by an American flag and a photograph of a hydrogen-bomb explosion, reduced the relation between national security and family preparedness to simple, if starkly brutal, terms. The "forces of Communism" were arrayed against the "forces of freedom." The Soviet Union was poised to launch a crushing nuclear assault against the United States. Although the main purpose of civil defense was said to be deterrence—"to assure that no nation, however, desperate, is likely to attack another that has the dual capacity to survive and to retaliate with annihilating power"—the United States must prepare itself for the possibility that deterrence might fail. Americans were called on to ready themselves for a nuclear war in which "only the self-sufficient will survive." Survival would be "a starkly personal matter." The family would not be able to count on the network of public and private institutions that sustained the home under normal conditions. Nor could it expect immediate help or emergency relief from civil defense and welfare organizations. Because "the strange menace of fallout" might drive the entire country underground for as long as a week, delaying rescue and relief operations, the survival of every family would be overwhelmingly dependent on its own resources and skills and its reserves of moral stamina and emotional stability.

Hoegh's observations served as a preface to the argument for family fallout shelters. In spite of the unsparing environment of the postattack world, the standards of comfort in a fallout shelter did not seem to differ appreciably from those of preattack domestic life. Even in the extremities of nuclear war, the family need not worry about giving up the amenities of middle-class existence. *This Is Your Civil Defense* depicted a couple in their thirties with a teen-age daughter and a younger son comfortably outfitted in a basement shelter with high ceilings and con-crete-block walls. In addition to fully stocked shelves and the large gar-bage can required by *Home Protection Exercises*, the shelter was furnished with upholstered chairs and a sofa. The family—smiling, purposeful, serenely confident, and equipped with enough supplies to survive for two weeks—practiced first-aid exercises in their well-appointed refuge. The wife, who wore open-toed shoes with two-inch heels, did not ap-pear to contemplate ultimate disaster. Perhaps it is not necessary to add that the inhabitants of this shelter were white middle-class household-ers. The poor, the working class, people of color, and even apartment dwellers and renters have been expelled from the world in which the family produces the conditions for its own survival.[20]

The FCDA film *Facts About Fallout* provided a more detailed account of the techniques such a family could employ to protect its home from radioactive contamination. Like *This Is Your Civil Defense*, *Facts About Fallout* linked the exigencies of family civil defense to the national se-curity crisis of the Cold War. The Soviet Union was represented as ut-terly ruthless, unprincipled, and dedicated to the universal domination of Communism. In light of this threat, the Soviet possession of nuclear weapons constituted an immediate danger for the United States and might even mean the end of the American experiment in democracy. The leaders of the Communist movement in Moscow were said to be clever and devious, masters of the dark arts of clandestine propaganda, fifth-column tactics, and sabotage. By recruiting dupes and sympathiz-ers who unwittingly carried out their perfidious schemes, they would be able to penetrate American society, weaken the American body pol-itic, and compromise the confidence of Americans in their own prin-ciples and way of life. Viewers were put on notice that the American response to the Soviet project of world domination could not rely on military power alone. It would also require civil defense designed to counter a thermonuclear offensive against the American home front.

Facts About Fallout opened dramatically and terrifyingly with the explosion of a hydrogen bomb. On the one hand, the facts about fallout seem profoundly discouraging: "Fallout could hurt you, might even kill you." The fallout produced by a single nuclear explosion could be lethal for days, weeks, or even longer. Fallout would endanger not only hu-man life, but also the ecostructure of the planet. Plants, animals, and even the earth itself could be poisoned by radioactivity. At home, view-ers were told, fallout could contaminate lawns, cars, and even the water supply, all of which would remain unusable and hazardous until de-contamination procedures were performed or the radiation decayed to what the film called an "acceptable level." On the other hand, viewers were also told that "knowledge of a few simple rules and precautions" could save their lives. Fallout, it turned out, was not a mysterious ca-tastrophe visited on its victims like a plague of unknown etiology, but ·

a problem that could be solved by means of techniques the ordinary householder could easily master. If Americans learned the relevant facts and took a few elementary precautions, they would be able to "cope" with fallout effectively. In short, the premises of nuclear crisis mastery also applied to the threat of nuclear fallout. The pragmatic logic and routine skills of domestic life could be transposed without loss of force or validity onto the marginal and emergency conditions of thermonuclear war.

In *Facts About Fallout*, the family that learned to cope with radioactive contamination also had the resources to maintain a substantial, well-kept, two-story house with a large yard. Fallout was represented as if it were light snow softly descending onto this comfortable middle-class haven. How should the inhabitants respond?

The film confidently asserted that weather forecasters would be able to chart the course and configuration of the "fallout pattern." As a result, householders were led to believe that the location of the "fallout area"—to be distinguished from the "actual bomb zone," a euphemism for the area of more or less total destruction—could be accurately predicted. Families threatened by fallout would have advance warning, not unlike people who face the prospects of dangerous weather such as a blizzard or a hurricane. Within the fallout area, the chances of survival were said to be excellent if one took suitable shelter. Simply remaining indoors could cut the danger of contamination in half, although the preferred mode of protection was an underground shelter. Ideally, the shelter should be constructed away from the family house so that it would not be subject to damage should the house collapse or burn. It should also be covered with at least three feet of earth to serve as a barrier against the penetration of radioactivity. *Facts About Fallout* depicted such a shelter occupied by a family of five. The shelves were well stocked, for, as the announcer blandly observed, it might be days or even a week before it was safe to emerge. A freestanding underground shelter presupposed that the family had the property and the income required to build such a structure. Should that not be the case, a basement shelter was recommended. Or if the house had no basement, one could at least close the windows and stay put on the first floor.[21]

Facts About Fallout characterized fallout as an uncommonly troublesome form of household dirt: "Dangerous radioactive fallout is like dust and can be removed like dust." Thus the metaphors of "fallout particles" and "radioactive dust," which suggested that fallout could be eliminated by cleaning—by brushing, washing, or scrubbing it away. Household fallout control was a problem of moderately advanced hygiene. Accordingly, *Facts About Fallout* recommended postattack housecleaning, including sweeping the roof and washing down the house with a hose. These measures obviously assumed that the municipal water supply had not been destroyed or contaminated. The effects of the runoff on the lawn and on those who ventured onto it were not considered. Contaminated clothing should be left outside and not washed "until radiation decays." Viewers were advised to take a bracing postattack shower, washing thoroughly with plenty of soap and water. Here, too, *Facts About Fallout* presumed an unlimited supply of uncontaminated water.

The announcer concluded with a confident reminder to viewers that the procedures recommended for fallout protection in the film were official and thus authoritative and incontestable. They were "the facts that should reassure and encourage you—and families all across America."

The most sophisticated attempt by the civil defense community to conceptualize fallout as a problem of nuclear housekeeping was a series of fifteen-minute television programs called "Retrospect," broadcast by CBS and sponsored by the OCDM.[22] The host of "Retrospect" was Douglas Edwards, known to millions of Americans as the man who read the evening news on the CBS television network. The format employed in each installment divided the program into three five-minute segments. The initial sequence used film and commentary by Edwards to sketch an important event, movement, or personality of the twentieth century. The second segment highlighted the government's civil defense program. The final segment returned to twentieth-century history. Frequently less portentous than the first, it was often devoted to entertainment or sports. The purpose of "Retrospect" was twofold: to give viewers the "facts" concerning the need for home preparedness in light of the dangers of nuclear war, and to provide authoritative information to families so that they would be able to fend for themselves in a nuclear attack. The stage setting of the civil defense sequence used a mock-up of a concrete-block fallout shelter, comfortably although not lavishly furnished with bunk beds and fully equipped with canned goods and bottled water, a radio, portable cooking equipment, and other survival gear prescribed by the FCDA's home-protection manuals.

In each installment, Edwards described "Retrospect" as a "film excursion" into past events that had proved decisive in their impact on contemporary life. The past determines, or at least forms, the present. In linking past and present, the principal strategy of "Retrospect" was to connect major crises of the past and the failure to prepare for them to the dangers of the Cold War and the importance of home-front readiness. The wars of the twentieth century were represented as inevitable, the necessary consequences of the irrationality of markets, the implacable struggle between states for power and assets, and the underlying violence and capriciousness of international relations, all of which must be taken as brute and unalterable facts. Nothing can be done to prevent wars, but precautions can be taken to protect oneself from the devastation they produce. In this manner, the logic of the format tied the inevitability and terrible destruction of recent wars and the folly of those who ignored their warning signals to the current American national security crisis and the importance of preparing for a nuclear war with the Soviet Union.

In one historical segment, the Soviet nuclear threat was compared with the audacious surprise attack by the Japanese that had destroyed the American Pacific fleet anchored at Pearl Harbor. In this comparison, "Retrospect" played on one of the darkest themes in American postwar culture: the fear of a nuclear Pearl Harbor. Once again caught off guard and defenseless, this time the United States would be annihilated by a single nuclear blow. In a spare narration, Edwards recounted the circumstances that had led to the Japanese attack. His principal theme was Japanese ruthlessness and duplicity. Because the Roosevelt government had trusted Japan's leaders, it took no measures to protect the fleet at Pearl Harbor and even discounted fugitive warnings and intelligence reports concerning an imminent Japanese attack. The Japanese use of surprise had brilliantly exploited American vulnerability and "worked to perfection." With only a small air force, Japan had destroyed a key outpost of "the greatest military power in the world." How much sooner would the war have ended, how many lives would have been saved, Edwards asked rhetorically, if Americans had been ready at Pearl Harbor?

The general lesson of Pearl Harbor is clear. Regardless of the strength of a nation's military forces, preparedness is essential to national security. In the Cold War, the more specific lesson for the United States, no longer protected from attack by its natural oceanic barriers, was also evident. Just as the Roosevelt government had made a catastrophic error in trusting the Japanese, so Americans would be fatally mistaken in trusting the Soviets. In both cases, a policy of reckless expansion and deceit made it impossible to achieve peace through conventional diplomacy and negotiation. In December 1941, the United States had risked defeat in the Pacific by failing to prepare for war. In the Cold War, the stakes were immeasurably higher and the margins of error had narrowed to the vanishing point. By failing to prepare for nuclear war, the United States risked much more than a military defeat: It stood to lose everything.

In shifting the format to the civil defense segment of the program, Edwards claimed that the United States had learned the bitter lesson of Pearl Harbor: "Today we realize that preparedness is our first line of defense." But exactly what did preparedness mean for the American family in the thermonuclear era? Above all, it required efforts taken in the home to protect the family from fallout. The links between national security and the danger of fallout and the translation of this danger into a household problem that could be managed by family self-protection were the major themes of the civil defense sequences of "Retrospect."

In one sequence, Edwards, making his way into the CBS fallout shelter, observed that all the critical problems facing the American public revolved around one central issue: survival—"yours, mine, the survival of the entire free world." Edwards reminded his viewers that the real objective of the Soviet Union was the subjugation of the entire world to Communist domination. Soviet leaders were prepared to use any means to achieve this aim: economic subversion, which would weaken the markets of the free world; a cynical campaign of propaganda, which would destroy the morale of freedom-loving peoples; and even their formidable arsenal of nuclear weapons, which would reduce to rubble any city in the United States. Americans needed to wake up to the stark realization that the Soviets were waging "total war" against the United States. Edwards admonished his audience that such a war required a total defense. Military forces alone, regardless of their strength and sophistication, were not sufficient to counter the Soviet threat: "This is why every American must prepare his home and family against possible attack."

But in view of the hazards of fallout, was survival actually possible in a nuclear war? In order to convince Americans that their efforts at nuclear household management would actually pay off, Edwards introduced a representative of state authority and scientific expertise in the person of Paul McGrath, the Director of Intelligence and National Security Affairs for the OCDM. Speaking in clipped and confident cadences, McGrath assured Edwards that despite of the danger of fallout, the survival of the American family in a nuclear attack was "substantiated by facts." Viewers learned that there was "one sensible answer" to the problem of fallout: home shelter. "Recent studies" were said to have "proved" that the simple addition of a shelter to the home would reduce American casualties in a nuclear war by 75 percent. Indeed, McGrath claimed that a shelter based on the CBS model would provide "excellent protection against radiation."

Returning from the CBS fallout shelter to face the television audience, Edwards offered an enthusiastic endorsement of McGrath's position. "We've heard the facts," Edwards observed. "Now we must do something about it" [*sic*]. Addressing the audience with a grave demeanor, Edwards reiterated the main point of the segment: "the importance of the fact that simple, inexpensive home shelters can save millions of lives in case of nuclear war." In the unlikely event that this point was not clear by the end of the program, the CBS announcer intoned in conclusion: "Survival in the nuclear age is a personal responsibility touching every American family. Make sure you take part.

Learn the facts about civil defense home preparedness. Start your home preparedness program today. A prepared family builds a prepared nation. Civil defense is an American tradition."

But suppose that Americans took shelter, protected themselves from fallout, and emerged at the all-clear signal only to discover that their food had been contaminated. Was it their fate to survive a week or more in a fallout shelter only to starve later? In order to get the "facts" on these questions in another installment of "Retrospect," Edwards moved to the kitchen work space of the CBS shelter, where he found Charles Shaeffer, the Director of Radiological Defense Plans for the OCDM. What was a mother to do, Edwards asked, when the family entered the postattack world after exhausting its two-week supply of specially protected food? In response to this problem, Shaeffer demonstrated radioactive-decontamination methods for the home kitchen, arguing that in the aftermath of a thermonuclear attack, family meals could be resumed as usual.

Shaeffer maintained that there were many simple ways to decontaminate food left in the refrigerator or on the kitchen shelves—food that, like the family itself, had survived a nuclear attack. To illustrate, Shaeffer "contaminated" a banana with what he described as a "radioactive solution." He then tested it with a Geiger counter to determine that it was indeed radioactive, peeled it, and tested the peeled banana to verify that it was safe for consumption. Finally, after showing that this was the case, he ate the banana. Because the peel was contaminated, he secured it in a plastic bag for "later disposal." Where this would take place, the audience was not told. This same procedure, Shaeffer added, could be used on any fruit or vegetable that has a thick skin, such as an orange, a grapefruit, or a melon.

Was the family ready for a fresh salad after two weeks entombed in a shelter? To decontaminate a head of lettuce, Shaeffer advised, simply strip away the outside leaves, "put them out of harm's way," and wash the head carefully, "as any housewife normally does." Shaeffer also demonstrated the proper postattack method for opening a can of Spam, wiping the can clean to remove any fallout particles before applying the can opener. After following these elementary decontamination procedures, the family could sit down to a delicious and nutritionally balanced 1950s lunch of Spam, iceberg lettuce, and fruit, without fear of radioactive poisoning. The lesson for the housewife in the thermonuclear era was clear. As the audience could see, "the radiation picture is not all black. In fact, if you do the proper things, it becomes quite manageable." Radiation was just another form of household dirt that could be managed by simple techniques and the addition of another kitchen appliance, a Geiger counter.

These assurances notwithstanding, would life in a fallout shelter actually be tolerable? "Have you ever wondered what it would be like for you and your family to spend seven days completely isolated from the outside world?" Edwards asked his audience. What happens to people when they are cut off from all outside contact? What problems do they face? What should ordinary Americans expect if they are forced to live under these conditions? As if in answer to these questions, Edwards escorted into the CBS shelter the Brown family of Topeka, Kansas, who conducted just such an exercise. The Browns, with a full complement of eight children, ranging in age from seven months to eleven years, shut themselves into their eight- by eleven-foot shelter for an entire week in order to undergo what Edwards called a "personal survival test." Speaking in the broad nasal tones of the Great Plains, Mr. Brown identified himself as a commercial builder of fallout shelters who wanted to give his family the experience of life under nuclear attack. Thus the Browns' family experiment consummated a synthesis of privatism and patriotism, domesticity and the profit motive, national security and the promotion of products for sale by means of public relations.

Mrs. Brown allowed that life in the austere eighty-eight-square-foot shelter was not altogether "homey." How to transform the shelter from a refuge for survival into a home? Mrs. Brown's solution was interior decorating. She put a cloth on the shelter table and decorated the walls with pictures torn from the children's coloring books. In this way, the shelter became a place for living rather than merely existing. The Browns stressed the importance to the success of their venture of elaborate advance planning, meticulous scheduling, and the close regimentation of shelter life. "We had regular times for everything that we did, and we did it together," Mrs. Brown explained. The main challenge for the Browns seems to have been the control of alienation and violence, which they characterized as the problem of preventing the children from getting bored and fighting. Their solution was organized recreation periods with toys and games. These sessions were carefully planned and regulated by means of what Edwards instructively called "police work." Sheltered domesticity depended on careful coordination and unremitting surveillance. "We controlled their play," Mrs. Brown observed of her eight children, and "we did it all together so that everybody was working with each other."

The Browns described their rehearsal for thermonuclear war as an adventure in family initiative, self-examination, and self-discovery. They emerged from isolation with a new and hard-won understanding of their family as a self-sufficient unit, resolute and psychologically tough, even under the conditions of nuclear attack. The experience of shelter life was also fun. As Edwards stressed, civil defense home protection was not only a patriotic duty and a domestic responsibility. It was an exciting and wholesome form of entertainment for the entire family.

The moral of the Browns' story for the American people was obvious. Domestic civil defense did not call for heroic feats or uncommon efforts. Ordinary people with very large families could protect themselves from the danger of fallout. They could embark on a journey of self-discovery and have a good time along the way. Edwards urged all American families to take their cue from the Browns: "The Browns are helping to ensure survival in this nuclear age. What about you?"

In many respects, "Retrospect" was an ideal vehicle for marketing civil defense home protection. Because it was produced by the Public Affairs Division of CBS News, "Retrospect" was able to take advantage of the conceptual and institutional separation between the press and the state, supposedly a fundamental principle of the American polity. CBS News was not a government agency, but an independent news organization that could be trusted to provide a reliable account of civil defense. Edwards was not an employee of OCDM or a minion of the civil defense community, but a news correspondent, committed by the ethics of his profession to maintain an uncompromising political neutrality. The format of "Retrospect" was drawn from the repertoire of familiar radio and television news programs. A journalist-narrator recites facts to an audience and tells a story the public needs to know. By the end of the program, the public has "the real facts" and knows "the whole story." Thus the warrant for the claims made on behalf of family civil defense was not the potentially partisan political requirements of national security policy, which could be contested on the basis of alternative positions, but the allegedly objective standards of reportage.

"Retrospect" also skillfully exploited the historical themes and the metahistorical assumptions built into the program. The positions on civil defense taken in "Retrospect" were represented as inescapable lessons of history. Because historical events have already happened and cannot be changed, they do not seem to be open to political debate. Civil defense was not a matter of policy—an unresolved set of issues about which there could be more than one legitimate opinion—but a historical fact.

In the same way that World War I had been a result of the hypernationalism of the late nineteenth century and the German ascendancy in Europe in the 1930s had been a product of the failures of the Western democracies, so the Cold War and the exigencies of American national security were inexorable consequences of the history of Soviet Communism and its project of world domination. In the monistic philosophy of history to which "Retrospect" was committed, there was only one valid account of historical events and only one true interpretation of history. Any interpretation that diverged from the privileged story could not be regarded as an alternative account, possibly legitimate if judged on its own premises. To the extent that it departed from the one true story, it was in error. It followed that there was only one valid account of the origins of the Cold War, the development of the American national security crisis, and the place of civil defense in American life. Any other version of this history was false and had to be rejected precisely for this reason. As a result, civil defense was insulated from criticism and protected from competing alternative views of the domestic requirements of American security. Because civil defense was an essential part of the current chapter in the one true history of the Cold War, there were no such alternatives.

Finally, "Retrospect" possessed a formidable public-relations asset in the person of Edwards himself, who was known to the television audience as the broadcaster who had read the news every weekday night since 1948 on "Douglas Edwards with the News." Edwards was cast as a narrator of impeccable reliability. He simply related information, read factual reports, or posed questions to expert interviewees and summarized their answers in an untendentious fashion. In fact, the civil defense community employed Edwards as an advocate of its own policies and an accomplished publicist who assisted OCDM officials in presenting questionable and controversial positions as if they were incontestable facts, guaranteed by the authority of science or history.

Thus a variety of factors—the impact of television on mass communications in the 1950s, the news format of "Retrospect," its historical and philosophical pretensions, the distinction between politics and journalism in American political discourse, and the use of a well-known television news broadcaster as host—made "Retrospect" a remarkably well designed instrument in the program to sell family civil defense.

The Cold War Ethic

American national security policy in the Cold War presupposed a civic ethic that would generate the toughness and determination without which the American people would be incapable of facing the risks of deterrence. This ethic would ensure that Americans fulfilled the responsibilities that the national security establishment had assigned them: the obligation to accept the dangers of deterrence and the task of making this strategy credible by preparing themselves for nuclear war. One of the chief objectives of the FCDA's home-protection program was to build into the family a commitment to the moral principles promoted by domestic civil defense as essential to meet the demands of the Cold War.

The main points of the Cold War ethic were outlined in a short speech dated October 22, 1951, and written for President Truman by the FCDA Public Affairs Office. This address was intended as an impressive introduction to a training film that would be shown to each entering class of the FCDA Staff College at Olney, Maryland, and also at its various technical schools throughout the country. Truman's speech began by stressing the unique threat to the American way of life posed by Soviet nuclear weapons. The new threat did not, however, call for a new ethic or a reform of American values. On the contrary, the moral qualities that Americans needed to prevail against the Soviets depended on a "revival of the old American tradition of community self defense."

Once upon a time, according to Truman, settlements along the American frontier were exposed to attacks by hostile Indian tribes. The pioneers responded by joining to form communities, all of whose members did their part to combat the common danger. When the Indians mounted their assaults, the men armed themselves with rifles and took up their positions on the communal stockade. Women loaded and reloaded rifles, and older children looked after their younger siblings. In securing the common defense, everyone had an important role to play, which meant that the fate of the community depended on the personal responsibility of each of its members.

This was the tradition that made the nation possible and provided the foundations for its security, from the Indian wars and the conquest of the frontier to the battles of World War II. The constituents of this tradition were also among the favorite quasi-historical materials for the construction of nuclear fantasies, in which they were recast and deployed in order to interpret the national security crisis of the Cold War and specify the conditions for its resolution.

In translating the Cold War national security crisis into the pioneer mythology, Truman argued that in a war with the Soviets, American cities would face the same challenges that had confronted the frontier settlements in the era of the Indian wars, when the question of American nationhood and the survival of entire communities also had been at stake. A Soviet nuclear offensive would attempt to destroy American cities one by one, in the same way that the Indians had undertaken the piecemeal destruction of pioneer blockhouses in the early American wilderness. It seemed to follow that contemporary Americans must counter the Soviets in the same way the that pioneers had fought off the Indians: "We can meet this danger, just as our forefathers did. We can set up a system of community defense, with all our citizens working together to protect our homes, our children, and our communities."[23]

Truman's speech imaginatively reconstructed the early history of the American national experience in Homeric proportions as the epic of the pioneers who had won the West. In this mythology, the old middle class of small-town America and the new middle class of suburbia were identified with their putative ancestors, the pioneer settlers of the frontier. America under the Soviet nuclear gun in the 1950s was identified with the outposts of the new nation under assault by the aboriginal Americans, the "Indians." The moral strengths of the pioneers were the virtues that contemporary Americans needed to defeat the Soviets. The Cold War would be won by Americans who recovered the ethic of their pioneer forebears.

The Cold War ethic, outlined in the Truman speech and reproduced in thousands of Cold War artifacts, may be reduced to four premises.

Even if deterrence failed and the Soviets launched a nuclear assault against the United States, the results would not be disastrous. The country, its definitive institutions, and the distinctive American way of life would survive. It was the obligation of the American people to think and act accordingly: the principle of optimism.

Survival was not, however, something that would happen fortuitously, nor was it a service that would be performed for the public by the government. On the contrary, the American people had to learn how to protect themselves. Survival was possible only if each household undertook the requisite preparations and all family members did their part, just as the pioneers had been able to defend their settlements against Indian attacks only because everyone had accepted responsibility for the enterprise of communal defense: the principle of personal responsibility.

Although training was important to preparing for World War III, it was not the paramount factor. In the final analysis, the key to civil defense was not technique, but the ethical character of the American people. Mastery of the skills of nuclear survival depended on self-mastery. Above all, the inner self had to be subjected to strict self-discipline so that doubts and fears could be expelled. Otherwise, the timely and proficient execution of coordinated operations under conditions of extreme stress would not be possible. As President Eisenhower observed during his first year in office, the most important desideratum of a civil defense program was that the public learn to discipline itself: the principle of self-control.[24]

Finally, civil defense appealed to the mythology of an earlier pristine era of solid moral values that had to be revived in order for America to pass the tests of the Cold War. These tests did not call for the formation of a new American character or fundamental changes in the American way of life. Instead, the objectives of civil defense could be achieved only by reclaiming the virtues of the early American republic and the old ties of family and community life. For Truman, civil defense was an American tradition, "dating back to the frontier days when all members of every family had a task to do in defending their homes and their stockades from marauding savages."[25] Leo Hoegh took the same view when he noted that in order to maintain the vitality of this tradition in his own home, he kept a Bible in his family shelter. "Our colonial ancestors built dual-purpose dwellings," Hoegh reminded a dinner audience of young businessmen in 1958. "Every home a fortress! That can well be our watchword as we strive to attain the freedom won so dearly by our pioneer forbears."[26] Early Americans had prevailed against their enemies only because of their uncompromising commitment to the original principles that defined the American character. The same principles must again come into play in order for Americans to win the Cold War and, if called on to do so, to emerge victorious in World War III: the principle of traditionalism.

In the 1950s, no one matched the tireless enthusiasm of Katherine Howard in her efforts to promote the Cold War ethic. R. J. Reynolds tobacco heiress, 1920 graduate of Smith College, and active Republican clubwoman in Massachusetts, she gained her entry into politics by marrying a Boston lawyer with ties to the Massachusetts State Republican party. Howard was a member of the Republican National Committee and served as its secretary during the volatile 1952 Republican National Convention. After switching her loyalties from Dewey to Eisenhower, she became the only female member of Eisenhower's 1952 campaign staff. In March 1953, President Eisenhower appointed Howard assistant administrator of the FCDA, and in June of the same year, she was advanced to deputy administrator.

Howard was a woman of remarkable enterprise and energy. Between March 1953 and August 1954, she gave sixty-three speeches, appeared on twenty-eight radio programs and fourteen television shows, and held twelve press conferences, logging almost 100,000 miles on behalf of civil defense. As the FCDA's deputy administrator, she served as its liaison with Congress, NATO, and federal agencies concerned with national security; she was in charge of the FCDA's ambitious women's affairs program, and when Val Peterson was not in Washington, she took his place as acting administrator of the FCDA. As Howard liked to remind her audiences, she was the first woman in any federal department or agency to become second in command. Because this agency was the FCDA, her official car was outfitted with special communications equipment designed for use in a nuclear attack. If the FCDA headquarters in Washington were destroyed, Howard's car would be designated as a mobile headquarters, linking her to the president and the FCDA secret command post that would be used in a nuclear war. Beginning in August 1954, Howard became a special consultant to the FCDA administrator and continued throughout the Eisenhower presidency to speak regularly on behalf of civil defense.

Because public relations at the FCDA were subject to strict oversight, all telephone calls were monitored, and no one was permitted to give extemporaneous speeches or hold unscheduled press conferences. Howard's speeches were generally written by Charles Ellsworth, a public-relations consultant for the FCDA based in New York. Ellsworth had an acute sense of Howard's chief strength as an advocate of civil defense: her unrivaled ability to translate the arcane complexities of nuclear war into simple and forceful concepts that would appeal to the ordinary householder. During her tenure at the FCDA, Howard also became quite adept at handling the public relations of civil defense advocacy. She made useful friendships with women in the Washington press corps and developed a deft touch in handling the press generally, courting and flattering correspondents with considerable success. A shrewd judge of her appeal to the press as a woman in an unusual and visible position in government, Howard was able to exploit her many opportunities for articles and interviews in order to promote the FCDA's objectives, shifting the interest of the press from her person and position to a discussion of the responsibilities of women in civil defense, the place of civil defense in the home, and the role of civil defense in the Cold War.

Howard was also sensitive to the importance of managing the public relations of femininity in Eisenhower's national security establishment. In responding to a survey concerning the news magazines she read regularly, she initially listed the *New Yorker, Ladies' Home Journal, House and Garden,* and *Vogue.* Then, on reflection, she struck out all these entries—none of which would qualify, even marginally, as news magazines—with the self-critical notation: "Sounds frivolous! Read the newspapers!" and contented herself with mentioning only *Life* and *U.S. News & World Report.*[27]

In many respects, Howard's career in Washington was a painful expression of her personal and institutional predicament, caught between a prefeminist ethic that prescribed separate spheres for men and women and a liberal feminism that demanded equality of opportunity and commensurate rewards for comparable performance. On the one hand, she was inordinately proud of her self-described "top policy-making job" in government and her status as a member of the Washington power elite. On the other hand, none of the thousands of pages of her personal papers provide a shred of evidence that Howard participated in civil defense policy making. Howard's own account of her life as a Washington bureaucrat is only superficially concerned with the philosophy, politics, and organization of civil defense. Her main interests seem to have been in her domestic affairs and the social life of Washington officialdom, especially ceremonial matters such as the seating arrangements at state dinners, who wore what, who poured tea and who poured coffee at which ends of the table, who was ritually favored, and who was diminished by the unspoken rules of White House protocol.

Taken as a whole, the speeches that Ellsworth wrote for Howard between 1953 and 1956 articulate the Cold War ethic in a clear, simple—perhaps even simple-minded—fashion, untroubled by careful qualifications and fine distinctions that would blunt their rhetorical force. A typical Howard performance began with an amusing but not frivolous anecdote and quickly turned to the gravity of the Soviet nuclear threat, the importance of civil defense, and what individuals, and

During Operation Alert 1955, Katherine Howard points out the importance of a home shelter. The exhibit shows what would happen to a wood frame house located 3,500 feet from a nuclear blast. The caption reads: "Another millisecond later, 'the shock wave rips across the desert.' The house front begins to sag and shingles fly from the roof." (Courtesy of Dwight D. Eisenhower Library)

especially individual families, could do to protect themselves, all this interlaced with inside Washington information, allusions to secret NSC meetings, and the details of the latest American nuclear-weapons tests. Howard concluded with a moral lesson drawn from a biblical text appropriate to the theme of personal responsibility for national security.

All of Howard's addresses were marked by a naive and unshakable optimism. Although nuclear war might hold the prospect of hitherto unknown and unimagined terrors, it posed no insurmountable threats to the American people once they were properly informed, trained, and motivated. One of Howard's early speeches, delivered in her third month at the FCDA, explored a single anecdote of small-town life in

How would the millions of urban Americans be fed who sought refuge in the relative safety of the suburbs in order to escape a nuclear attack? Katherine Howard poses some questions about cooking skills for the postattack world. (Courtesy of Dwight D. Eisenhower Library)

the nuclear era. In 1951, a large meteorite exploded above Norfolk, Virginia. Some four hours after the incident, a busy housewife called her local newspaper to learn whether the explosion and the bright light had been caused by an atomic bomb and, if so, what steps she should take. She would have called earlier, the housewife explained, but a large washing had to be sorted and pinned to the clothesline. According to Howard, the priorities of the Norfolk housewife were in order. Even if a nuclear attack had occurred, there would still be meals to cook, beds to make, and clothes to wash.

Civil defense did not assume that nuclear war would create a disaster of such proportions that these mundane chores and the life in which they were embedded would be suspended or perhaps even terminated. On the contrary, one of its main objectives was to enable people to continue with the simple tasks of life, regardless of what happened. Howard confidently asserted that no number of enemy bombs could interrupt for long the American way of life. American homes, or at least some of them, might perish, but not American homemakers. American factories, some of them at least, might be destroyed, but not the heads of American families. What was the job of civil defense?

> To prepare people to live through an atomic attack, not to die in one; to keep their homes, not to lose them; to protect and preserve their families, not to scatter and dissolve them; to hold and work at the jobs of their breadwinners, not to give them up; to survive and win over any attacks that may be launched against our home communities, not to collapse under them in abject helplessness.[28]

This was a job the American people could expect to have for the next ten to twenty years, perhaps even for the rest of their lives. This was why it must be incorporated into the routines of the world it was intended to protect. Most important, Howard assured her audience, civil defense was a job the American people could do.

In another speech, delivered in October 1953, Howard even found encouragement in the terrible demographics of atomic-bomb destruction. In contemplating nuclear war, she urged her audience to take "comfort and strength from the many living in our burial of the fewer dead." Instead of regarding the large number of casualties as a cause for despair, Howard took cheer in the fact that the number of survivors would be even larger, appealing to the utilitarian argument that if the numbers are on your side, you must be right. More Americans would live than die in a nuclear attack. More people would be physically untouched than even the hydrogen bomb could possibly injure. Although Americans would suffer serious deprivations, they could not be wiped out. Even if the estimates of the greatest possible damage the United

States could sustain were doubled, tripled, or increased "an inconceivable five times," Howard would not be disheartened by the consequences: "You will **still** have left one of the most potentially powerful nations on earth." Therefore, the outlook for American survival in a nuclear war justified confidence and not despair, effort and not apathy: "We will not be destroyed—indeed, we cannot be destroyed—once we face up to the fact that there are ways to guard ourselves as civilians against even the most terrible weapons of modern warfare."[29]

Howard's speeches were characterized by an enthusiastic and unqualified embrace of the conventionalization argument. The atomic bomb was not a weapon of absolute destruction against which no defense was possible. On the contrary, an atomic attack could be survived by ordinary citizens as long as they were adequately trained and prepared. As Howard noted in a radio interview, the atomic bomb appeared to be so terrifying that any attempt at self-protection seemed futile. This was a mistake. In fact, the bomb was just another weapon, with the limitations that applied to any bomb. It could not kill everyone, not even everyone within sight of its detonation. The more Americans learned about nuclear weapons, the more reason they had to be encouraged. What has been learned, Howard assured her listeners, proved that the destructive effects of the atomic bomb "can be broken down to manageable proportions, like those of any other disaster, and fought by determined civilians."[30]

Howard extended the trivialization of nuclear weapons to the hydrogen bomb, which was nothing more than "a bigger A-bomb." This meant that it represented "the same problem, only more so."[31] Therefore, not even the hydrogen bomb was sufficient to dampen Howard's optimism about the chances of American survival in a nuclear war.

In a series of speeches following the television broadcast of the film *Operation Ivy*, Howard informed her audiences that the hydrogen bomb was merely another addition to the American nuclear stockpile, larger than the atomic bomb, but "neither particularly new nor particularly astonishing." In an effort to counter the public perception of the hydrogen bomb as a qualitatively new weapon of ultimate terror against which any defense was unimaginable, Howard stressed its limits. It could not kill all life over a radius of hundreds of miles, nor could it contaminate the atmosphere or poison all the water in the seas, much less set entire continents ablaze. In fact, Howard claimed, the radius of total destruction produced by the first hydrogen bomb was a mere three miles. For Howard, this was a virtual cause for celebration: "There are more than three million square miles of solid ground in this great country of ours. That's a lot of area to cover with death and devastation—H-bomb or no H-bomb." Employing the utilitarian and demographic reasoning often favored in her speeches, Howard argued that no weapon, not even an arsenal of hydrogen bombs, could obliterate so vast a territory. Even if the United States were obliged to absorb the worst the Soviets could do, Howard saw plenty of space left for the survivors: "And most of these people would never actually have seen or felt an atomic blast at first hand!"[32]

It followed that the hydrogen bomb would not end the prospects for survival and render obsolete the policies of civil defense developed in the early 1950s. On the contrary, it reaffirmed the value of these policies. America needed more civil defense, not less. The civil defense planning and organization the United States had undertaken and the skills Americans had learned would be even more necessary in a thermonuclear war. In the final analysis, the development of the hydrogen bomb meant that America needed "many more well-informed and well-prepared homes, because our American homes would be our most critical defense redoubts if attack should come. And the important thing is: most of these homes would survive."[33]

Survival, however, would not be possible unless Americans made themselves personally accountable for their own protection. In her addresses, Howard generally stressed the obligation of every family to secure its own home against nuclear attack. In a prepublication speech on *Home Protection Exercises,* she noted that the main theme of the booklet was individual and family initiatives that would ensure survival. *Home Protection Exercises* was a response to the concerned citizen who asked, "The A-bomb is terrible but what can I do about it?"[34] It was based on the principle that civil defense would be helpful only to those who took responsibility for helping themselves. Howard maintained that Americans were prepared to accept this responsibility.

In a speech to the exclusive Sulgrave Club in Washington, she discussed President Eisenhower's conception of a nuclear "age of peril" and its impact on American life. Howard argued that in concentrating on the analysis of attack capabilities and the prediction of casualty ratios, the national security establishment had failed to grasp the most important consequence of this new age of peril: "a long overdue return of individual responsibility to its all-important place in the life of the family, and the community, and the Nation." The outcome of the Cold War was tied to this "renaissance of individual responsibility." As in no other period of American history, the fate of the country depended less on the government than on the "character and spiritual strength of its people." The ultimate response to Soviet nuclear weapons was the American Cold War ethic and its commitment to what Howard called a "high order of citizenship that asks only, 'What can I do to help?'."[35]

In order to specify what this ethic required of the American people, Howard used a rhetorical device often favored by advocates of civil defense in the 1950s. She asked what would happen to the survivors of a nuclear attack on a particular city. If an atomic bomb exploded at the intersection of Broad and Wharton Streets in Philadelphia, what would this mean for Philadelphia suburbanites and residents of the Delaware Valley? The bomb would destroy only one-half of 1 percent of the buildings in the Delaware Valley and kill only 8 percent of its inhabitants. But these figures did not capture the real dimensions of the damage, which would be magnified by the concentration of all essential enterprises and services in the Delaware Valley area within Philadelphia itself. The offices of 1,301 doctors would be destroyed, along with many of their homes, 17 hospitals, and 4 large residences for nurses. Twelve newspapers and 4 radio stations, 23 banks together with all their records, 119 drugstores, 722 foodstores, 77 gasoline and oil distributors, and virtually every important office of the federal government in Philadelphia would be wiped out. In short, the commercial, financial, professional, and governmental center of the city would disappear.

But what about the remaining 92 percent of the people in the Delaware Valley, who would survive the attack with their bodies and homes more or less intact? Without essential utilities, medical care, and police and fire protection and isolated by the destruction of metropolitan communication and transportation networks, what would their chances be? They would be helpless, Howard claimed, "unless, of course—and this is a big unless—their sense of individual responsibility had prepared them in part for the blow."[36]

What would it mean for Philadelphia suburbanites to take individual responsibility for their survival? Personal responsibility in a nuclear emergency entailed an imposing list of obligations. Because there might be only a few minutes' warning before the attack, everyone would have to learn standardized civil defense alert signals and take shelter promptly at the sound of the siren. Because utility plants would be destroyed, water cut off, and food unobtainable for several days, emergency supplies would have to be stored. Fire departments would not respond to calls, and, in any case, there would probably be no postattack telephone service. Therefore, families would be obliged to learn essential home fire-prevention measures and fire-fighting techniques. Because no one could count on the availability of medical services, households would have to provide their own emergency first-aid care. Sewage systems would be inoperable, and garbage collection would obviously be suspended. Because the lapse of sanitation services would threaten the entire area with epidemics, every home would have to see to the safe disposal of its own wastes. The interruption of telephone service would encourage the circulation of dangerous rumors that could confuse, demoralize, and panic survivors. In order to ensure adequate postattack emotion management, every family would be responsible for monitoring the behavior of its neighbors and maintaining rigorous self-censorship.

Howard linked these daunting responsibilities to the special moral qualities they required. Americans' home-front assets included more than the economic and technological resources necessary to maintain production. In the end, the decisive factor in the Cold War was the spiritual vitality of the American people, which Howard saw as the critical element of the Cold War ethic. The Norfolk housewife was emblematic of this spiritual vitality. In responding to a possible nuclear attack, she did not panic or collapse into an irrational display of hysteria or apathy. On the contrary, she demonstrated remarkable poise and "a personal willingness, after fulfilling her own domestic responsibilities, to come to the assistance of others." This determination to stand up under the demands of a nuclear crisis was the "inner resource" of the American people. It was grounded in the "sheer personal faith" that Americans had in themselves, their communities, and ultimately the American way of life and its promise.[37]

The true repositories of the virtues required by civil defense were "the housewives and homemakers of the land." They supplied the "stabilizing influence" and the self-control needed to combat moral weakness, the fear of imagined dangers, and a lack of confidence. "Their spiritual strength—their faiths, their convictions, their strong moral characters—have never been in short supply in any emergency in our history, local or national, and never will be." The United States would triumph in the Cold War, but not primarily because of its size or material resources. The real secret weapon in the struggle against Communism was the American greatness of soul. Americans possessed a courage and a faith that had been tested and proved by history. Above all, they had the strength of their homes and the spirit of their women: "feminine courage, and strength of mind and heart."[38] In the end, Howard maintained, Americans could depend on "motherhood qualities" to save the country in a nuclear attack.[39]

In the moral psychology of American civil defense, there were three views concerning the relative strengths and weaknesses of men and women: their capacity to withstand the rigors of nuclear war and their ability to assume civil defense responsibilities and carry out tasks essential to survival.

Howard maintained that because of their uniquely feminine strengths and skills, women could be expected to make a distinctive and perhaps superior contribution to civil defense. Women's singular capacities for civil defense work were due to their position in the social division of labor as homemakers—mothers and keepers of the hearth. Although this view was not entirely ignored in the FCDA's promotional material, it represented a decidedly minority position.

Even more marginal were the views expressed in Val Peterson's *Collier's* article, which held that women were more prone to panic than men were, precisely because of their role as homemakers and their relative isolation from the forces of the polity and the economy. The role of housewife, the factor to which Howard attributed women's strength, was regarded as the source of their weakness. Because of the importance of women in civil defense, these remarks about their relative moral and psychological inferiority constituted an obvious tactical error in propaganda, especially ironic in view of their attribution to the FCDA's chief.

The dominant view, articulated most fully in the several editions of *Home Protection Exercises* and in the FCDA films on family preparedness, held that there were no important gender distinctions relevant to civil defense. When civil defense posters and films depicted the administration of first aid following a nuclear attack, more often than not the caregiver was a women. However, women were also represented fighting fires, performing rescue operations, transporting emergency supplies, and serving as armed auxiliary police, in some cases on motorcycles. Although *Home Protection Exercises* occasionally referred to "homemakers," none of its various editions distributed domestic civil defense responsibilities according to traditional gender criteria. Furthermore, as early as 1950, the Office of Civil Defense Planning in the NSRB took a general position on women's role in civil defense that corresponded roughly to the view of contemporary liberal feminism: Given the same training, men and woman could do the same jobs. This position was stated by William A. Gill, Coordinator of Civil Defense Planning for the NSRB, in a memorandum dated July 18, 1950, "Women's Role in Civil Defense:"

> In considering the role of women in mobilization, the Resources Board has in the past usually treated the question of manpower without regard to sex. Recognition has been given to the principle that a woman can do almost any wartime task for which men are capable, on the assumption that women are given the same amount of training or have equivalent backgrounds of experience.[40]

Why did civil defense depart from American institutions and conventions of the 1950s that reinforced a rigidly stereotypical distribution of roles based on gender? Civil defense was obliged to come to terms with the expected distribution of human resources on the home front. In the event of a nuclear attack, the military establishment would make heavy demands on American manpower, which meant that most civil defense jobs would have to be filled by women. Considered from the standpoint of the division of labor in the postattack world, the assumption that women were competent to perform all civil defense tasks was tantamount to making a virtue of a necessity, comparable to the celebration of female industrial labor in World War II.

Although the outcome of the Cold War would ultimately be decided by the moral qualities of the American people, the Cold War ethic did not require new moral armaments. On the contrary, it called for a return to what were represented as older American values. The moral traditionalism of civil defense is a theme to which Howard repeatedly returned in her addresses.

In one of her most interesting speeches, "The Power of Women in Civil Defense," Howard discussed the concept of a national heritage and its role in American life, by comparing a national heritage and a family heirloom. Like a family heirloom, a national heritage is not sold in shops. Indeed, it cannot be purchased under any conditions or bought at any price. A national heritage has a value that cannot be manufactured or fabricated. In this regard, it resembles a cherished possession that has been in a family for generations. The practical purposes served by an heirloom cannot be detached from its spiritual significance, which ties the family to its own past. Because of the meanings that an heirloom accumulates over the generations, it creates a feeling of comfort and appropriateness. Like a family heirloom, a national heritage is an irreplaceable element of contemporary life as well as a link to "the security of the past and the promise of the future."[41]

Not surprisingly, Howard included civil defense among the great American national heritages. It was grounded in the traditions of the sanctity of the home and the family—"the true pioneer feeling," which Howard characterized as "the home-loving spirit of the early days, complete with family traditions and all the inner securities that go with them." Like these traditions, civil defense had no price. It could not be bought or delivered to the household, factory assembled and ready for use. Rather, like any national heritage, it depended upon care and dedication. In Howard's conception of American history, the early Americans had their own version of civil defense. Moreover, the strength of character on which it depended had not been lost. It was only "hidden away, perhaps, in the backs of our minds—waiting to be pressed into service again."[42] It followed that civil defense was not something Americans had to discover, invent, or produce anew. Because civil defense was a part of their national heritage, they needed only to rediscover it and recapture its spirit.

Howard linked the recovery of the spirit of home-front defense to the reclamation of the spirit of 1776, the ideals that inspired the original Americans of Cold War mythology. In a speech to an organization of women's club officers, she recalled the image of the great pamphleteer of the Revolutionary War, Thomas Paine, pulling up a drumhead near a campfire and composing his "stirring last-ditch appeal to the Colonists." Howard asked her audience to remember the tribulations of the colonists during the War of Independence, when they had defended the values that became the spiritual basis of the new nation. With little food and money, families had been forced to abandon their homes in order to survive and carry on the fight. In the long run, they had prevailed in a war in which their militia had been defeated in every battle but the last—"the one that brought victory." Because of this formative experience, Howard argued, the United States had a finer appreciation than did most nations of the indissoluble bond between security and preparedness and a deeper understanding of the bitter truth that there could be no final victory over "the powers of darkness." Once again, Howard warned, American homes were in danger of being attacked. "Once more the front lines of freedom lie at our very doorsteps." Because of the American tradition of self-defense and personal responsibility for national security, the American people did not leave to the president the decision of whether to defend their homes against nuclear attack. "That decision was made for us generations ago by the Pilgrims, and the Minute Men, and the Western pioneers."[43]

In a beautifully crafted speech delivered in 1954 to the sixty-third Continental Congress of the Daughters of the American Revolution—with the inspired title "The Ramparts We Watch"—Howard connected the American Revolution to the Cold War, the colonial homesteads of the eighteenth century to the suburbs of the 1950s, and the spirit of 1776 to the Cold War ethic. The speech was conceived within the mythology of a timeless American fireside, where the values that underpin the security of the American nation are passed from generation to generation. Because of the tradition of home defense embedded in American life, wives and mothers would not flinch from the horrible prospect of a nuclear war. Nor would they falter when they were required to protect their own homes and families. American women would take World War III in stride precisely because of the tradition of self-defense that stemmed from the Revolution. "We women have faced such problems since Colonial times," Howard reminded her audience. "We know how to help others as well as ourselves, and what we don't know, we are ready to learn." Soviet nuclear weapons might be new and terrible. But American defenses against these weapons are "as old as our first homesteads." They have been transmitted from one generation to another "at every American fireside." In defending the home front against the Soviet hydrogen bomb, what were the main weapons of the American family? They were the constituents of the indestructible heritage passed down from their ancestors: "love of family, loyalty to country, aid to others, faith in God, a fierce regard for freedom—and the will to work together in the traditional American ways."[44]

What would happen if Cold War Americans failed to recapture the values of the American past? What consequences could be expected if the suburbanites of the 1950s strayed from the path struck by the Minute Men of Concord and Lexington and ignored the call to form "the citizen army of our times"? Howard had no doubts about the answer to this question. If the moral standards that made America great were not revived, the American people would be unable to "uphold the beacon light of freedom." If the light that shines from the city built on a hill were extinguished, "the Dark Ages could once again settle upon the world." In the end, "Christian civilization as we know it would vanish from all the lands of the earth." In Howard's Cold War eschatology, the failure to reclaim traditional American values could hardly be more spectacularly catastrophic. It was not merely the conflict between the United States and the Soviet Union that would be decided by the moral character of the American people. The failure of American will in the Cold War would determine the fate of Western civilization and mark one of the great turning points in world history. "If our morale were shattered," Howard admonished her audience, "the forces of atheistic Communism would almost certainly engulf, all of Free Europe, what remains of free Asia—and perhaps even this beloved Land as well."[45]

5

The Antinomies of
Cold War Culture

The civil defense programs of the 1950s reveal several contradictions, two of which will be considered here. Neither is the product of a theoretical or academic exercise disconnected from actual civil defense plans. On the contrary, both emerged in the earliest stages of Cold War civil defense planning, and both were explored in detail by the national security establishment during the Eisenhower presidency, when they were the subject of sober, but ultimately inconsequential, debate.

The Dilemma of Emotion Management

The doctrine of nuclear terror held that without civil defense, the public response to the prospect of a nuclear attack would defeat the objectives of American national security policy. Either Americans would be paralyzed by fear and collapse into a state of stupefaction, or the horror of impending total destruction would drive them into a frenzy. Both reactions were incompatible with the steady resolve regarded as essential to the credibility of deterrence. The solution to this problem was civil defense, which would enlighten Americans concerning the true dangers of nuclear war and teach them how to survive. When they learned how to beat the bomb, nuclear terror would vanish.

There seemed to be a basic flaw in this solution, for the more people learned about nuclear war, the more terrified they became. Civil defense information would not lead to self-control and pragmatic measures of self-protection. On the contrary, it would magnify public fears by confirming that they had a sound basis in reality. FCDA propaganda held that nuclear terror was irrational because it was based on mistaken apprehensions and irresponsible speculation. Civil defense would give the people the facts about nuclear weapons, but these facts would only substantiate some of their worst fears. A nuclear attack really would be as bad as many people imagined and incalculably worse than the uninformed and apathetic supposed. Therefore, nuclear terror seemed a reasonable response to the government's public-information program.

The result was a dilemma. On the premises of their own theory of emotion management, civil defense strategists faced two equally intolerable alternatives. In the absence of civil defense, the public would be gripped by nuclear terror. But once civil defense had done its work, the public would be even more terrified. It apparently followed that the problem of nuclear terror—the extreme form in which civil defense planners framed the problem of national will—had no solution. Civil defense, which was necessary in order to solve the problem of national will, seemed to guarantee that this problem could not be solved.

The paradox that civil defense could defeat its most important objective emerged as early as 1947, when the JCS Evaluation Board responsible for analyzing the results of OPERATION CROSSROADS sent its top secret report to President Truman. In its assessment of how effectively the atomic bomb would perform in a war against the United States, the Evaluation Board argued that the bomb's chief value in such a war was not the physical destruction and death it could produce, but its impact on mass psychology and national morale. The main threat of the atomic bomb in the hands of an enemy of the United States was its capacity to create nuclear terror and weaken, or perhaps destroy, the national morale: "the bomb's potentiality to break the will of nations and of peoples." The Evaluation Board maintained that the American communications network, its huge media industry, and its vast national market for news made the United States much more vulnerable than other nations to these psychological and moral dangers.[1]

How serious was the problem of nuclear terror, and what could be done about it? In considering these questions, the Evaluation Board rejected one of the received premises of American civil defense doctrine: the assumption that reassuring hypotheses about the emotional and moral impact of a nuclear attack on the United States could be supported by the study of Japanese reactions to the Hiroshima and Nagasaki bombings made by the United States Strategic Bombing Survey. Unlike Americans in a possible World War III, the Japanese had no prior knowledge of the bomb's effects. With no idea of what the bomb could do, the Japanese had no opportunity to exhibit what the Evaluation Board called "anticipatory panic." In addition, the "mental makeup peculiar to the Japanese" would invalidate any inferences from the bombing of Hiroshima and Nagasaki to atomic attacks on

American cities. Finally, in World War II the atomic bomb was used only twice. On both occasions, a single mission delivered a single bomb over a single city. Any analysis of these two missions would be irrelevant to the mass psychology of a future nuclear war, in which hundreds of bombs might be detonated in quick succession over scores of cities.[2]

In stark contrast with the optimistic program of emotion management later implemented by the civil defense community, the Evaluation Board seemed to regard nuclear terror as a problem without a solution. A policy of informing the American people about the real effects of an atomic attack—a public-information program, which the FCDA later embraced with unreserved enthusiasm—would only exacerbate the problem:

> Paradoxically, it would seem that, within some limits, the greater the knowledge of nuclear fission phenomena, the greater the fear it engenders. Dwellers of a city who are aware of the nature of the calamities being inflicted upon their fellow countrymen of another city, will identify themselves with these calamities and may, the more easily, translate early fear into ultimate alarm and panic.[3]

Americans who were not so well informed about nuclear weapons would presumably be less affected by the logic of nuclear terror. Precisely because of their ignorance, however, they would be subject to what the Evaluation Board called "primordial fears" of the unknown, the invisible, and the mysterious.[4] As a result, both the enlightened and the unenlightened seemed likely victims of nuclear terror. In either case, it appeared that no solution to the problem of nuclear terror was possible.

Millard Caldwell, Truman's administrator of the FCDA, took a similar view in a letter to Philip Wylie dated July 13, 1951. In earlier correspondence, Wylie had expressed his doubts that any population under nuclear attack could maintain the discipline necessary for civil defense. Incapable of withstanding the stresses of an atomic attack, the public would panic. Although Caldwell did not share Wylie's pessimism, he agreed that in civil defense planning, the main problem was not the nuclear attack itself, but public anxiety about its possibility: "Fear represents the big danger—a far greater danger than the physical effects." To Caldwell, this meant that even if Wylie's position were correct, it should remain a closely held state secret. On this question of emotion management, Caldwell compared the American public in the Cold War with the predicament of a cancer patient: "Sometimes, when a situation is utterly hopeless, it may be better not to say so. The doctors often conclude against telling the hopeless cancer patient what the situation is."[5]

Caldwell's physicians faced a dilemma. If they withheld information about the patient's true condition, she would be petrified by the fear that she might die. But if they told her exactly how bad her disease really was, she might become even more terrified. In Caldwell's analogy, the state and its national security apparatus occupied the position of the physicians, an interestingly antidemocratic observation on the character of American democracy and the relation between the government and the public that seems much closer to the political philosophy of Dostoevsky's Grand Inquisitor than to that of Truman's Fair Deal. In their ignorance, the American people were horrified by the possibility of nuclear war. But if they were enlightened by civil defense information, their fears would become more reasonable and therefore more powerful. In consequence, emotion management seemed to provide no solution to the problem of panic.

During the Truman presidency, the dilemma of emotion management remained the subject of incidental and desultory reflections, but this changed quite dramatically during Eisenhower's first term. Beginning in 1954, the yearly Operation Alert exercises provided the occasion for a periodic reexamination of the assumptions and implications of civil defense planning.

Each year from 1954 through 1960, top-secret, preexercise planning sessions and postexercise evaluations were held in which both the NSC and the cabinet participated. These assessments were generally forthright and unsparing. The unofficial positions on civil defense taken by the Eisenhower national security team were invariably more nuanced and qualified than the bland assurances of FCDA propaganda. The highest officials—Eisenhower, Vice President Richard Nixon, John Foster Dulles, Secretary of Defense Wilson, Secretary of the Treasury Humphrey, and JCS Chairman Admiral Radford—were brutally realistic in their judgments and increasingly cynical about the actual prospects of surviving a nuclear attack. They demonstrated little patience for the public objectives of their own civil defense program, which they regarded as naive and hopelessly optimistic. The president himself had an acute sense of the link between emotion management and national security. Therefore, during the Eisenhower presidency, the dilemma of emotion management was regarded as a serious anomaly in American national security policy. However, the perception of this anomaly, even at the highest levels of government, did not lead to significant changes or even minor adjustments in civil defense programs.

Val Peterson first broached the possibility of a national civil defense alert in the NSC meeting of January 28, 1954. His proposal to test the government's plans for handling a nuclear emergency was introduced in a seemingly paradoxical fashion. The issue of a national civil defense alert should be considered by the NSC, Peterson argued, because the exercise might prove to be an international embarrassment. In particular, it might lend credence to the charge that Americans were "subject to hysteria." Admiral Radford was also troubled by the "psychological impact," both international and domestic, of such a test. His main concern was that a large-scale event could create "public alarm or panic."[6]

These considerations suggested that the American people, already anxious about the possibility of nuclear war, would become still more disturbed by an exercise in which civil defense plans were put to a realistic test. Perhaps such an exercise would even push them over the threshold from fear to panic. This reasoning implied that the more Americans knew about the realities of nuclear war, the more terrified they would become, an inference that contradicted the main psychological premise of the government's civil defense program.

No one drew this inference in the January 28 NSC meeting. Nor was it expressed in the NSC meeting held some three weeks later, in which release of the film *Operation Ivy* was the chief item on the agenda. The AEC's secret film of the first American hydrogen-bomb test had been cut from one hour to twenty-eight minutes for possible broadcast on television and in movie theaters. *Operation Ivy* included quite dramatic shots of the explosion: the huge blast in the sea, the shock waves it produced, and the gigantic mushroom-shaped cloud. In addition, a diagram indicated how many Pentagon-sized buildings would be required to fill the crater created by the blast.

Several members of the NSC maintained that even this expurgated version of the film was too sensational. Public showings, it was feared, would create "anxiety and disturbance." When Robert Cutler, the President's Special Assistant for National Security Affairs, argued on behalf of Peterson's proposal that the FCDA needed something to "scare the American people out of their indifference" and frighten them into taking civil defense seriously, Eisenhower's response was vehement. The president declared himself unconditionally opposed to fear tactics and rejected any attempt to gain support for civil defense by "scaring people to death." The film would be acceptable only if it provided "real and substantial knowledge to the people."[7] In this meeting, the NSC did not consider whether Americans could digest real and substantial knowledge about the hydrogen bomb without becoming scared to death. Nor did it ask what would happen if publication or broadcast of information about nuclear weapons intensified precisely those fears it was intended to calm.

At this juncture, Eisenhower and his advisers seem to have assumed an absolute dichotomy of types of civil defense propaganda and modes of emotion management. Substantive information about nuclear weapons and their effects would not terrify the American people. On the contrary, such information was indispensable to teaching Americans how to protect themselves in a nuclear attack. Nonsubstantive and emotionally charged accounts, however, would panic the public. Suppose that this were a false dichotomy. What consequences would follow for the Cold War system of emotion management if accurate information about nuclear weapons and "scare tactics" were ultimately indistinguishable? What conclusions should be drawn if liberal propaganda in the guise of public information inevitably led to nuclear terror?

National security officials began to consider these perplexing issues in the more detailed and comprehensive discussions that were devoted to assessing Operation Alert 1955. In the cabinet meeting of June 17, 1955, Undersecretary of Labor Arthur Larson speculated on how decisions concerning the allocation of labor power might be made in the postattack world. Who would decide whether a given worker should be assigned to a given work site? A civilian official or a military authority? Peterson suggested that these decisions should be made by state governors and city mayors. They would be on the scene and in command of the most recent information about local conditions following an attack. Eisenhower disagreed. Public officials "would probably be as scared as anyone else."[8] Eisenhower's conjecture implied that the Cold War system of emotion management might be unduly optimistic. If the authorities were incapable of exercising emotional control over themselves, how could they expect to control the public?

The president's implicit skepticism about the possibility of solving the problem of panic became an explicit conviction by the following summer. In the expanded cabinet meeting of July 25, 1956, on the assessment of Operation Alert 1956—attended by AEC Chairman Lewis Strauss, CIA Director Allen Dulles, and FBI Director J. Edgar Hoover—Eisenhower listened as Sinclair Weeks of the Commerce Department reaffirmed the official ideology of nuclear crisis mastery. Noting how he had "smoothly" evacuated some 450 of his employees to one of the secret Operation Alert relocation sites, Weeks provided a confident account of the government's plans for managing a nuclear emergency. In response to Weeks's unreserved enthusiasm, the president found it necessary to warn those attending the meeting that in an actual attack, government officials would not be "normal people." Like everyone else, they would be scared, even "hysterical," and "absolutely nuts." In Eisenhower's judgment, it was preposterous to suppose that the Cold War system of emotion management could deal effectively with the disorder of the postattack world and its impact on the moral and psychological equilibrium of the survivors. Because the problem of panic had no solution, "we are simply going to have to be prepared to operate with people who are 'nuts.' " Eisenhower emphasized his conviction that the terrified, the hysterics, and the absolute nutters would not be confined to the general public and the lower echelons of officialdom. Heads of government departments and even the president himself all would be "completely bewildered."[9]

Eisenhower's position constituted a sweeping rejection of the doctrine of emotion management promoted in films such as *Operation Alert* and *The Day Called X*, in which the entire country—from the president at his secret White House to elementary schoolchildren in their class-rooms—calmly executed their assignments as if a thermonuclear attack on the United States were a routine occurrence. Notwithstanding the best-laid plans and the most sophisticated training, in a nuclear crisis the real task of emotion management would be to "preserve some com-mon sense in a situation where everybody is going crazy." Who would bury the dead? Eisenhower demanded. And in the nightmare of pos-tattack life, how could such an endeavor be organized? On the unlikely assumption that workers could be recruited, where would they find the tools they needed? Eisenhower argued that it would be "completely unrealistic" to suppose that these and other postattack tasks could be performed with the facility and efficiency required by the government's emotion management program. Survivors would be emotionally over-whelmed by the experience of the attack, stunned by grief, and trau-matized by fears concerning the fate of their families. Yet they would still be expected to "carry on and do something which will be of use."[10]

Would even this minimalist conception of emotion management, radically reduced from the ideal of robotlike discipline and icy self-control advanced by FCDA propaganda, be feasible in an actual nuclear attack? Eisenhower and his advisers were uncertain. In the cabinet discussion of Operation Alert 1957, Wilson observed that because of the flurry of emergency-government activity connected with the ex-ercise, "the people were panic stricken in large cities and were paying no attention to Government orders." Attempts to manage the public response during a simulated nuclear crisis seem to have backfired, pro-ducing results antithetical to those the government intended.

Working on the assumption that the public panic during Operation Alert 1957 had been caused by confusion concerning the actual cir-cumstances the exercise, Lewis Berry of the FCDA reported that no satisfactory solution to this problem seemed possible. True, the presi-dent might make an announcement to clarify the objectives and as-sumptions of the exercise. Although the American public would be its intended audience, it was obvious that such an announcement would not be ignored by the Soviets. How would they interpret the president's remarks? Possibly as an indication that the United States was preparing a nuclear attack. In that case, how could the Soviets be expected to respond? Mistaking the presidential clarification as evidence of Amer-ican mobilization for nuclear war, they might reasonably employ what they regarded as a brief period of tactical warning to launch a preemp-tive attack, thereby forestalling the presumed American nuclear offen-sive. As a result, Berry concluded, "a war that might be avoided would be triggered."[11]

In short, it seemed that the efforts at emotion management un-dertaken in Operation Alert would produce either of two unacceptable consequences. If the public were left in confusion, the result would be panic, which would defeat the specific objectives of Operation Alert as well as the more general purposes of emotion management. But if the president attempted to eliminate this confusion by a public explanation of the aims of Operation Alert, the result might be nuclear war.

Midway through his second term, Eisenhower remarked that he had long been undecided about the wisdom of building a shelter on his farm at Gettysburg. On the one hand, this seemed to be a good idea, since it would set the right example for the public. On the other hand, if it were generally known that the president had built a fallout shelter, this might "scare other people to death."[12] In Eisenhower's bleak assessment, the Cold War system of emotion management seemed incapable of resolving a "tremendous psychological problem." The American people would refuse to take measures necessary for their own protection unless they were motivated to do so by fear. But if Americans were terrified by government propaganda, then they would be unable to take these measures in any case.[13]

The government wanted to tell the people what they needed to know about nuclear war so that they could control their fears and go about the serious business of protecting themselves. But suppose that the government's story or the manner of its telling terrified the people by leading them to believe that nuclear war was imminent. In Eisenhower's judgment, civil defense planning was on a "knife edge." The Cold War system of emotion management could cut in either of two ways. If the public was left in uncertainty, the aims of emotion management could not be achieved. But if the government took steps to eliminate public doubts, the aims of emotion management would be defeated. In either case, there seemed to be no escape from the dilemma.[14]

The Paradoxes of Nuclear Crisis Management

In the Cold War conception of nuclear reality, there is a paradoxical relation between the aims of nuclear crisis management and the actual results of the programs based on this doctrine. Operation Alert was intended to demonstrate that the United States would be able to survive a nuclear attack. Indeed, with careful planning, sound organization, and competent execution, the country would quickly be back on its feet. Moreover, all this would occur without draconian measures, heroic exertions, or excessive sacrifice. However, in their assessment of these yearly rituals, national security planners discovered, to their surprise and vexation, that the performance of Operation Alert seemed to defeat its own objectives. Instead of proving that the nation was capable of effective nuclear crisis management, the exercise seemed to show that a large-scale nuclear attack would nullify the assumptions of the

Cold War conception of nuclear reality. Contrary to planning assumptions, the routines of the preattack world would not be swiftly reestablished by the application of managerial rationality. On the contrary, the effects of a nuclear attack would be so massive and incalculable that no judgments about when, or even whether, the United States might be able to operate on the basis of preattack practices could be ventured with confidence.

Operation Alert seemed to produce two disturbing anomalies. The first was a paradox of crisis management. The purpose of Operation Alert was to show how brilliantly nuclear crisis management would work, but the actual exercise suggested that it would not work at all. The second was a paradox of normalization. Operation Alert was designed to prove how easily the familiar securities of everyday life could be reestablished. But its performance suggested that in the postattack world, the idea of a return to preattack norms and standards was an illusion. As a result, Operation Alert was self-defeating. Not only did it fail to realize its objectives, but it seemed to demonstrate that their realization was impossible.

The assumption that a nuclear attack could be mastered by the exercise of managerial rationality was questioned as early as the report of the JCS Evaluation Board on OPERATION CROSSROADS. The fiction of nuclear crisis mastery was based on the premise that the scope of a nuclear attack would remain within the limits of planning and control. The Evaluation Board rejected this premise, chiefly on the grounds that the problems created by radioactive contamination were neither manageable nor even predictable.

In the Evaluation Board's chilling picture of a modern city emerging from an atomic bombardment and "enveloped by radioactive mists," indeterminate areas, irregular in size and shape and without visible boundaries, would be contaminated by radioactivity. Many survivors—including, of course, civil defense workers—would be doomed to die of radiation sickness. Rescue parties could not enter any part of the city without risking their own lives. Therefore, nuclear crisis management would be out of the question. In 1951 and 1952, the FCDA developed plans to deploy specialized civil defense cadres in damaged areas immediately after the attack. Damage would be repaired, and the norms of preattack life would be reinstituted. According to the Evaluation Board, such plans were hopelessly naive: "The dead would remain unburied and the wounded uncared for in the areas of heaviest contamination where certain death would lurk for many days and, in which, for many years to come, continuous habitation would be unsafe."[15]

Throughout the Eisenhower presidency, the FCDA's public-relations line glibly promised the American people that they could survive nuclear war by keeping their heads and following a few simple rules. Privately, the Eisenhower national security team recognized the futility of nuclear crisis mastery, even as it promoted this doctrine to the country as the only means of survival.

During the first three years of the Eisenhower presidency, the view of the Cold War conception of nuclear reality held by senior government officials changed significantly. Although questions about the feasibility of nuclear crisis management were raised in 1953 and 1954, confidence in its basic premises remained unshaken. Planning for the continuity of government, the protection of the economy, and the survival of the American people proceeded accordingly. By the summer of 1955, however, Eisenhower and his chief advisers began to question the principal assumptions of nuclear crisis management. The crucial event in this shift from confidence to doubt seems to have been the experience of planning and evaluating Operation Alert 1955. Although this was the second Operation Alert, it was the first large-scale simulation of a nuclear attack. It was also the first exercise that called for the participation of thousands of government officials as well as millions of American citizens. Beginning in the summer of 1955, the officials responsible for assessing Operation Alert were gradually pressed to the conclusion that its objectives could not be achieved. The performance of Operation Alert appeared to refute the Cold War conception of nuclear reality on which it was based.

On January 28, 1954, the NSC considered the issue of how to maintain the essential wartime functions of the government's executive branch during a nuclear assault. Its plans were based on the assumption that Washington would be totally destroyed in a surprise attack. Did this also mean the destruction of the federal government? Not at all. "Permanent facilities would be conveniently situated on the periphery of the City to carry out essential functions."[16] In this meeting, the NSC seemed engaged in a bizarre undertaking. Much of the discussion covered concrete measures for operating the executive branch during a nuclear crisis. At the same time, however, the NSC placed in question the prerequisites for these very measures. It even considered, albeit tentatively, the possibility that an actual attack might invalidate not merely a specific set of plans, such as those under discussion, but also the premises on which all nuclear crisis planning made sense. On the one hand, the January 28 NSC meeting seemed to be a straightforward exercise in policy planning, which assumed that the prerequisites for planning could be met. On the other hand, it seemed to be an exercise in metaplanning, which dismantled the framework of planning by placing in doubt the premises on which planning rested.

In this meeting, Eisenhower and Humphrey pondered how the Treasury Department might arrange to print new war bonds following the destruction of Washington. After the attack, it would be necessary to pay for World War III by selling war bonds to the American public, just as World War II had been financed by issuing war bonds. Humphrey assured the president that even if the capital were "knocked out," the Treasury Department could quickly set up operations in another city and have a new bond issue printed in a short time. Indeed, Humphrey claimed that "we could take fifteen people and run Treasury for ninety days."[17]

FCDA Administrator Peterson cautioned, however, that the premises of this discussion might be unrealistic. If the Soviets bombed Washington, they would attack some sixty-five other important American cities at the same time. Moreover, FCDA studies projected that after 1960, these attacks would be carried out not only by long-range bombers, but by intercontinental ballistic missiles (ICBMs) as well. Peterson also suggested that on the morning after the attack, the military establishment might be "immobilized," in which case maintaining the civil order necessary for the continuity of the state and the economy might become problematic. These considerations implied that the effects of a Soviet nuclear attack could not be contained in the way that Eisenhower and Humphrey supposed. On the contrary, if the United States became the battleground in World War III, this would have a serious impact on virtually every sphere of American life. Peterson even went so far as to claim that "if we had a major attack, dictatorship is the answer you have to come to, even if you couldn't talk about it."[18]

Thus the administrator of the FCDA, which was zealously promoting nuclear crisis mastery to the public as the only possible means of surviving a nuclear attack, seemed to reject the major assumptions on which this doctrine was based. If the sixty-five largest American cities were reduced to rubble, it was difficult to imagine how the FCDA's plans for managing the postattack emergency could be executed. The FCDA assumed that American industry as well as communication and transportation networks would continue to operate after the attack, a premise that was hardly consistent with the destruction of every large industrial city and communications center. Furthermore, if the military could not be counted on in a nuclear crisis, a postattack crime wave, widespread social disorder, and even civil war might ensue, eventualities that would thwart any plans for recovery. Finally, suppose that Peterson's political solution for the nuclear crisis were adopted. The Constitution would be shelved, liberal-democratic institutions and procedures would be suspended, and the American state would be converted into a dictatorship. Such a transformation would produce changes in American society so multitudinous and fundamental that they could not even be anticipated. If Peterson were right, then the basic premises of the Cold War conception of nuclear reality would have to be jettisoned.

The president immediately grasped the consequences of this apocalyptic argument. Peterson's position had to be rejected; otherwise, any discussion of nuclear survival plans would be meaningless. Civil defense was not consistent with the assumption of nuclear strikes by ICBMs. Eisenhower contended that if the technology of nuclear warfare reached that level, "we would be beyond the point of keeping the nation together," in which case civil defense and national security planning would be pointless. Using the same reasoning, Eisenhower maintained that if the NSC proceeded on the assumption that the military could be immobilized by a nuclear attack, "there was no sense in doing anything."[19]

Unless military control of the postattack environment were regarded as beyond question, planning for a nuclear emergency would be futile, since political and economic stability could not be guaranteed. In reflecting on the conditions under which it made sense to plan for a nuclear crisis, the president explained that the project of planning required certain premises and ruled out others. Peterson's premises made nuclear crisis planning impossible. In order to prepare for an attack, it was necessary to "determine the scale of destruction, set a maximum level of destruction, and plan accordingly."[20] These steps were dictated by what Eisenhower called "the rule of reason" on which all meaningful planning was based. The president did not further define the import of this rule. As a contribution to planning along these lines, however, he instructed the NSC to "think in terms of possibly 25 or 30 cities being shellacked." Then the measures necessary to secure the survival of the nation under these conditions could be specified.[21]

By June 1955, when the cabinet began to sift out what had been learned from Operation Alert 1955, Eisenhower and his senior advisers found it much more difficult to assume that it was possible to plan for a nuclear crisis. Because of the magnitude of a nuclear attack and the number of imponderable variables it introduced, the idea of managing a nuclear crisis seemed absurd. Because the norms of the preattack world would not apply to postattack conditions, it would be profoundly mistaken to represent these conditions by extrapolating the logic of preattack existence to postattack life. This position amounted to a repudiation of the Cold War conception of nuclear reality.

As a result, much of the discussion of new initiatives to be taken in light of Operation Alert 1955 has a dreamlike quality. At the same time that the cabinet considered how the government might indemnify property owners for damage suffered in a nuclear war, it rejected the premises on which this discussion made sense. The president observed that under the conditions of "chaos" entailed by the planning assumptions of Operation Alert, it would be necessary to govern the country as one big, closely regimented camp. This meant that the postattack world would realize one of the ultimate nightmares of Cold War planners in both the Truman and the Eisenhower presidencies: America as a garrison state, in which the basic rights and liberties that the United States was prepared to defend by risking nuclear war would be destroyed from within by the very measures required to wage such a war. According to Eisenhower:

> No longer would only the armed services bear the brunt of war. Millions of homeless people would have to be sustained and helped and fed in soup kitchens and, compared with this responsibility, the objective of indemnifying property loss seemed rather insignificant. People will be lucky if their losses are only property—and not their own lives.[22]

As Wilson added, "if we lose the war, the people will lose all their property anyway."[23]

Eisenhower seemed convinced that in the postattack world, the routines of American life would no longer apply. Commenting on Operation Alert 1955, he warned that "we must stop depending on things that sustain usual life in a State." Even the planning assumptions of Operation Alert—which would reduce American life to "chaos"—were unreasonably sanguine. Operation Alert assumed a single massive nuclear strike against the United States, but there was no reason to suppose that a first strike would be the last: "All the ordinary processes by which we run this country will simply not work under the circumstances we have assumed here. Our great fundamental problem will be how to mobilize what is left of 165 million people and win a war."[24]

The Cold War conception of nuclear reality presupposed a general plan for managing a nuclear crisis that could be adjusted to the local conditions of each part of the country. However, the scale of a nuclear attack, the impossibility of predicting its effects, and the inability to determine whether a first strike would be followed by others and, if so, what the consequences of these latter attacks might be invalidated this presupposition. Exploring the many contingencies of nuclear war, Eisenhower argued that "in logic one could say that we ought to have an infinite number of plans to cover all the contingencies."[25] But an infinite number of plans is an absurdity, the logical equivalent of no plan at all. Thus the president seemed forced to conclude that a nuclear attack was not a possible managerial problem. Rather, planning would become a hopeless undertaking, since the conditions for the formation and execution of plans would no longer be satisfied. Although not given to metaphor, Eisenhower suggested that this was "'the new face' that war was wearing."[26] It seemed to be a face without a visage. The dimensions of a nuclear war were indeterminate. Its character was indefinable. Therefore, it was impossible to say what it would really look like.

Eisenhower ended the cabinet meeting with a piercing observation on the real value of civil defense and exercises such as Operation Alert. In the summary of the Secretary to the Cabinet:

> The President concluded by reflecting aloud on the deterrent effect of a test of this nature on the Soviet General Staff. War seen in this light would reveal itself to anyone as only an unmitigated catastrophe. Our test would

probably not impress the Russians, but if they, knowing full well that we would hit them back in the event of such aggression upon us, ran such a test of their own, their eyes would be opened. If they should ever play out any of these problems for themselves, as we have done, such an exercise might well give them pause.[27]

It followed that the rhetoric of the FCDA's public-information program was profoundly misleading. Because a nuclear attack would constitute an "unmitigated catastrophe," it could not be handled by careful planning and organization. Civil defense as nuclear crisis mastery was out of the question—a deception practiced on the American people for reasons of state and justifiable only on the higher logic and metaphysics of national security. This meant that the deterrent value that national security strategists ascribed to civil defense was also worthless. The conception of civil defense as a deterrent assumed that Americans would be able to protect themselves from the worst the Soviets could do. Convinced of this assumption, the Soviets would conclude that the costs of nuclear aggression outweighed its benefits. But if civil defense as self-protection turned out to be nothing more than an elaborate marketing strategy, it obviously could not qualify as a deterrent by demonstrating the American capacity to survive a nuclear attack.

Despite these considerations, Eisenhower argued that civil defense might function as a deterrent in a quite different, ironic, and morbid sense. Although Operation Alert was represented as a demonstration of virtually effortless nuclear crisis mastery, in fact it showed that there was no possible protection against a nuclear attack. Nuclear war would visit unimaginable horrors on its victims, who could do nothing to escape them. In their examination of Operation Alert, the Soviets would be forced to arrive at the same conclusion. More important, they would reflexively apply this proof of the failure of nuclear crisis mastery to their own situation. Soviet society would thus become the object of a hypothetical Operation Alert, a conceptual experiment that would open the eyes of Soviet war planners in the same way that Operation Alert had shattered the illusions of Eisenhower and his advisers. Once Soviet strategists caught a glimpse of "the new face of war," they would see why it was impossible to protect themselves against an American counterstrike. The terrible consequences they would suffer should they decide to strike first would be apparent. In the final analysis, civil defense did constitute a deterrent, but only by proving its own futility.

Perhaps Eisenhower's most disconsolate reflections on the fallacies of the Cold War conception of nuclear reality were his personal diary entries. On January 23, 1956, he recorded his impressions of a report concerning the damage that could be anticipated in the initial stage of a nuclear war between the United States and the Soviet Union. The report analyzed two scenarios. The first assumed no strategic warning and only the tactical warning provided by the American Distant Early

Warning line, the point in their flight at which Soviet aircraft could be detected by American radar. The second assumed a strategic warning of one month, but no specific information about the date of the attack.

In the first scenario, the United States suffered virtually a complete economic collapse. The federal government was wiped out, and new political arrangements were improvised by the states. The casualties were, of course, much higher than the government's public predictions indicated. Although 65 percent of the population required medical care, most injuries went unattended. What was the impact of civil defense planning on limiting the destruction produced by this hypothetical attack? What would nuclear crisis management achieve? It seemed that civil defense would accomplish nothing. Eisenhower noted that "the limiting factor on the damage inflicted was not so much our own defense arrangements as the limitations on the Soviet stockpile of atomic weapons." The crucial factor in defining the level of destruction was not civil defense, the effects of which would be negligible. Instead, the brute fact of the size of the Soviet nuclear arsenal would determine the amount of damage. Regardless of the United States' efforts, the destruction produced by a Soviet nuclear offensive would be a simple function of the number of nuclear weapons delivered on target. In the aftermath of such an attack, "it would literally be a business of digging ourselves out of ashes, of starting again."[28]

In the second scenario, the Soviets favored strikes on air bases over attacks against cities. Yet the analysis of this scenario indicated that American losses would not differ significantly from those produced in the first scenario. This meant that in the month between the warning and the attack, civil defense efforts to limit damage would be inconsequential.

Eisenhower concluded that there was only one way the United States could reduce its losses. During the month of strategic warning, America would have to take the initiative and launch a surprise attack against the Soviet Union. However, a preemptive attack was contrary to American traditions. In addition, it would require Congress to meet in a secret session and vote a declaration of war that would be carried out even before the session ended. The president regarded such an extraordinary emergency procedure as an impossibility and rejected it as a serious planning option.[29]

The yearly Operation Alert exercises nonetheless continued, even though Eisenhower and his lieutenants had concluded that they were self-defeating. Although the exercises were intended to show how well the American people could protect themselves in a nuclear attack, in the judgment of the national security elite they demonstrated exactly the contrary: Self-protection was impossible. But the FCDA and the White House persisted in promoting the project of nuclear crisis mastery to the public, as well as the view that the United States would remain essentially unchanged by nuclear war. After the debris was cleared, the familiar American institutions would remain in place. They remained steadfast in their advocacy of these positions despite their private assessment that a nuclear attack would constitute a unique catastrophe, transforming the country in ways that could not even be imagined.

As a result, discussion of civil defense in the cabinet and the NSC assumed a disconcertingly surreal character. Policy makers seem to have lost their footing. In some cases, they appear to have been engaged in the impossible task of thinking in multiple realities, as if they were attempting to consummate an intellectually insupportable but morally defensible commitment to mutually inconsistent principles. On other occasions, they seemed to travel, with astonishing alacrity and apparent obliviousness, from one ontological framework to another. A single issue might be considered in the same meeting on the basis of conflicting ontological assumptions, without any apparent awareness by the nation's leaders of the course of their thinking. Despite these dizzying shifts in framework, policymakers did not seem to experience intellectual vertigo.

Between the summer of 1955 and the end of the Eisenhower presidency, deliberation about civil defense at the highest levels of government took place within two quite different conceptions of a nuclear attack on the United States. According to one view, the assumptions of the Cold War conception of nuclear reality remained in force. The disruptions in American life caused by nuclear war would be repaired by the exercise of nuclear crisis management, and the return to preattack normality would be swiftly negotiated. This was the optimistic ontology, which the government consistently promoted in public. The second position held that although the vast scope and indeterminate consequences of a nuclear attack made self-protection impossible, it was still necessary to plan on the basis of a policy that presupposed self-protection. According to this view, the Cold War conception of nuclear reality was an inevitable pretense, required by the connection between home-front morale and the credibility of nuclear deterrence. Civil defense was a fraud. But because of the importance of convincing the public that a nuclear war was tolerable, it was an indispensable fraud. If Americans could be persuaded that the risks of World War III were acceptable, they would also accept the dangers of nuclear deterrence. In that case, the moral foundations of national security policy would be in place. But if the illusions of nuclear crisis mastery were exposed, the emotion management strategies developed to solve the problem of national will would lose their credibility as well. The public would panic and refuse to live with the uncertainties of deterrence. As a result, the Cold War would be lost, and the American century would come to a premature and ignominious end. This was the cynical ontology, which became the unofficial view of the Eisenhower national security establishment.

In spite of their lost illusions about civil defense, it is not astonishing that Eisenhower and his advisers perpetuated the public myth of the Cold War conception of nuclear reality. In their view, this was what the demands of national security required. It is somewhat more surprising that in their confidential deliberations, they continued to entertain the merits of plans based on this ontology. In the NSC meeting of August 16 and 17, 1956, Val Peterson presented the FCDA proposal for a federally supported $13 billion public-fallout-shelter program. The FCDA's recommendation was based on the assumption that in a nuclear war, the Soviet Union would be able to deliver hundreds of nuclear weapons on their targets, destroying every major American city. After a perfunctory question to Allen Dulles concerning Soviet civil defense policy—the director of the CIA allowed that he had no clear idea about this matter, but promised to "look into the question"— Eisenhower reflected on the problem of how far civil defense–planning assumptions could be pushed before they became self-defeating. How far could we go, he asked, "until we reached a state of complete futility?"

Although Eisenhower was confident that the United States could withstand a heavy attack, he was not sure when a threshold would be reached beyond which planning for survival no longer made sense. He seemed convinced, however, that the scenario for nuclear war used in the FCDA shelter program would reduce civil defense policy to an absurdity. In planning for nuclear war, Eisenhower argued, "we always reach the point of realizing that an attack on any such scale contemplated in Governor Peterson's presentation would result in the paralysis of both sides." Therefore, Peterson's proposals would render the problem of nuclear crisis mastery "virtually unsolvable."[30]

Peterson presented the shelter program within the framework of the optimistic ontology. It was intended as a genuine effort at nuclear crisis management. The president assessed the proposal from the standpoint of the cynical ontology. The program would not work because its assumptions concerning nuclear crisis management were unsound. Nevertheless, Eisenhower was still willing to consider the merits of plans based on the optimistic ontology. It was not only the NSC that continued to entertain such proposals; the president himself repeatedly stressed their importance. But at the same time that the NSC debated civil defense plans from the standpoint of the optimistic ontology, it seemed to reject the conditions under which these debates made sense.

In deliberations on a national fallout-shelter program in the NSC meeting on March 27, 1958, Eisenhower maintained that "when we talk about a vast nuclear exchange between the United States and the enemy, we are in fact talking about something the results of which are almost impossible to conceive of." Yet discussion of these results and the measures for recovery that they called for remained on the agenda of the NSC.[31] Eisenhower and his advisers, feeling the ground give way beneath them, appeared helpless. Their civil defense proposals seemed to be the desperate fabrications of frightened men, a means of satisfying themselves that it was neither necessary nor even possible to do what they, at least on some occasions, were convinced had to be done.

Even in the closing weeks of the Eisenhower presidency, the NSC was still debating the wisdom of a fallout-shelter program. In a planning document entitled "Measures for the Passive Defense of the Population, with Particular Regard to Fallout Shelter," the OCDM defended fallout shelters within the framework of the optimistic ontology. OCDM Director Leo Hoegh pointed out that fallout shelters were "the key element" of civil defense. They would deter a Soviet attack and, if deterrence failed, protect the American population, "enabling the nation to survive and win the war."[32] On the one hand, Eisenhower praised the OCDM's proposal as an effort to rouse the American people to action without driving them to hysteria. In addition, it demonstrated that the government was serious about fallout protection. The president even suggested that if Americans could be persuaded to take the requisite precautionary measures, the policies advocated in the paper might actually work. On the other hand, discussion of the paper's concept of recovery led both Eisenhower and other members of the NSC to pursue a quite different line of argument.

Hoegh explained that the OCDM understood recovery to include more than the bare fact of physical survival following a nuclear strike. It also rested on political and economic conditions. Politically, recovery would be possible only if preattack liberal-democratic institutions were reinstated. Economically, survival depended on stockpiling the goods necessary to resume production at levels sufficient to sustain the surviving population and "support continued viability of the country." In response to this analysis, Eisenhower voiced his doubts that the preattack institutions of the American polity could be restored "very soon after a nuclear attack." He also regarded the OCDM's plan to rebuild the postattack economy on the foundation of preattack stockpiles as a vain fantasy. The reconstruction of the American economy following a nuclear attack was a problem that had "no real solution." Postattack crisis management of the economy was not possible because "no one knows in what condition a nuclear attack will leave the country." How could the United States conceivably stockpile enough supplies to restart the economy? Even if enough materials could be stored before the bombs began to fall, what reason was there to believe that the stockpile itself would survive? And in the unlikely event of its survival, what was the basis for supposing that the distribution and transportation facilities needed to ship the stockpiled goods would still exist?[33]

The president's skepticism seems to have been infectious. Hoegh, retracting the optimistic OCDM concept of recovery, conceded that after a nuclear attack, the American living standard could be restored perhaps only to the level of 1920. Thomas Gates, Secretary of the Navy, interjected that a return to the living standard of 1776 was more likely. Eisenhower anticipated even more abysmal consequences. A nuclear war might destroy the economy beyond foreseeable recovery. As a result, "we would all be nomads." In the final analysis, the fallout-shelter plan proposed in the OCDM paper was futile: "Our imagination could not encompass the situation which would result from an attack on this country involving the explosion of 2000 megatons." "War," the president concluded, "no longer has any logic whatsoever."[34]

In the end, perhaps Eisenhower and his advisers grasped, however tenuously, that the Cold War conception of nuclear reality was refuted by its own premises. Civil defense depended on precisely the state of affairs it was intended to reestablish: an ensemble of functioning social, economic, and political institutions. In the absence of a viable institutional order, civil defense organizations could not be formed, nor, of course, could their operations be carried out. But in a functioning social order, civil defense would seem to be unnecessary. Therefore, civil defense was either impossible or redundant.

Nuclear crisis management rested on certain tacit conditions that were never mentioned in the civil defense program, even though they were essential to its objectives. These conditions specify an implicit minimum level of social order that must obtain if the public is to carry out civil defense procedures. Even the ability to take unlimited hot showers to eliminate the danger of radioactive contamination—which the civil defense classic *Survival Under Atomic Attack* assumed without further comment—was based on the supposition that a nuclear attack would leave American society fundamentally unchanged. Highways would be open and streets would be cleared of debris so that workers could make their way to utility plants. Plants would be in operating condition, the homes of workers and managers would remain standing, and the communications systems necessary to inform workers of the postattack work schedule would function. The financial apparatus and the reward structure of the economy would remain in place. Plants would not be abandoned by managers looking out for themselves and their families. Workers on the way to their jobs would not be threatened by rioting mobs. Members of the labor force would be not only alive and uninjured, but also psychologically and morally prepared to appear at work at the appropriate time and perform more or less as usual. Fear of further attacks would not keep the work force at home, perhaps boarding up the house, maintaining a furtive lookout for postattack looters, mounting a machine gun at the entrance of the family shelter in order to fend off invaders, or preparing an escape to safer ground. On the contrary, the American people would maintain their everyday roles and fulfill their preattack responsibilities. All these requirements and others as well had to be met in order for the water to flow when the American public turned on the faucet for the first postattack shower.

These conditions were not secured by civil defense; rather, they formed the unsecured basis on which civil defense rested. In their absence, the measures required by civil defense could not be taken. If they obtained, then the United States would have succeeded in demonstrating its ability to survive and recover, in which case civil defense was not needed. Paradoxically, if civil defense was necessary, then it was impossible. If it was possible, then it was not necessary.

Epilogue

Liberal Propaganda and the Exigencies of National Security

While the FCDA was making films that extolled the virtues of nuclear crisis management and civil defense strategists were fine-tuning their emotion management techniques and streamlining Operation Alert, the highest officials of the government were engaged in discussions that led them to reject the principal assumptions of the civil defense program that had been zealously promoted to the public since 1950. And yet Eisenhower and his lieutenants remained advocates of civil defense to the bitter end, even as they quietly dismantled the conceptual apparatus on which it was based. This should occasion no surprise. The actual protection of the public in a nuclear attack was not crucial to the role of civil defense in American national security. It was necessary only for Americans to believe that they could be protected. Appearance and not reality, conviction and not fact, credibility and not performance were the critical desiderata of the strategy that linked civil defense, national morale, and national security. Fortified by their belief in civil defense, Americans would accept the dangers of nuclear deterrence. The solution to the problem of national will—the key to achieving domestic tolerance for the logic of keeping the peace by threatening nuclear war—was the only truly indispensable objective of civil defense. Civil defense would achieve this objective if the American people could be convinced that even if deterrence backfired into World War III, the consequences would still be bearable, and the United States would emerge victorious. Without a solution to the problem of national will, the risks of deterrence would be intolerable. Therefore civil defense could not be abandoned.

This meant that authorities could not afford to be candid about their loss of confidence in the public objectives of civil defense. As a result, civil defense was inevitably based on deceit, mythmaking, and illusion. The fallacies of nuclear crisis management, the impossibility of self-protection, and the dilemma of emotion management remained state secrets. Eisenhower and his national security team were obliged to maintain a posture of public enthusiasm for the official ideals of civil defense. Their skepticism was necessarily confined to confidential deliberations. Although officials might agree privately that the prospects for American survival under nuclear attack were marginal or even hopeless, publicly they exhibited an unclouded optimism and the pretense of unconditional commitment.

In the 1950s, no one in government was more ruthlessly clearsighted than Vice President Richard Nixon in his understanding of the connection between a civil defense policy of deception and mendacity and the higher moral exigencies of the Cold War. In the NSC meeting on March 27, 1958, Nixon dissected with brutal consistency the rationale and limits of government support for fallout shelters. Speculative calculations concerning how many millions of Americans would die in a nuclear war, Nixon observed coolly, were beside the point. From the perspective of national survival, did it really matter whether the casualties numbered 30 million or 50 million? According to Nixon, this was a distinction without a difference. If 30 million Americans failed to survive a nuclear attack, "there would be no hope of the United States surviving."

American security rested not on the passive defenses of civil defense, but on the active defense provided by the American nuclear deterrent. Therefore, why waste any money at all on civil defense? Nixon's answer was that the government had to make some gesture in the direction of a shelter program "because the country demands it." It was necessary to maintain the public illusion of security through civil defense. Otherwise, the tolerance for deterrence would collapse. Accordingly, the government's civil defense policy was clear: The state should spend whatever was necessary, but not a penny more, to sustain this illusion. Because a shelter program could produce only the appearance of security and not security itself, "we should do as little as we can to satisfy this demand."[1] On these grounds, civil defense was marketed to the American people as self-protection for survival. It was a necessary illusion: indispensable to the moral underpinning of national security, but ultimately irrelevant to survival under nuclear attack.

In the 1950s, the national security establishment officially embraced a liberal conception of propaganda as public information. This view may be reduced to two premises, both of which have their origins in the Enlightenment: the idea that democracy depends on truth and the idea that public opinion is a product of knowledge, that on any issue, the public will take the best course of action if it is properly informed. The first premise seemed to imply that civil defense propaganda should be limited to a faithful representation of government policy and its intentions. Since democratic politics is based on the consent of the governed, the public had to be persuaded, by credible means, to accept the government's national security policy. Credibility rests on reputation, however—above all, a reputation for veracity. This meant that if the government failed to keep faith with the public and misrepresented its policy, the public would withdraw its support because it could not trust the government. According to this view, truth was a necessary condition for the acceptability of policy. The second premise seemed to imply that if the American people were given the facts about nuclear war, they would do their part to support the grand strategy of national security, that truth was a sufficient condition for the acceptability the policy.

Given this conception of propaganda, the government needed to produce what it had repeatedly promised: a full and frank account of the facts of nuclear war and the prospects for survival. However, officials also held that the American people were emotionally unstable, morally irresponsible, and corrupted by leisure, pleasure, and the postwar explosion of commodity consumption. Therefore, Americans lacked the character to face the hard truths of the Cold War. In addition, these truths proved to be even more bitter than the public had been led to believe. National security officials were eventually persuaded that a nuclear attack was not a problem that could be solved by nuclear crisis management.

Although millions of Americans would survive a nuclear war, millions would also die, and the country itself might collapse. It followed that propaganda as full disclosure would defeat its own purpose: to convince the public that the impact of nuclear war on the American home front would be bearable. Without this conviction, the American people would refuse to accept the risks of deterrence, in which case they would be incapable of filling the role that national security planners had reserved for them in fighting the Cold War. These considerations required the government to choose between its liberal principles of propaganda as public enlightenment and its view of the exigencies of national security.

The choice was easy. Without the strategy of nuclear deterrence, the intellectual structure in which national security officials interpreted the postwar international system would fall to pieces. Without a coherent conception of the international order, it would be impossible to frame the plans that would keep America strong and secure. In the end, the principles of liberalism were sacrificed to the exigencies of national security.

Notes

Introduction

1. All civil defense films discussed in this book are in the National Archives.

2. John Morton Blum, *V Was for Victory: Politics and Culture During World War II* (New York: Harcourt Brace Jovanovich, 1976), p. 16. The problem of making World War II real on the American home front is also considered in William H. Chafe, *The Unfinished Journey: America Since World War II* (New York: Oxford University Press, 1986), pp. 4–7.

3. The literature on Cold War national security planning from 1945 to 1950 is voluminous. An especially useful recent synthesis is Melvyn P. Leffler, *A Preponderance of Power: National Security, the Truman Administration, and the Cold War* (Stanford, Calif.: Stanford University Press, 1992).

4. On the domestic political and economic requirements of American Cold War mobilization, see, for example, Charles S. Maier, "The Politics of Productivity: Foundations of American International Economic Policy After World War II," in Peter Katzenstein, ed., *Between Power and Plenty* (Madison: University of Wisconsin Press, 1978), pp. 23–50; Robert Pollard, *Economic Security and the Origins of the Cold War, 1945–1950* (New York: Columbia University Press, 1985); Michael J. Hogan, *The Marshall Plan: America, Britain, and the Reconstruction of Western Europe, 1947–1952* (New York: Cambridge University Press, 1987); and Aaron L. Friedberg, "Why Didn't the United States Become a Garrison State?" *International Security* 16 (1992): 109–42.

5. Scholarly literature on civil defense in the 1950s falls under roughly three headings: public policy studies of federal civil defense agencies and the

development of civil defense programs and legislation; interpretations of the impact of the atomic bomb on American life, in which civil defense is represented as as element of an American nuclear culture; and investigations of the relations between civil defense and important American social institutions. Under the first heading, see Nehemiah Jordan, *U.S. Civil Defense Before 1950* (Washington, D.C.: Institute for Defense Analyses, 1966); Lyon G. Tyler, Jr., "Civil Defense: The Impact of the Planning Years, 1945–1950" (Ph.D. diss., Duke University, 1967); and Thomas J. Kerr, *Civil Defense in the U.S.: Bandaid for a Holocaust?* (Boulder, Colo.: Westview Press, 1983). Under the second, see Paul Boyer, *By the Bomb's Early Light: American Thought and Culture at the Dawn of the Atomic Age* (New York: Pantheon, 1985); Spencer R. Weart, *Nuclear Fear: A History of Images* (Cambridge, Mass.: Harvard University Press, 1988); and Allan M. Winkler, *Life Under a Cloud: American Anxiety About the Atom* (New York: Oxford University Press, 1993). Under the third, see Michael J. Carey, "The Schools and Civil Defense: The Fifties Revisited," *Teacher's College Record* 84 (1982): 115–27; JoAnne Brown, "A Is for Atomic, and B Is for Bomb: Civil Defense in American Public Education," *Journal of American History* 75 (1988): 68–90; and Elaine Tyler May, *Homeward Bound: American Families in the Cold War Era* (New York: Basic Books, 1988).

6. Here and in the following chapters, propaganda is understood in a non-pejorative fashion as political marketing—that is, the packaging, advertising, promotion, and distribution of political policies and programs.

Chapter 1

1. W. Phillips Davison, *The Berlin Blockade* (Princeton, N.J.: Princeton University Press, 1958), p. 64. See also Avi Shlaim, *The United States and the Berlin Blockade, 1948–1949* (Berkeley: University of California Press, 1983).

2. See Richard G. Hewlett and Francis Duncan, *A History of the United States Atomic Energy Commission*, vol. 2: *1947/1952: Atomic Shield* (Washington, D.C.: U.S. Atomic Energy Commission, 1972), p. 159.

3. Davison, *Berlin Blockade*, p. 117; Walter Millis, ed., *The Forrestal Diaries* (New York: Viking Press, 1951), p. 457; and *Foreign Relations of the United States* [hereafter *FRUS*], *1948* (Washington, D.C.: Government Printing Office, 1973), vol. 2, pp. 927–28.

4. "60 B-29s Ordered to Fly to Britain," *New York Times*, July 16, 1948, p. 4.

5. Davison, *Berlin Blockade*, p. 285.

6. *FRUS, 1948*, vol. 2, p. 972.

7. "JCS 1952/1, December 21, 1948: Evaluation of Current Strategic Air Offensive Plans," in Thomas H. Etzold and John Lewis Gaddis, eds., *Containment: Documents on American Policy and Strategy, 1945–1950* (New York: Columbia University Press, 1978), pp. 357–58.

8. See John Lewis Gaddis, *The Long Peace: Inquiries into the History of the Cold War* (New York: Oxford University Press, 1987), p. 4.

9. Walter H. Waggone, "Truman Orders Reserves Strengthened and Trained, but His Peace Hopes Gain," *New York Times*, October 17, 1948, p. 1. On the efforts in 1948 to achieve national security without producing fiscal breakdown, see Millis, ed., *The Forrestal Diaries*; Warner A. Schilling, "The Pol-

itics of National Defense: Fiscal 1950," in Warner A. Schilling, Paul Y. Hammond, and Glenn H. Snyder, *Strategy, Politics, and Defense Budgets* (New York: Columbia University Press, 1962), pp. 1–266; *FRUS, 1948* (Washington, D.C.: Government Printing Office, 1976), vol. 1, pt. 2, pp. 644–47, 670–71; Robert A. Pollard, "The National Security State Reconsidered: Truman and Economic Containment, 1945–1950," in Michael J. Lacey, ed., *The Truman Presidency* (New York: Cambridge University Press, 1989), pp. 205–34; and Townsend Hoopes and Douglas Brinkley, *Driven Patriot: The Life and Times of James Forrestal* (New York: Knopf, 1992), pp. 415–21.

10. See Hewlett and Duncan, *Atomic Shield*, pp. 176–79; David Alan Rosenberg, "American Atomic Strategy and the Hydrogen Bomb Decision," *Journal of American History* 66 (1979): 62–87, and "U.S. Nuclear Stockpile, 1945–1950," *Bulletin of the Atomic Scientists* 38 (1982): 25–30; Lynn Eden, "Capitalist Conflict and the State: The Making of United States Military Policy in 1948," in Charles Bright and Susan Harding, eds., *Statemaking and Social Movements: Essays in History and Theory* (Ann Arbor: University of Michigan Press, 1984), pp. 233–61; and Frank Kofsky, *Harry S. Truman and the War Scare of 1948* (New York: St. Martin's Press, 1993).

11. See Robert L. Messer, *The End of an Alliance: James F. Byrnes, Roosevelt, Truman, and the Origins of the Cold War* (Chapel Hill: University of North Carolina Press, 1982), p. 89.

12. *FRUS, 1948*, vol. 1, pt. 2, p. 626.

13. See Gregg Herken, *The Winning Weapon: The Atomic Bomb in the Cold War* (New York: Knopf, 1980), pp. 256–60.

14. *FRUS, 1948* (Washington, D.C.: Government Printing Office, 1974), vol. 3, p. 281.

15. Millis, ed., *Forrestal Diaries*, p. 502.

16. David E. Lilienthal, *The Journals of David E. Lilienthal: The Atomic Energy Years, 1945–1950* (New York: Harper & Row), vol. 2, p. 464.

17. Millis, ed., *Forrestal Diaries*, pp. 350–51.

18. Joint Strategic Plans Committee, "Estimate of Probable Developments in the World Political Situation up to 1957," in Etzold and Gaddis, eds., *Containment*, p. 290, which reprints only the appendix of the "Estimate."

19. Hewlett and Duncan, *Atomic Shield*, p. 366. On the detection of the Soviet atomic explosion, see Harry S Truman Library [hereafter HSTL], Papers of Harry S Truman [hereafter HST], President's Secretary's Files, Subject File: National Security Council—Atomic, Box 199, Folder: Atomic Bomb—Reports. According to General Hoyt Vandenberg's official memo to President Truman, the Soviet atomic test was carried out between August 26 and August 29. On White House efforts to control the public relations of the announcement of the Soviet explosion, see HSTL, Papers of Eban A. Ayers, Box 4, Folder: Atomic Energy Commission, "Russian Atomic Bomb." For the text of Truman's announcement of the Soviet atomic bomb, see "Atom Blast in Russia Disclosed," *New York Times*, September 24, 1949, p. 1.

20. Arnold Wolfers, "The Atomic Bomb in Soviet–American Relations," in Bernard Brodie, ed., *The Absolute Weapon* (New York: Harcourt, Brace, 1946), p. 125.

21. *FRUS, 1949* (Washington, D.C.: Government Printing Office, 1976), vol. 1, p. 192.

22. Steven T. Ross, *American War Plans, 1945–1950* (New York: Garland, 1988), p. 108.

23. Samuel F. Wells, "Sounding the Tocsin: NSC 68 and the Soviet Threat," *International Security* 4 (1979–1980): 126.

24. Ibid., p. 127.

25. *FRUS, 1950* (Washington, D.C.: Government Printing Office, 1977), vol. 1, p. 142. Two days after Truman's directive, Paul Nitze, director of the State Department Policy Planning Staff, reported to its members the judgment of Secretary of State Dean Acheson that the possibility of war with the Soviet Union was "considerably greater" than in the previous autumn. Acheson's pessimism was based on signs of a new "toughness" on the part of the Kremlin and also on the view of the JCS that the Soviet Union was now capable of mounting a full-scale surprise attack "from a standing start," which meant that the usual indices of war preparation and mobilization would not be in evidence (pp. 142–43). Only six days later, Nitze himself summarized the near-term probabilities of war with the Soviet Union for the principal officers of the State Department. Emphasizing his sense of a new militancy and audacity in the Soviet conduct of foreign affairs, Nitze argued that the Soviet willingness to risk the use of force in local conflicts could easily lead to "nuclear war through miscalculation." This was also "the profound lesson of Korea": The Soviets now had the confidence to take actions that risked World War III. According to this view, the attack on South Korea in June 1950 was the Soviet Union's first major military move in a conflict that could be expected to end in nuclear war (pp. 324–47, 395–96).

26. Ibid., pp. 251–52.

27. Ibid., p. 263. By the end of 1950, this conception of Soviet intransigence, malevolence, and virtual omnipotence led to near-hysterical predictions of an imminent nuclear attack on the United States. See, for example, Memorandum, "Estimates of Moscow–Peiping Time-Table for War," O. Edmund Clubb, director of the State Department Office of Chinese Affairs, to Dean Rusk, Assistant Secretary of State for Far Eastern Affairs, December 18, 1950. Following a résumé of factors indicating that the conditions for an early surprise attack by the "Moscow–Peiping axis" were satisfied, Clubb concluded that war with the Soviet Union was probable in the very near future. Indeed, the attack might be expected on Christmas Day, 1950, only a week after the dispatch of his memo. "For our defense moves," Clubb urged, "we have left to us only days and hours, not months and years" (p. 141).

28. HSTL, "Statement by the Secretary of War at the Cabinet Meeting of September 7, 1945, in re Military Training," Henry L. Stimson Diaries, vols. 47–52, May 1, 1944–September 21, 1945, pp. 106–8.

29. John Foster Dulles, "Thoughts on Soviet Foreign Policy and What to Do About It," *Life*, June 3, 1946, pp. 112–26, and June 10, 1946, pp. 119–30.

30. Dulles, "Thoughts on Soviet Foreign Policy," *Life*, June 10, 1946, p. 118. On the same page, the editors of *Life* noted with some uneasiness that about only a quarter of adult Americans attended church. Thus on a single page, *Life* managed to link Dulles's conception of the Puritan vision of the American destiny and the foundation of the American nation by God; the fear that Americans would not fulfill their duties as citizens because they had failed in their religious obligations; the inference that because of these moral and

spiritual lapses, the vital interests of the United States would suffer; and the importance to the national interest of a renewed commitment to divinely ordained moral principles.

31. John Foster Dulles, *War or Peace* (New York: Macmillan, 1950), p. 255.

32. Ibid.

33. Max Weber, *The Protestant Ethic and the Spirit of Capitalism*, trans. Talcott Parsons (New York: Scribner, 1958), p. 175.

34. George F. Kennan, *Memoirs, 1950–1965* (Boston: Little, Brown, 1972), p. 84.

35. See Kennan's observations on the idyllic life that he and his family enjoyed on their Pennsylvania farm, in *Memoirs, 1925–1950* (Boston: Little, Brown, 1967), pp. 304–5, and *Memoirs, 1950–1965*, pp. 64–65.

36. Kennan, *Memoirs, 1950–1965*, p. 67.

37. Ibid., pp. 68–69.

38. Ibid., p. 73.

39. Ibid., pp. 67–68, 70.

40. Ibid., p. 62. On the banality, hedonism, and moral vacuity of life in California, see also Kennan's observations in *Sketches from a Life* (New York: Pantheon, 1989), pp. 169–70.

41. Kennan, *Sketches from a Life*, p. 172, where these pessimistic reflections are inspired by yet another view of the outskirts of St. Louis from a passing train.

42. Kennan, *Memoirs, 1925–1950*, p. 559.

43. George Kennan, "The Sources of Soviet Conduct," in Etzold and Gaddis, eds., *Containment*, pp. 90–91.

44. *FRUS, 1949*, vol. 1, p. 404.

45. Ibid., p. 405.

46. *FRUS, 1950*, vol. 1, pp. 169–72.

47. Ibid., p. 191.

48. Ibid., pp. 220–21.

49. Ibid., pp. 225–26.

50. At this point, some remarks on the types of actors in the civil defense program and their organizational loci may be useful as a way of providing a general orientation to the institutional production of civil defense in the 1950s. In any institution that produces ideas—regardless of whether they are scientific theories, theological doctrines, advertising campaigns, or political programs— it is essential to distinguish at least three types of actors: the theoreticians and strategists who generate the ideas; the planners and tacticians who translate these ideas into programs; and the purveyors, distributors, or marketers who interpret, package, and promote these programs. Civil defense theorists were typically located in major universities such as Yale, Princeton, and the University of Michigan. They were sometimes academic intellectuals on loan to think tanks or special projects such as Project East River and the Social Science Research Council Committee on Social Aspects of Atomic Energy, both of which are discussed later. Civil defense planners were typically situated in federal agencies responsible for civil defense: first in the War Department, in 1948 at the Office of Civil Defense Planning in the Department of Defense, in 1949 at the National Security Resources Board, from 1950 to 1958 at the Federal Civil Defense Administration, and from 1958 to 1960 in the Office of Civil and

Defense Mobilization. Civil defense marketers were typically public-relations and advertising specialists who worked in the Public Affairs Office of the Federal Civil Defense Administration; government officials in the Federal Civil Defense Administration who had received patronage appointments from President Truman or Eisenhower; Madison Avenue advertisers who, through their agencies, worked with the Advertising Council to promote civil defense; and executives in the communications industry who made decisions on how to feature civil defense in newspapers and magazines and on radio and television.

Chapter 2

1. Harold C. Urey, as told to Michael Amrine, "I'm a Frightened Man," *Collier's*, January 5, 1946, p. 18. See also Dexter Masters and Katherine Way, eds., *One World or None* (New York: McGraw-Hill, 1946).

2. On the planning of OPERATION CROSSROADS, see HSTL, HST, President's Secretary's Files, Subject File: National Security Council—Atomic, Box 201, Folder: Atomic Test—Miscellaneous. The question of interpreting the results of OPERATION CROSSROADS was of considerable import, since it would decide the issue of how to fight a nuclear war. The interpretation of the tests was the occasion for a major strategic and bureaucratic struggle between the navy and the air force. The air force argued that the navy had become obsolete because it could not develop a war-fighting role for sea power in the atomic age. The navy, of course, rejected this view and was determined that OPERATION CROSSROADS should make a conclusive case for the viability of seagoing forces in a nuclear war. The implications for both services were enormous, since they concerned the power to define strategy and command resources in preparation for World War III.

3. HSTL, HST, President's Secretary's Files, "The Evaluation of the Atomic Bomb as a Military Weapon: The Final Report of the Joint Chiefs of Staff Evaluation Board for OPERATION CROSSROADS," June 30, 1947. The doctrine that the strategic bombing of cities would panic urban populations and destroy the will of an adversary to wage war was not, of course, a product of the Cold War. On the same fears expressed by both British and German leaders during the infancy of aerial bombing in World War I, see Nehemiah Jordan, *U.S. Civil Defense Before 1950* (Washington, D.C.: Institute for Defense Analyses, 1966), pp. 1, 9–10; and Michael S. Sherry, *The Rise of Air Power* (New Haven, Conn.: Yale University Press, 1987), pp. 12–21. The effect of aerial bombardment on civilian morale was also an important strategic issue in the years immediately before World War II. War planners hypothesized that sudden, massive, and utterly catastrophic air raids would produce panic, a collapse of public resolve to fight, and a swift surrender (Sherry, *Rise of Air Power*, pp. 64–69).

4. Gregg Herken, *The Winning Weapon: The Atomic Bomb in the Cold War* (New York: Knopf, 1980), p. 228.

5. Ansley J. Coale, *The Problem of Reducing Vulnerability to Atomic Bombs* (Princeton, N.J.: Princeton University Press, 1947), p. 24 and also pp. 41–42, 106.

6. *A Study of Civil Defense* (Washington, D.C.: National Military Establish-

ment, Office of the Secretary of Defense, 1948), p. 3. On the history of the Bull Board and the details of its recommendations, see Jordan, *U.S. Civil Defense Before 1950*, pp. 64–69; and Lyon G. Tyler, "Civil Defense: The Impact of the Planning Years, 1945–1950" (Ph.D. diss., Duke University, 1967), pp. 41–64.

7. *Study of Civil Defense*, p. 19.

8. *Civil Defense for National Security* (Washington, D.C.: Government Printing Office, 1948), p. 186. On the background and substance of the Hopley Report, see Jordan, *U.S. Civil Defense Before 1950*, pp. 73–77; and Tyler, "Civil Defense," pp. 79–116.

9. *Civil Defense for National Security*, p. 101. See also p. 260 on the importance of public information as a means of maintaining national morale by preventing panic and confusion.

10. Executive Office of the President, National Security Resources Board, *United States Civil Defense* (Washington, D.C.: Government Printing Office, 1950), p. 56.

11. Letter, Dean R. Brimhall and L. Dewey Anderson to L. Edward Scriven, November 3, 1950, National Archives, Record Group 304, OCDM/NSRB, Box 1: Records Relating to Civil Defense, 1949–1953.

12. HSTL, HST, Files of Spencer R. Quick, Address by James J. Wadsworth, "Preparedness, the Price of Peace," November 20, 1952.

13. Dwight D. Eisenhower Library [hereafter DDEL], Federal Civil Defense Administration, "Civil Defense Implications of the Psychological Impact and Morale Effect of Attacks on the People of the United States," April 1953.

14. Frederick "Val" Peterson, "Panic: The Ultimate Weapon?" *Collier's*, August 21, 1953, pp. 99–100 [ellipsis in original]. According to Peterson, less intelligent people were more panic prone than were the more intelligent. Furthermore, women were more panic prone—by almost 30 percent—than men. The latter datum was explained by the routines of female life, which were said to pose fewer hazards than did the work world of men. As a result, women did not have as much practice in "conquering fear" (pp. 106–7).

15. Ibid., pp. 100–101.

16. DDEL, Papers of Katherine Howard, Box 11, Folder: Television (1), Letter, Charles Ellsworth to Katherine Howard, June 19, 1953.

17. Edward Shils, *The Torment of Secrecy: The Background and Consequences of American Security Policies* (Glencoe, Ill.: Free Press, 1956), p. 68. On the exhilaration of the earliest American response to the bombing of Hiroshima and Nagasaki, see also Allan M. Winkler, *Life Under a Cloud: American Anxiety About the Atom* (New York: Oxford University Press, 1993), pp. 26–29.

18. Hanson A. Baldwin, "The Atomic Weapon," *New York Times*, August 7, 1945, p. 10.

19. See "Text of Statement by Truman," *New York Times*, August 7, 1945, p. 4. On the background of the Truman announcement, apparently based on a draft prepared in May 1945 by William Laurence, the *New York Times* science reporter for whom General Leslie Groves had reserved exclusive access to the coverage of the Manhattan Project, see Spencer R. Weart, *Nuclear Fear: A History of Images* (Cambridge, Mass.: Harvard University Press, 1988), p. 103.

20. For a comprehensive account of the press response to the atomic bomb between 1945 and 1947, see Paul Boyer, *By the Bomb's Early Light: American*

Thought and Culture at the Dawn of the Atomic Age (New York: Pantheon, 1985), pp. 3–32, 59–75; and Michael John Yavenditti, "American Reactions to the Use of Atomic Bombs on Japan, 1945–1947" (Ph.D. diss., University of California, Berkeley, 1970).

21. Hearst Metrotone Newsreels, UCLA Film and Television Archive, Tape VA–6786.

22. Cousins's widely read essay in the *Saturday Review*, August 18, 1945, was quickly reprinted as a book. See Norman Cousins, *Modern Man Is Obsolete* (New York: Viking Press, 1945), p. 37.

23. See "Scientists Scare Congress," *Life*, December 31, 1945, p. 18. On the Federation of Atomic Scientists, see Alice Kimball Smith, *A Peril and a Hope: The Scientists' Movement in America, 1945–1947* (Chicago: University of Chicago Press, 1965).

24. "A Report to the Secretary of War," *Bulletin of the Atomic Scientists* 1 (1946): 2.

25. On Langmuir's testimony, see "Langmuir Warns of Danger to U.S.," *New York Times*, October 9, 1945, p. 9.

26. Urey, "I'm a Frightened Man," p. 18.

27. Charles Poore, "The Most Spectacular Explosion in the Time of Man," *New York Times Book Review*, November 10, 1946, p. 7. On the response to the publication of "Hiroshima," see Yavenditti, "American Reactions," pp. 356–71.

28. John Hersey, *Hiroshima* (New York: Knopf, 1946), p. 39.

29. Ibid., pp. 44, 68.

30. On the management of emotions, see Arlie Russell Hochschild, *The Managed Heart: The Commercialization of Human Feeling* (Berkeley: University of California Press, 1983); Carol Zisowitz Stearns and Peter N. Stearns, *Anger: The Struggle for Emotional Control in America's History* (Chicago: University of Chicago Press, 1986); Peter N. Stearns, *Jealousy: The Evolution of an Emotion in American History* (New York: New York University Press, 1989), and "Suppressing Unpleasant Emotions: The Development of a Twentieth Century American Emotional Style," in Andrew E. Barnes and Peter N. Stearns, eds., *Social History and Issues in Human Consciousness* (New York: New York University Press, 1989), pp. 230–61; and Peter N. Stearns and Timothy Haggerty, "The Role of Fear: Transitions in American Emotional Standards for Children, 1850–1950," *American Historical Review* 96 (1991): 63–94.

31. On emotions as cultural artifacts, see E. Doyle McCarthy, "Emotions Are Social Things: An Essay in the Sociology of Emotions," in David D. Franks and E. Doyle McCarthy, eds., *The Sociology of Emotions: Original Essays and Research Papers* (Greenwich, Conn.: JAI Press, 1989), pp. 51–72.

32. DDEL, Papers of Katherine Howard, Box 9, Folder: Project East River.

33. For details concerning the history of Project East River, a complete list of personnel, and the phasing of the various stages of planning, briefings, research, and writing, see "Historical Summary of Project East River Operations," app. IA of *Report of the Project East River: General Report, Part I* (New York: Associated Universities, 1952).

34. *Report of the Project East River: General Report, Part I*, p. i.

35. Ibid., p. 2

36. Ibid., p. i.

37. HSTL, HST, Staff Member Office Files, Psychological Strategy Board Files, Box 34, Folder 384.51: Project East River, Project East River Panel on Public Information and Training, "Basic Problems for C.D. Information and Training," January 4, 1952.

38. On the Psychological Strategy Board, see Sallie Pisani, *The CIA and the Marshall Plan* (Lawrence: University Press of Kansas, 1991), pp. 128–33. In the internecine struggles within the national security apparatus for the power to frame policy and command resources, the Psychological Strategy Board was quickly outmaneuvered by the NSC, the CIA, and the Policy Planning Staff of the State Department.

39. See HSTL, HST, Staff Member Office Files, Psychological Strategy Board Files, Box 34, Folder 384.51: Project East River, Memoranda, Irwin to Godel, January 8, 1952, and Irwin to Godel, January 10, 1952; Letter, Joseph McLean to Raymond Allen, January 12, 1952. On Allen's credentials as a cold warrior, see Sigmund Diamond's richly detailed study, *Compromised Campus: The Collaboration of Universities with the Intelligence Community, 1945–1955* (New York: Oxford University Press, 1992), pp. 247–56. The FCDA also attempted to interest the Psychological Strategy Board in a collaboration along the same lines. In 1952, FCDA Administrator Millard Caldwell asked the Psychological Strategy Board for a briefing concerning psychological warfare and its bearing on American civil defense. The FCDA was also interested in the course on psychological warfare that the Psychological Strategy Board conducted in Georgetown. Psychological Strategy Board files indicate that a date for the briefing would be arranged. In addition, John DeChant, director of the FCDA Public Affairs Office, would receive a résumé of the Georgetown course (HSTL, HST, Staff Member Office Files, Psychological Strategy Board Files, Box 27, Folder 377: Staff Meetings, Report of Staff Meeting, April 2, 1952). Like Project East River, the FCDA hoped to modify the tools of psychological warfare that the Psychological Strategy Board had fashioned for use abroad and put them to work in the domestic civil defense program. Theories of emotion management deployed against the Communists would be employed to prosecute the objectives of the Cold War in the United States. Propaganda techniques devised to confuse and weaken the Soviets would be applied to the problem of strengthening American resolve.

40. On the concept of conventionalization, see Hans Morganthau, "The Fallacy of Thinking Conventionally About Nuclear Weapons," in David Carlton and Carlo Schaerf, eds., *Arms Control and Technological Innovation* (New York: Wiley, 1976), pp. 256–64; Robert Jervis, *The Illogic of American Nuclear Strategy* (Ithaca, N.Y.: Cornell University Press, 1984); and Steven Kull, *Minds at War: Nuclear Reality and the Inner Conflicts of Defense Policymakers* (New York: Basic Books, 1988).

41. These circulation and distribution figures were achieved through the FCDA's efforts to persuade the private sector to assume costs for civil defense that Congress was unwilling to fund, a fiscal strategy used by civil defense officials throughout the 1950s. For example, the film industry in Hollywood and New York produced and distributed films under an agreement with the FCDA, which supplied basic information and technical consultation. As a result, civil defense propaganda films were produced by the motion picture industry at minimal cost to the federal government.

42. Federal Civil Defense Administration, *Survival Under Atomic Attack* (Washington, D.C.: Government Printing Office, 1950), p. 1 [emphasis in original].

43. Ibid., p. 7.

44. Ibid., pp. 4–5.

45. Ibid., pp. 24–25.

46. Ibid., pp. 21, 26. In its advice on postattack ablutions, *Survival Under Atomic Attack* warned that it might be necessary to return to the showers for another scrubbing and perhaps even a third washing. However, in carrying out this routine, there was no cause for alarm: "You can remove practically all of the radioactivity if you keep at it" (p. 26).

47. United States Strategic Bombing Survey, *The Effects of Atomic Bombs on Hiroshima and Nagasaki* (Washington, D.C.: Government Printing Office, 1946), and *Summary Report (Pacific War)* (Washington, D.C.: Government Printing Office, 1946). On the survey, see David MacIsaac, *Strategic Bombing in World War II: The Story of the United States Strategic Bombing Survey* (New York: Garland, 1976).

48. Strategic Bombing Survey, *Effects of Atomic Bombs on Hiroshima and Nagasaki*, pp. 3, 15, 38, 41. See also Strategic Bombing Survey, *Summary Report (Pacific War)*, pp. 29–31; and MacIsaac, *Strategic Bombing in World War II*, p. 106.

49. R. E. Lapp, *Must We Hide?* (Cambridge, Mass.: Addison-Wesley, 1949), pp. 48–49. Lapp added the hazards of modern conventional warfare to this catalog and asked rhetorically: "Who can say that the victim of an atomic attack suffers more than the victim of a flamethrower or a person who has broken down mentally under the stress of combat?" (p. 18).

50. Ibid., p. 14.

51. Irving L. Janis, "Psychological Problems of A-Bomb Defense," *Bulletin of the Atomic Scientists* 6 (1950): 259. See also his *Air War and Emotional Stress* (New York: McGraw-Hill, 1951), pp. 23, 44–45, 59.

52. The Editors, "The Unwanted War," *Collier's*, October 27, 1951, p. 17.

53. Hal Boyle, "Washington Under the Bomb," *Collier's*, October 27, 1951, p. 20.

54. Robert E. Sherwood, "The Third World War," *Collier's*, October 27, 1951, p. 30.

55. The Editors, "Operation Eggnog," *Collier's*, October 27, 1951, p. 6.

56. *FRUS, 1952–54* (Washington, D.C.: Government Printing Office, 1984), vol. 2, pt. 1, p. 590.

57. Ibid., p. 593.

58. DDEL, Papers of Dwight D. Eisenhower as President [hereafter DDE], White House Central Files, Official Files, Box 195, Folder 20: Releases, "Background Memorandum for All Media: OPERATION IVY," FCDA Public Affairs Office, April 7, 1954.

59. DDEL, DDE, White House Central Files, Official Files, Box 195, Folder 20: Releases, "Public Release of Motion Picture on OPERATION IVY," FCDA Press Information, March 31, 1954.

60. See Ralph E. Lapp, *The Voyage of the Lucky Dragon* (New York: Harper, 1958). The hydrogen bomb converted some proponents of civil defense into critics. Lapp became an important convert.

61. William L. Laurence, "H-Bomb Can Wipe Out Any City," *New York Times*, April 1, 1954, p. 1. The Hearst Metrotone "News of the Day" includes segments of this press conference, but omits questions from reporters (Hearst Metrotone Newsreels, UCLA Film and Television Archive, Tape VA–3704). See also Robert A. Divine, *Blowing on the Wind: The Nuclear Test Ban Debate, 1954–1960* (New York: Oxford University Press, 1978), pp. 3–13.

62. Even in his confidential briefings to other members of Eisenhower's inner circle of national security advisers, Strauss denied the dangers of fallout produced by the BRAVO test. In this regard, his disingenuous attempts to reassure Secretary of State John Foster Dulles are interesting (Seely G. Mudd Library, Princeton University, Papers of John Foster Dulles, Telephone Box 2: Conversation Memoranda, telephone conversation with Admiral Strauss, March 29, 1954, 10:30 A.M.).

63. Ralph Lapp, "Fall-out—Another Dimension in Atomic Killing Power," *New Republic*, February 14, 1955, pp. 8–12, and "Radioactive Fall-out," *Bulletin of the Atomic Scientists* 11 (1955): 45–51. For the AEC report, see "H-Bomb Tests—They're Safe," *U.S. News & World Report*, February 25, 1955, pp. 128–34.

64. DDEL, DDE, White House Central Files, Official Files, Box 658, Folder OF 133-B-2 (2): Remarks of Val Peterson, Administrator, Federal Civil Defense Administration, A Report on the Washington Conference of Mayors on National Security, December 2–3, 1954.

65. "Panic Prevention and Control," app. IXB of *Report of the Project East River: Information and Training for Civil Defense, Part IX*, pp. 56–57. The authors of this appendix were Dwight W. Chapman, Jr., Department of Psychology, University of Michigan, who chaired the research panel; Dale C. Cameron, U.S. Public Health Service; Leonard Logan, director, Institute of Community Development, University of Oklahoma; and Stephen B. Withey, Institute for Social Research, University of Michigan.

66. Ibid., p. 64.

67. Ibid.

68. Ibid., p. 61.

69. Ibid., pp. 58–59.

70. *Report of the Project East River: Information and Training for Civil Defense, Part IX*, p. 30.

71. Ibid., p. 31.

72. Ibid.

73. Ibid., p. 32.

74. "Panic Prevention and Control," pp. 61–62.

75. *Information and Training for Civil Defense*, p. 25. The April 1953 FCDA study, "Civil Defense Implications of the Psychological Impact and Morale Effects of Attacks on the People of the United States," followed the theory of home-front mobilization as emotion management worked out by Project East River.

76. The FCDA collected an extensive body of correspondence documenting that the problem of panic was indeed a source of worry to many Americans. This correspondence constituted evidence that the public embraced one of the main axioms of the Cold War system of emotion management: The main danger posed by the Cold War was not a Soviet nuclear attack but American panic

in the face of such an attack (National Archives, Record Group 304, OCDM, Box 5, Folder: Comments and Queries).

77. Peterson, "Panic," pp. 106–7.

78. Ibid., pp. 101, 108.

79. Janis, *Air War and Emotional Stress*, p. 195.

80. Ibid., p. 250.

81. Ibid., p. 202.

82. Ibid.

83. Philip Wylie, *Tomorrow!* (New York: Rinehart, 1954). On Wylie's career, see Truman Frederick Keefer, *Philip Wylie* (Boston: Twayne, 1977). On the background of *Tomorrow!* see Lewis Nichols, "Talk with Philip Wylie," *New York Times Book Review*, February 21, 1954, p. 12.

84. Rampant and stampeding mobs reappear throughout Wylie's Cold War writing. In a later novel, ironically entitled *Triumph*, the United States and the Soviet Union engage in a no-holds-barred thermonuclear exchange that ends in mutual annihilation. Huge crowds press to the entrances of the few available shelters. Here as well, limbs are crushed or broken off, rib cages are cracked, and internal organs are smashed in what Wylie pictures as "gouting blood vomits or a last explosive belch of red-frothed air." Desperate suburbanites lay siege to the only owner of a shelter on the block. He responds by mowing down his neighbors with a machine gun, which he had prudently installed in the shelter before the attack. When this form of civil defense proves inadequate, he tosses out hand grenades, blasting out the intestines and tearing off the heads of local children. During the excitement, a young woman is chased through the streets by a crowd of pursuing males and repeatedly raped. In sum, when nuclear terror breaks the power of the police and the force of legal sanctions, the social order collapses (*Triumph* [Garden City, N.Y.: Doubleday, 1963]). Wylie's worries about the irrational and self-destructive response of the American people to a nuclear attack and his suggestions on preventing and controlling it are fully documented in the Philip Wylie Collection, Firestone Library, Princeton University. See especially "Civil Defense and a Third War" (Box 121, Folder 2), and "Civil Defense Suggestion" (Box 121, Folder 4).

Chapter 3

1. *Report of the Project East River: General Report, Part I* (New York: Associated Universities, 1952), p. 4.

2. HSTL, HST, Files of Spencer R. Quick, Box 5, Folder 1: Civil Defense Campaign—General; Box 1, Civil Defense Programs; Box 5, Folder: Civil Defense Campaign Correspondence. The advertising agency assigned by the Advertising Council to develop the Alert America campaign was Batten, Barton, Durstine & Osborn. The convoys were declared a popular success. In April 1952, the advertising magazine *Tide* observed, perhaps with some exaggeration: "So far, the response has been terrific, with mobs thronging the exhibits wherever they appear" (p. 38).

3. On early plans to maintain the continuity of the federal government under nuclear attack, see HSTL, HST, Staff Member Office Files, Psychological Strategy Board Files, Box 34, Folder 384.51: Project East River, Department of

Defense Directive on Disaster Planning, November 10, 1951, and NSRB Bulletin 53–1 on Continuity of Government, September 10, 1952. On early plans to maintain industrial production under the same conditions, see National Archives, Record Group 304, NSRB Central Files, July 1949–April 1953, Box 102, Folder: Publicity for Post-Attack Rehabilitation Program.

4. National Archives, Record Group 304, NSRB Central Files, July 1949– April 1953, Box 101, Folders: Labor Supply and Manpower, and Post-Attack Rehabilitation, General.

5. See William V. Reed, "A Study of Housing Problems in Post-Attack Industrial Rehabilitation," January 16, 1952, and "A Study of Housing Problems in Post-Attack Industrial Rehabilitation: Phase Two," August 19, 1952, National Archives, Record Group 304, NSRB Central Files, July 1949–April 1953, Box 102.

6. DDEL, DDE, Ann Whitman File, NSC Series, Box 5, Folder: 182nd meeting of NSC, January 28, 1954.

7. These efforts to control press coverage of Operation Alert 1955 met with some success. See "Civil Defense: So Much to Be Done," *Newsweek*, June 27, 1955, pp. 21–22; "Civil Defense: Best Defense? Prayer," *Time*, June 27, 1955, pp. 17–18; and "When Ike 'Fled' Washington," *U.S. News & World Report*, June 24, 1955, pp. 66–69. Hearst Metrotone "News of the Day" rebroadcast film footage produced by the FCDA in movie theaters throughout the country, thereby investing the Cold War conception of nuclear reality with the authority of objective reportage. State propaganda and the news became indistinguishable (Hearst Metrotone Newsreels, UCLA Film and Television Archive, Tape VA–5723).

8. DDEL, DDE, White House Central Files, Official Files, Box 658, Folder OF 113-B-5; Letter, Bryson Rash to James Hagerty, June 2, 1955.

9. On the planning of Operation Alert 1955, see DDEL, DDE, White House Central Files, Confidential File, Box 16, Folder CD 1.

10. Hearst Metrotone "News of the Day" broadcast part of Eisenhower's speech for movie audiences (Hearst Metrotone Newsreels, UCLA Film and Television Archive, Tape VA–5723).

11. On the plans for Operation Alert 1956, see DDEL, DDE, Ann Whitman File, Cabinet Series, Box 7, Folder: Cabinet Meeting of July 13, 1956, Cabinet Paper—Privileged (April 2, 1956).

12. DDEL, DDE, White House Central Files, Official Files, Box 658, Folder OF 133-B-5: Telegram, George Meany to the President, July 20, 1956.

13. *Newsletter: By, for and About Women in Civil Defense*, no. 16 (Battle Creek, Mich.: FCDA, n.d. [1956]), p. 4.

14. Ibid., p. 5. In the same *Newsletter*, see Barbara Beene, "Edgewood Goes to Head of Class in H-Bomb Exam," which covered the evacuation of the Edgewood, Alabama, school by 250 local matrons. Following the rhetoric of nuclear crisis mastery, the importance of organization, training, efficiency, and moral and emotional self-control was stressed: "Split second timing" and "clockwork precision" were held to be crucial to the success of the evacuation. In the conduct of the exercise, "there was no noise, no pushing or shoving, as the youngsters hastily but orderly, went to their places, following drill instructions" (p. 9).

15. On the plans for Operation Alert 1957, see DDEL, DDE, Ann Whitman File, Cabinet Series, Box 8, Folder: Cabinet Meeting of February 1, 1957, Cabinet Paper—Privileged (January 28, 1957).

16. On the plans for Operation Alert 1958, see DDEL, DDE, Ann Whitman File, Cabinet Series, Box 11, Folder: Cabinet Meeting of June 6, 1958, Cabinet Paper—Privileged (January 13, 1958).

17. Cabinet Meeting of July 13, 1956, Cabinet Paper—Privileged (April 2, 1956).

18. The National Archives has a copy of *Operation Alert*, but no information concerning its broadcast dates and distribution.

19. Hearst Metrotone "News of the Day" reproduced clips of *Operation Alert* for commercial broadcast under the headline "Nation-Wide Test of Civil Defense." Consistent with the premises of the Cold War conception of nuclear reality, Manhattan is evacuated without incident. Traffic police, clothed in what appear to be transparent, knee-length plastic bags, monitor the exercise in Times Square during the final minutes before the simulated attack, as drivers dutifully abandon their vehicles and seek shelter along with pedestrians (Hearst Metrotone Newsreels, UCLA Film and Television Archive, Tape VA–5723).

20. The ubiquitous suburban station wagon of the 1950s is also deployed in Washington, D.C., where bureaucrats load documents into waiting vehicles and "key federal officials" are transported to the secret emergency relocation centers of Operation Alert. Although a nuclear crisis may pose new and terrifying dangers for the American nation, it can be managed with equipment and know-how drawn from everyday life.

21. The National Archives has a copy of *The Day Called X*, but neither the National Archives nor the CBS News Film and Video Tape Archive has information on its broadcast dates and distribution.

Chapter 4

1. DDEL, Papers of Katherine Howard, Box 11, Folder: Television (1), "Excerpts from the Text of President Eisenhower's Address at the Forty-Fifth Annual Governor's Conference," August 4, 1953.

2. Ibid.

3. DDEL, DDE, Staff Files of James M. Lambie, Jr., Box 3, Folder: Civil Defense Campaign 1953 (1), Letter, J. M. Chambers to Allan M. Wilson, February 27, 1953.

4. DDEL, DDE, Central Files, Official Files, Box 195, Folder 20 (Releases): Val Peterson, Address at the Eighth Annual Home Safety Awards Dinner, April 22, 1953 [emphasis in original].

5. Ibid.

6. Ibid.

7. Ibid [emphasis in original].

8. For these figures, see Steven Mintz and Susan Kellogg, *Domestic Revolutions: A Social History of American Family Life* (New York: Free Press, 1988), pp. 182–84.

9. Civil defense home-protection manuals fall within the mainstream

of the self-help and self-made happiness literature of the 1950s. Self-improvement manuals are among the oldest and most characteristic literary artifacts of American culture. See John Cawelti, *Apostles of the Self-Made Man* (Chicago: University of Chicago Press, 1965); Richard Weiss, *The American Myth of Success* (1969; Urbana: University of Illinois Press, 1988); Richard M. Huber, *The American Idea of Success* (New York: McGraw-Hill, 1971); and Nicole Woolsey Biggart, "Rationality, Meaning, and Self-Management: Success Manuals, 1950–1980," *Social Problems* 30 (1983): 298–311. Just as there have been self-help manuals on succeeding in all manner of enterprises and improving performance in virtually every arena of human endeavor, so it is not surprising that anxieties about nuclear war and the fear of atomic attack during the early years of the Cold War provided the occasion for comparable manuals on surviving World War III.

10. Federal Civil Defense Administration, *Home Protection Exercises* (Washington, D.C.: Government Printing Office, 1953), p. 14.

11. Ibid., p. 23.

12. On the relations between technological innovation and changes in the family as a domestic labor force, see Ruth Schwartz Cowan, "The 'Industrial Revolution' in the Home: Household Technology and Social Change in the 20th Century," *Technology and Culture* 17 (1976): 1–23; and Joann Vanek, "Household Technology and Social Status: Rising Living Standards and Status and Residence Differences in Housework," *Technology and Culture* 19 (1978): 361–75.

13. On Weber's concept of rationalization, see especially Wolfgang Schluchter, *The Rise of Western Rationalism: Max Weber's Developmental History*, trans. Guenther Roth (Berkeley: University of California Press, 1981); and Wolfgang Schluchter, *Rationalism, Religion, and Domination: A Weberian Perspective*, trans. Neil Solomon (Berkeley: University of California Press, 1989). See also Stephen Kalberg, "Max Weber's Types of Rationality: Cornerstones for the Analysis of Rationalization Processes in History," *American Journal of Sociology* 85 (1980): 1147–79; Mahmoud Sadri, "Reconstruction of Max Weber's Notion of Rationality: An Immanent Model," *Social Research* 9 (1982): 616–33; and Donald N. Levine, *The Flight from Ambiguity: Essays in Social and Cultural Theory* (Chicago: University of Chicago Press, 1985).

14. FCDA, *Home Protection Exercises*, p. 8.

15. See the section "How Well Prepared Is Your Family?" and the accompanying sample scorecard in ibid., p. 26.

16. On dirt as a threat to purity and order, see Mary Douglas, *Purity and Danger* (London: Routledge & Kegan Paul, 1966). On American fears of fallout in the 1950's, see Allan M. Winkler, *Life Under a Cloud: American Anxiety About The Atom* (New York: Oxford University Press, 1993), pp. 96–108.

17. Federal Civil Defense Administration *Shelter From Radioactive Fallout* (Washington, D.C.: Government Printing Office, n.d.), and *Facts About Fallout* (Washington, D.C.: Government Printing Office, 1955).

18. Federal Civil Defense Administration, *Home Protection Exercises*, rev. ed. (Washington, D.C.: Government Printing Office, 1956), p. 8.

19. Ibid., p. 25.

20. On the comfort of family fallout shelters, see Hearst Metrotone Newsreels, UCLA Film and Television Archive, Tapes VA–4157, VA–5723; and Elaine

Tyler May, *Homeward Bound: American Families in the Cold War Era* (New York: Basic Books, 1988), pp. 3–5.

21. However, suppose one has the bad luck to be caught in the open country when the radioactive rain begins to fall. *Facts About Fallout* pictures a couple blithely strolling hand in hand along a country lane that passes a barn nearby. What should they do? They should take advantage of any shelter available, most obviously the barn. Or they should return to the car and roll up the windows. What about the worse possible case, when no shelter is readily available, and there is no time to seek it out? The best advice, which the film proposes in dead seriousness, is to dig a hole and cover it with branches or boards. The couple is pictured—quite implausibly, since they are not equipped with tools for digging or cutting—engaged in these efforts. With an ordinary piece of lumber, the man digs a hole large enough to conceal the pair while his companion drags up a small tree to cover it. How did he dig a large hole with a flat-ended board? How did she cut down the tree? The film does not pause to consider these details. Instead, as the couple peers warily out of their tree-covered redoubt, the light of a brilliant blue sky glimmering through the branches, the announcer advises them not to let radioactive dust touch their skin. How they could follow this advice under the protection offered by the foxhole remains obscure.

22. The National Archives has thirteen installments of "Retrospect," but neither the National Archives nor the CBS News Film and Video Tape Archive has information on their broadcast dates.

23. HSTL, HST, Official File, Box 1671, File 1591: "Welcome Film by President Truman to Students at CD Staff College and CD Technical Training Centers," October 22, 1951.

24. DDEL, DDE, Ann Whitman File, Cabinet Series, Box 2, Cabinet Meetings of May 1, 1953.

25. HSTL, HST, Official File, Box 1671, Folder 1591: Speech at the Alert America Exhibit in Washington, D.C., which Truman attended on January 1, 1952.

26. DDEL, DDE, Central Files, Official Files, Box 195, Folder OF 20 1958, Address of Leo A. Hoegh, January 21, 1958.

27. The Katherine Howard Papers (1917–1974) are housed in the Eisenhower Library in thirty-one archival Boxes. Boxes 1–13 cover her career in civil defense. On Howard's responsibilities and work as the FCDA's deputy administrator, see Box 1, Folder: Activities and Engagements, 1953–1954; Box 3, Folder: Correspondence—Miscellaneous (1953). On her responsibilities as the "special adviser" to the FCDA administrator, see Box 3, Folder: Correspondence—Miscellaneous (1954–1955), Letter, Val Peterson to Katherine Howard, July 16, 1954. On Howard's management of her own press and public relations, see Box 9, Folders: Press (Miscellaneous) (1), Press (Miscellaneous) (2), Press (Miscellaneous) (3), Radio (1), Radio (2), Radio (3); and Box 11, Folders: Television (1) and Television (2). On Howard's response to the news magazine survey, see Box 9, Folder: Press (Miscellaneous) (2), Document, July 6, 1955. See also Howard's autobiography, *With My Shoes Off* (New York: Vantage Press, 1977).

28. DDEL, Katherine Howard Papers, Box 1, Folder: American Women in Radio and TV, "A Great Light," June 6, 1953, p. 2.

29. Katherine Howard Papers, Box 4, Folder: General Federation of Women's Clubs, "The Distaff Side of Civil Defense," October 15, 1953, p. 6.

30. Katherine Howard Papers, Box 9, Folder: Radio (1), Recorded Broadcast by Mrs. Howard with Leanor Sullivan, n.d. [summer 1953].

31. Katherine Howard Papers, Box 9, Folder: Press (Miscellaneous) (2), United Press Radio Service Interview with Helen Thomas, April 2, 1954.

32. Katherine Howard Papers, Box 4, Folder: Federation of Republican Women's Organizations, "We Will Survive," May 15, 1954, p. 4.

33. Ibid., p. 5.

34. Katherine Howard Papers, "Distaff Side of Civil Defense," p. 8.

35. Katherine Howard Papers, Box 11, Folder: Sulgrave Club, "Civil Defense in an Age of Peril," January 18, 1954, p. 2.

36. Ibid., pp. 5–6.

37. Katherine Howard Papers, "Great Light," pp. 9–10.

38. Katherine Howard Papers, Box 5, Folder: Kappa Kappa Gamma Fraternity Alumna Group, "The First Steps," May 22, 1954, pp. 1, 5.

39. Katherine Howard Papers, "Distaff Side of Civil Defense," p. 4.

40. National Archives, Record Group 304, OCDM, Box 1: Records Relating to Civil Defense, 1949–1953. Howard's position that civil defense was committed to defining roles based on gender is defended in May, *Homeward Bound*, pp. 92–113, although from a feminist perspective that Howard did not share. According to Howard, civil defense exhibits women's strengths and virtues. From May's standpoint, it constitutes yet another strategy of the 1950s for taming the dangerous and destructive forces represented by "uncontained" women (p. 109).

41. Katherine Howard Papers, Box 10, Folder: Regional Conference on Civil Defense, "The Power of Women in Civil Defense," September 28, 1954, p. 1.

42. Ibid., p. 3.

43. Katherine Howard Papers, "Distaff Side of Civil Defense," pp. 10–11.

44. Katherine Howard Papers, Box 3, Folder: Daughters of the American Revolution, "The Ramparts We Watch," April 20, 1954, p. 5.

45. Katherine Howard Papers, Box 12, Folder: Women's Patriotic Conference on National Defense, "Freedom's Holy Light," February 16, 1956, p. 2.

Chapter 5

1. HSTL, HST, President's Secretary's Files, "The Evaluation of the Atomic Bomb as a Military Weapon: The Final Report of the Joint Chiefs of Staff Evaluation Board for OPERATION CROSSROADS," June 30, 1947, p. 36.

2. Ibid.

3. Ibid., p. 37.

4. Ibid., p. 36.

5. Firestone Library, Princeton University, Philip Wylie Collection, Box 184, Folder 3: FCDA, Letter, Millard Caldwell to Philip Wylie, July 13, 1951.

6. DDEL, DDE, Ann Whitman File, NSC Series, Box 5, Folder: 182nd Meeting of NSC, January 28, 1954, p. 12.

7. DDEL, DDE, Ann Whitman File, NSC Series, Box 5, Folder: 185th Meeting of NSC, February 17, 1954, p. 12.

8. DDEL, DDE, Ann Whitman File, Cabinet Series, Box 5, Folder: Cabinet Meeting of June 17, 1955, p. 6.

9. DDEL, DDE, Ann Whitman File, Cabinet Series, Box 7, Folder: Cabinet Meeting of July 25, 1956, pp. 8–10.

10. Ibid., pp. 9–10.

11. DDEL, DDE, Ann Whitman File, Cabinet Series, Box 9, Folder: Cabinet Meeting of July 12, 1957, p. 2.

12. DDEL, DDE, Ann Whitman File, NSC Series, Box 10, Folder: 390th Meeting of NSC, December 11, 1958, p. 2.

13. DDEL, DDE, Ann Whitman File, Cabinet Series, Box 12, Folder: Cabinet Meeting of October 9, 1958, p. 3.

14. 390th Meeting of NSC, December 11, 1958, p. 3.

15. "Evaluation of the Atomic Bomb as a Military Weapon," p. 34.

16. 182nd Meeting of NSC, January 28, 1954, p. 3.

17. Ibid., p. 7.

18. Ibid., p. 5. On the prospects for a constitutional dictatorship in the United States as a consequence of the exigencies of the Cold War, see Clinton L. Rossiter, *Constitutional Dictatorship: Crisis Government in the Modern Democracies* (Princeton, N.J.: Princeton University Press, 1948), pp. 288–314.

19. 182nd Meeting of NSC, January 28, 1954, p. 7.

20. Ibid., p. 5.

21. Ibid., p. 4. Even Eisenhower's more permissive assumptions seemed to rule out a substantial range of proposals for managing a nuclear crisis. As Treasury Secretary Humphrey observed, if twenty-five major cities were destroyed, it would seem pointless to relocate income tax collectors. Since normal economic activity would be suspended, there would be no income to tax.

For the Federal Reserve's plans to create an emergency fiscal and credit system that would operate in the postattack and reconstruction phases of a nuclear crisis, see DDEL, DDE, White House Central Files, Official Files, Box 659, File 133-B-7 Post-Attack Mobilization, Folder: "Preattack Planning for Postattack Financial and Economic Rehabilitation," March 14, 1957.

22. Cabinet Meeting of June 17, 1955, p. 1.

23. Ibid., p. 2.

24. Ibid.

25. Ibid., p. 5.

26. Ibid., p. 6.

27. Ibid., p. 8.

28. DDEL, DDE, Ann Whitman File, Dwight D. Eisenhower Diaries Series, Box 12, Folder: January 1956 Diary, pp. 1–2.

29. Ibid., p. 2.

30. DDEL, DDE, Ann Whitman File, NSC Series, Box 8, Folder: 293rd and 294th Meetings of NSC, August 16 and 17, 1956, pp. 7–8.

31. DDEL, DDE, Ann Whitman File, NSC Series, Box 10, Folder: 360th Meeting of NSC, March 27, 1958, p. 6. See also Folder: 372nd Meeting of NSC, July 14, 1958.

32. DDEL, DDE, Ann Whitman File, NSC Series, Box 13, Folder: 471st

Meeting of NSC, December 22, 1960, p. 5. The financing requested in the OCDM's proposal was much more modest than the earlier $13 billion recommended by the FCDA, which the White House had rejected. The purpose of the OCDM's program was to provide fallout protection for every American by 1965. This would be achieved by encouraging both families and industry to construct their own shelters, but "without undue panic or haste." According to Hoegh, 25 percent of the population had adequate fallout protection in existing buildings. In addition, more than 1 million families had already built their own home shelters.

33. Ibid., pp. 11–12.
34. Ibid., p. 11.

Epilogue

1. DDEL, DDE, Ann Whitman File, NSC Series, Box 10, Folder: 360th Meeting of NSC, March 27, 1958, p. 9.

Index

Advertising Council, 82, 106, 174n.50
Alert America, 82–83, 106
Alert Today–Alive Tomorrow (film), 3, 4, 5
Allen, Raymond, 50–51
American character, 21–23
American Red Cross, 94, 112
Anderson, L. Dewey, 38
Army Signal Corps, 48
Atomic bomb. *See also*
    Conventionalization argument
    American monopoly of, 13, 16, 44
    American tests of, 34–35
    assembly teams, 11
    Berlin blockade and, 12–13, 17
    early press coverage of, 43–47, 52
    first newsreel of test of, 43
    futility of protection against, 44
    implications of, for civil defense, 35–36
    Katherine Howard on, 137–39
    loss of American monopoly of, 17–18, 49
    mass-producible, 11
    nuclear deterrence and, 6
    nuclear terror and, 35–36, 38
    public information about, 31, 38
    as response to Soviet expansion, 13, 15–16
    Soviet, 17–20, 31
    use of, in war, 16, 19
Atomic Energy Commission (AEC), 92, 118, 149
    Berlin crisis and, 11

BRAVO test and, 60–61
OPERATION IVY and, 58

Baldwin, Hanson, 43
Berlin blockade, 16
    B-29s and, 12–13, 16–17
    Cold War and, 10
    imminence of World War III and, 10–13
Bernard, Chester, 31
Berry, Lewis, 151
Blast shelters, 70–71, 110, 119. *See also*
    Fallout shelters
B'nai B'rith, 94
Boyle, Hal, 57
Boy Scouts, 94, 98
BRAVO hydrogen-bomb test, 60–61, 119
Brimmhall, Dean R., 38
Brodie, Bernard, 36
BROILER, 35–36
Bull, Harold, 36–37
Byrnes, James F., 16

Caldwell, Millard, 147–48, 177n.39
CBS, 100
    "Retrospect" and, 123–28 passim
Central Intelligence Agency (CIA), 20, 91, 92, 150, 161
Chambers, J. M., 106
Civic ethics, 23, 129. *See also* Cold War
    ethic
    civil defense and, 7–8
    propaganda, marketing, and, 9

Civil defense, 48–49, 55, 67–68. *See also* Cold War conception of nuclear reality; Cold War ethic; Cold War system of emotion management; Federal Civil Defense Administration; *Home Protection Exercises*; Nuclear crisis management; Project East River
   advertising and, 106
   American communal ethic and, 3–5
   contradictions of, 145–64 passim
   family and, 105–29 passim, 128–29
   home-protection manuals and, 9
   marketers and, 174n.50
   national will and, 40
   nuclear deterrence and, 6–7, 34, 165–66
   official, optimistic version of, 6–8. *See also* Optimistic ontology
   planners and, 173n.50
   in Portland, Oregon, 101–4
   in Reading, Pennsylvania, 4–5
   self-protection and, 6–7, 34, 165–66
   television and, 120, 129
   theorists of, 173n.50
   unofficial, cynical version of, 7–8. *See also* Cynical ontology
Civil Defense Board (Bull Board), 36–37
Civil Defense for National Security (Hopley Report), 37–38, 55
Clay, Lucius, 12
Coale, Ansley, 36
Cold War. *See also* Cold War conception of nuclear reality; Cold War ethic; Cold War system of emotion management
   American national security and, 7, 33–34
   American way of life and, 15
   civil defense planning and, 6
   culture of, 9
   end of, 9
   family civil defense and, 105–24 passim
   George Kennan on, 25–26, 29
   moral assumptions of, 22, 49
   mythology of, 12
   nuclear war and, 19
   problem of American national will and, 21
   problem of panic and, 34–46 passim
Cold War conception of nuclear reality, 78–104 passim. *See also* Nuclear crisis management; Operation Alert
   concept of nuclear crisis and, 79–84
   definition of, 78–79
   experience of nuclear attack and, 104
   family civil defense and, 113–14
   paradoxes of nuclear crisis management and, 152–54
   as self-refuting, 163–64

Cold War ethic, 31, 129–44 passim. *See also* Howard, Katherine
   American national security and, 7–8, 129
   the home and, 8–9
   premises of, 131
   Truman's speech on, 129–31
Cold War system of emotion management, 46–71 passim. *See also* Emotion management; Janis, Irving L.; Nuclear fear; Nuclear terror; Operation Alert; Panic; Project East River
   atomic bomb and, 62–63
   civil defense and, 47
   nuclear fear and, 62–63
   nuclear terror and, 47, 62
Columbia University, 47
Committee on Social Aspects of Atomic Energy (Social Science Research Council), 36, 173n.50
Communism, 50–51, 107, 128, 144
   emotion management and, 62–63, 177n.39
   in Europe, 12, 14
   George Kennan on, 26, 29
   ideology of, 20
   infiltration of U.S. by agents of, 67
   John Foster Dulles on, 23
   threat of, 15, 120–21, 125
Compton, Karl, 35
CONELRAD, 101–2, 111
Containment, 6, 18, 25–29, 33
Conventionalization argument
   atomic bomb and, 51–52, 54–56
   Cold War system of emotion management and, 51–52
   hydrogen bomb and, 58–62
   nuclear terror and, 51–52
   psychological effects of atomic attack and, 56
   radioactive fallout and, 58–62
   in speeches of Katherine Howard, 137–38
   trivialization of radioactivity and, 55–56
Cornell University, 47
Cousins, Norman, 43–44
Cutler, Robert, 149
Cynical ontology, 160–61
Czechoslovakia, 16

Day Called X, The (film), 101–4, 151
DeChant, John, 177n.39
Dewey, Thomas E., 23, 132
Distant Early Warning Line, 158–59
Department of Defense, 48–49, 87
"Duck and cover," 53
Dulles, Allen, 91, 92, 150, 161
Dulles, John Foster, 148
   on decline of American spirituality, 23–25

on national will and American national
security, 23–25, 30

Edwards, Douglas, 123–29 passim
Eisenhower, Dwight D., 8, 41, 109, 132
broadcast of speech of, during
Operation Alert 1955, 88, 90
on civil defense and self–discipline,
105–6, 131
on conflicting conceptions of civil
defense, 8
on emotion management, 148–49,
150–52
on financing World War III, 154–55
Harold Bull and, 36–37
Katherine Howard and, 132–33
on nuclear "age of peril," 138
on nuclear crisis management, 155–59
on Operation Alert, 157–58
in Operation Alert 1955, 89, 90
on paradox of nuclear crisis
management, 156–57, 161–63
press conference of March 31, 1954, 60
telegram of George Meany to, 93, 94
Ellsworth, Charles, 42, 132–33
Emotion management, 49–59, 66–71
passim, 165
dilemma of, 145–50 passim, 166
nuclear terror and, 33, 46
system of, 47

Facts About Fallout (film), 121–23,
184n.21
Fallout shelters, 61–62, 105–24 passim
Federal Civil Defense Act of 1950, 38
Federal Civil Defense Administration
(FCDA), 3, 47–48, 165
Alert America and, 82
civil defense planners in, 173n.50
civil defense propaganda of, 148
civil defense theorists in, 173n.50
Cold War ethic and, 129–44 passim
contradictions in civil defense and,
145–64 passim
The Day Called X (film), 100–101
emotion management and, 47–73
passim, 147, 151, 177n.39
family civil defense and, 106–29 passim
formation of, 38
on hydrogen bomb, 7, 59
on nuclear crisis management, 153–54,
159–60
on nuclear terror, 146
OCDM and, 118
Operation Alert and, 85–95 passim
Operation Alert (film) and, 96
OPERATION IVY and, 58
on *Operation Ivy* (film), 59
problem of panic and, 39–42

Public Affairs Office of, 39, 41, 129,
174n.50, 177n.39
Psychological Strategy Board and,
177n.39
Federation of Atomic Scientists (League
of Frightened Men), 44
Fifth-column subversion, 37, 41, 107
Flemming, Arthur, 89, 90
Ford, Glenn, 100, 101, 104
Forrestal, James A., 14, 17
Franck, James, 44

Garrison state, 10, 15, 156
Gates, Thomas, 163
Geiger counter, 52, 74, 100, 126
Gender differences and civil defense, 5
FCDA on, 140–41
Home Protection Exercises on, 141
Katherine Howard on, 140–41
NSRB on, 141
Val Peterson on, 140–41, 175n.14
Gill, William A., 141
Girl Scouts, 94

Harvard University, 47
Hersey, John, 45–46
Hiroshima, 54–55, 101
atomic bomb designed for, 11
atomic bombing of, 43, 46, 52, 146
John Hersey on, 45–46
Soviet atomic bomb compared to attack
on, 20
victims of bombing of, 56
Hiroshima (Hersey), 45–46
Hitchcock, Alfred, 5
Hoegh, Leo, 120, 131, 162–63
Home Protection Exercises (FCDA), 109–20
passim, 138
Hoover, J. Edgar, 150
Hopley, Russell J., 37
Howard, Katherine, 42, 132–45 passim
Humphrey, George, 89, 148, 154–55
Hydrogen bomb, 4. *See also*
Conventionalization argument
first test of, 58
implications of, for family civil defense,
117–29 passim
Katherine Howard on, 136–38

Invasion of the Body Snatchers (film), 97
Isolationism, 22

Janis, Irving L., 56, 69–71
Johns Hopkins University, 47
Joint Chiefs of Staff
Berlin blockade and, 13
Evaluation Board for OPERATION
CROSSROADS, 35–36, 146–47, 153
Joint Strategic Plans Committee of,
18

Joint Chiefs of Staff (*continued*)
    on Soviet atomic bomb, 19–20
    Truman's military budget and, 15

Kennan, George F., 23–30 passim
    "Long Telegram" of, 29
    "X" article of, 29
Kennedy, John F., 6

Langmuir, Irving, 44
Lapp, Ralph, 55–56, 61
Larson, Arthur, 91, 92, 150
Liberalism, American, 28–29
Lucky Dragon (Japanese fishing boat), 60

McGrath, Paul, 125
McLean, Joseph E., 50–51
McMahon, Brian, 71
Manhattan Project, 35, 43–44, 55
Marshall, George C., 13, 17
Massachusetts Institute of Technology
    (MIT), 35, 47
Meany, George, 93, 94
Middle class, American
    civil defense and, 3, 5, 121–22, 130
    Cold War conception of nuclear reality
        and, 96, 101, 104
    George Kennan on, 25, 27
Molotov, V. M., 13
Murrow, Edward R., 57

Nagasaki, 54–55
    atomic bomb designed for, 11
    atomic bombing of, 43, 46, 52, 146
    victims of bombing of, 56
National security, American. *See also* Civil
        defense; Nuclear deterrence
    economic prosperity and, 14–15
    moral basis of, 7–9, 21, 25–30 passim
    national will and, 18
    new conception of, 6, 106
    nuclear deterrence and, 8, 167
    permanent crisis in, 18
    traditional bases of, 18–19
National Security Act of 1947, 38
National Security Council (NSC)
    Berlin blockade and, 16
    discussion of civil defense in, 160
    meeting of August 16/17, 1956, 161
    meeting of January 28, 1954, 148–49,
        154–56
    meeting of March 27, 1958, 161–62,
        166
National Security Resources Board
    (NSRB), 38, 48–49, 52, 141
    civil defense planners in, 173n.50
    postattack rehabilitation plans of, 83–84
National will. *See also* Dulles, John Foster;
        Kennan, George F.; Stimson, Henry L.
    American national security and, 7, 14,
        39

economic prosperity and, 14
    problem of, 20–21, 165
Nitze, Paul, 30
Nixon, Richard, 148, 166
Normalization, paradox of, 153
NSC 30, 16
NSC 68, 20, 26, 30–31
NSC 162/2, 58
Nuclear crisis management (mastery),
        79–84 passim, 163–65, 167. *See also*
        Operation Alert
    civil defense as, 7
    methodology of, 80
    official ideology of, 150
    paradox of, 152–66 passim
    rhetoric of, 181n.14
    self-protection and, 8
Nuclear deterrence, 160. *See also* Nuclear
        terror
    implications of Soviet nuclear weapons
        for, 20–21
    moral foundations of, 6, 31–34
    shelter program and, 166
Nuclear fear
    civil defense and, 62, 72
    national will and, 33
    subjectification of nuclear threat and,
        62–63
Nuclear Pearl Harbor, 21–22, 44, 124
Nuclear terror
    early press coverage of atomic bomb
        and, 43–47
    implications of, 34
    national will and, 33, 146
    nuclear deterrence and, 34, 46, 145

Office of Civil and Defense Mobilization
    (OCDM), 118–29 passim
    civil defense planners in, 174n.50
    fallout shelter program of, 162–63
Office of Civil Defense Planning, 37
Office of Defense Mobilization (ODM),
    89, 93, 118
Ogburn, William, 36
"One world or none," 34
Operation Alert, 84–95 passim, 104, 165
    dilemma of emotion management and,
        148–52
    paradox of nuclear crisis management
        and, 156–59
    protocol of, 85
    purpose of, 84–85, 96
    self-defeating character of, 152–54, 159
    telescoping in, 85, 93
Operation Alert (film), 102, 104, 150,
    182nn.19–20
    American society in, 96–100
    future as past in, 104
    radioactive fallout in, 99–100
Operation Alert 1954, 85–86

Operation Alert 1955
    emotion management and, 90
    home shelters and, 135
    NEWPOINT and, 87–89
    press and public relations and, 85–89,
        92
Operation Alert 1956, 92–93, 95
    in Canton, Ohio, 94–95
    in Wright City, Missouri, 94–95
Operation Alert 1957, 95, 151
Operation Alert 1958, 95
OPERATION CROSSROADS, 35, 146–47
Operation Ivy, 58–59, 149
Operation Ivy (film), 59, 137, 149
Oppenheimer, Robert, 18, 30
Optimistic ontology, 160–62, 166

Panic, 5, 81, 117
    American propensity for, 41–42, 49, 68
    nuclear terror and, 33–34
    possibility of, in nuclear attack, 64–67
    problem of, 34, 36–38, 69–70
Pearl Harbor, 20, 22, 124
Peterson, Val, 132
    on civil defense and hydrogen bomb,
        59, 61–62
    on civil defense as emotion
        management, 68–69
    on fallout shelters, 61–62
    on family civil defense, 106–8
    on federal shelter program, 161
    in *Operation Alert* (film), 99
    in Operation Alert 1955, 89, 90
    on panic, 41–42, 68
    plans of, concerning Operation Alert,
        148, 150
    skepticism of, concerning nuclear crisis
        management, 155–56
"Preview of the War We Do Not Want"
    (*Collier's*), 56–58
Princeton University, 36, 50, 177n.50
Project East River, 47–69 passim, 81,
    173n.50
Propaganda, 125, 170n.6
    American moral resolve and, 31
    civil defense, 5, 148, 151
    Cold War, 50, 108
    Communist, 29
    control of postattack rumors and, 66–
        67
    liberal, 8, 166–67
    marketing and, 9
Protestant ethic, 24–25
Psychological Strategy Board, 50–51,
    177n.39
Puritan paradox, 24–25

Rabb, Max, 91, 92
Rabi, Isidor, 36
Radford, Arthur, 148

Radioactive fallout, 58–59
    absence of, in Operation Alert, 89, 92
    first publication of danger of, 61
    implications of, for family civil defense,
        118–29 passim
    information on, from AEC and FCDA,
        118
Rand Corporation, 56
Report of the Project East River, 48
"Retrospect" (television series), 123–29
    passim
Rockefeller, Nelson, 91, 92
Rockefeller Foundation, 31
Rockwell, Norman, 74
RKO, 3
Roosevelt, Franklin D., 54

SANDSTONE nuclear tests, 11
Scapegoats, 40, 64, 67
Schaeffer, Charles, 126
Siegel, Don, 97
Smith, Merriman, 60
Social order and nuclear attack, 5, 37,
    39–40
State Department Policy Planning Staff,
    19, 29–30
Stewart, Elaine, 73
Stimson, Henry L., 22–23
Strauss, Lewis, 60, 150
Study of Civil Defense, A (Bull Report), 37–
    38, 55
Sulgrave Club, 138
Survival Under Atomic Attack (NSRB), 52–
    54, 80, 163

This Is Your Civil Defense (film), 120–21
Tokyo, bombing of, 54–55
Tomorrow! (Wylie), 71–77 passim
Truman, Harry S, 9, 109, 146, 148
    announcement of Hiroshima bombing
        and, 43
    Berlin blockade and, 12–13
    formation of FCDA and, 38
    on limiting military budget, 14–15
    NSC 68 and, 20, 30
    speech by, October 22, 1951, 129–31
    United States Strategic Bombing Survey
        and, 54

United States Civil Defense (Blue Book), 38,
    55
United States Information Agency, 87
United States Strategic Bombing Survey,
    54–56, 146
University of Michigan, 173n.50
University of Pennsylvania, 47
University of Rochester, 47
Urey, Harold C., 34, 44

Vandenberg, Hoyt, 19

Wadsworth, James J., 39
Washington Conference of Mayors on
    National Security, 61
Weber, Max, 24–25, 113–14
Weeks, Sinclair, 150
Wesley, John, 24
Wilson, Allan, 106
Wilson, Charles, 148, 151, 157
Wilson, Richard, 60
Wolfers, Arnold, 18–19
World War I, 22, 128
World War II, 11, 20, 43, 109, 130
    air raids in, 54
    American civil defense doctrine and,
        61
    American home front in, 5
    American national will and, 7
    atomic bomb in, 147
    challenges posed by end of, 23, 48–49
    collapse of distinction between front
        lines and home front in, 46
    conventional bombs used in, 52, 62
    conventionalization argument and, 56–
        57, 59
    European recovery from, 14
    female labor in, 141
    financing of, 155
    Hollywood version of, 57

incarceration of Japanese-Americans
    in, 64
military secrecy in, 68
World War III, 8, 62, 104, 131
    American society in, 71–77 passim
    American women in, 143
    atomic attacks of World War II and,
        146
    Collier's version of, 56–57
    in *The Day Called X* (film), 102
    family civil defense and, 105, 107–9,
        117
    mobilization of public for, 5
    nuclear deterrence and, 165
    nuclear terror and, 35
    Operation Alert and, 85
    in *Operation Alert* (film), 100
    United States as theater of, 79–80, 92,
        155
Wylie, Philip, 57–58
    background of, in civil defense, 71–72
    on civil defense training, 74–77
    correspondence of, with Millard
        Caldwell, 147
    on nuclear terror and moral chaos, 72–
        74, 180n.84

Yale University, 47, 56, 173n.50